To the End of the Road

– RAY KING –

FASTPRINT PUBLISHING
PETERBOROUGH, ENGLAND

FastPrint

www.fast-print.net/store.php

To the End of the Road

ISBN 978-184426-950-1

First published 2011 by
FASTPRINT PUBLISHING
Peterborough, England.

An environmentally friendly book printed and bound in England by
www.printondemand-worldwide.com

Mixed Sources
Product group from well-managed
forests, and other controlled sources
www.fsc.org Cert no. TT-COC-002641
© 1996 Forest Stewardship Council
FSC

PEFC Certified
This product is
from sustainably
managed forests
and controlled
sources
PEFC
PEFC/16-33-415
www.pefc.org

This book is made entirely of chain-of-custody materials

Contents

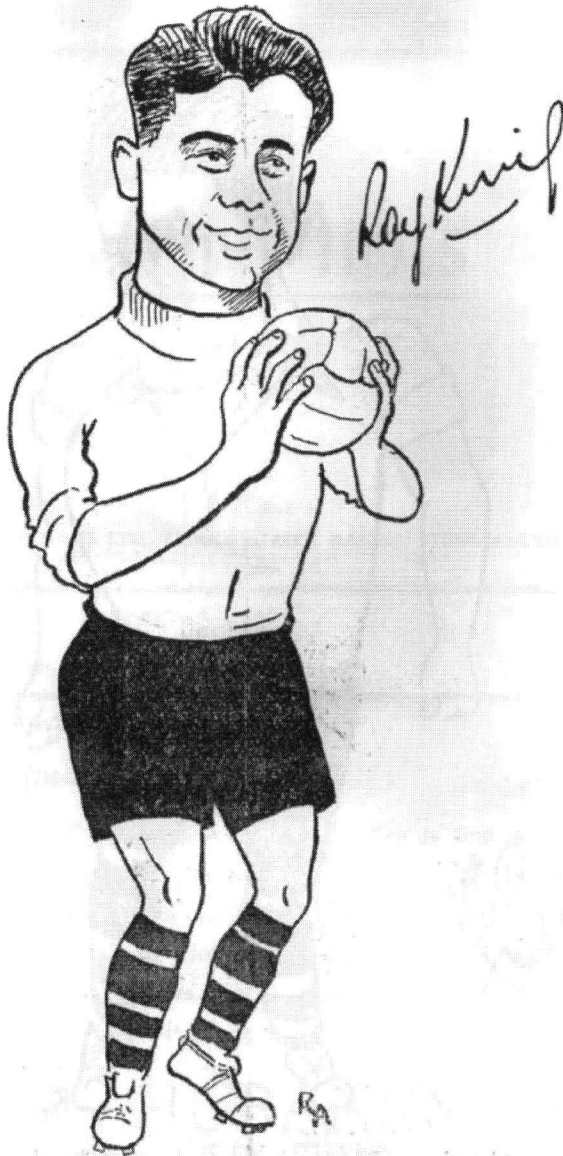

RAY KING—(Goalkeeper)

Ray joined Port Vale five seasons ago from Ashington Colliery after a spell during the war seasons with Newcastle United. He is of excellent physique and is an ever present this season. His brother, George, is a professional footballer—centre forward—and after a term with Port Vale joined Barrow and then Gillingham.

Image taken from Port Vale season 1953-54 souvenir programme

Ray King – a Son's Perspective

One of the many topics of conversation that I share with my father, Ray King, is how football has become so popular with young people the world over. When I first moved to New York in the 1980s, football, or soccer as they refer to the beautiful game there, was that strange game played with a round ball that was played just about everywhere else in the world. In Thailand the kids and the adults are "football daft!"

I often strike up conversation with the locals in Bangkok, especially the cab drivers. Almost always when they know where I come from they ask be which team I support – most of them support Man U as they call it. In this new millennium soccer has taken on a life hitherto unknown. I work with many young people as an educational consultant and it never fails to amaze me just how often they ask me about the latest results, which is my favourite team and which players' careers I follow. This last question is an easy one.

I still follow my Dad's illustrious career and have been as proud as any son can be of a father who was not only successful in his own right as a footballer but loved the game for what it was, not for how much money he could make (£14 per week at the height of his career!!).

Gary King
Director
Cambridge Academics
Educational Consultancy
Bangkok, THAILAND

Mam & Dad (c) Gary King

Another Book?

"**R**ay, when are you going to write another book?"
This question was thrown at me constantly after I wrote
""*Hands, Feet and Balls*"". The simple answer was that it was easier said
than done!

It may come as a surprise to most readers when I divulge the fact
(one I find difficult to believe) that ""*Hands, Feet and Balls*"" was written
in one month. All 365 pages.

Setting my memoirs on paper was the easy part. Although I had
never kept a diary, my long-term memory served me well with
incredibly accurate experiences and images, but assembling the whole
project was a mammoth task. Without a publishing company to finance
the proposed book, I sought the aid of my nephew David White, who,
with his almost clapped-out computer, agreed to work alongside me on
the difficult task ahead. Achieving this required a round journey of 20
miles on a narrow winding road to the village of Shilbottle almost every
day. There were many moments when I was deep in despair, especially
when the computer broke down and we almost lost the whole
manuscript! Suicide wasn't far away! After two and a half years of trials
and tribulations the project was complete, and without David's editing
expertise the book would never have reached the printing press.

The next decision was the small matter of printing and distribution.
We settled on an order of 1,600 books – not a great many by normal
standards, but even that cost £5,000 and David had to be paid on top of
that. Not having the financial clout myself I borrowed £2,000 from my
son Gary and a further £2,000 from my brother Frank – a sad
indictment for someone who'd been involved in professional football as
a player, manager, coach and physio over a period of 30 years.

Writing ""*Hands, Feet and Balls*"" gave me an opportunity to express my thoughts and opinions on every aspect of the beautiful game as I knew it in the 1940s and 50s – a stark contrast to the millionaire status of those connected with football today. In an effort to publicise my book copies were sent to several top sports writers at national and regional newspapers. Many of them gave rave reviews, including Ian Wooldridge of the *Daily Mail*, who devoted almost his full column to my book.

Ian told me he receives an average of 200 books a year from hopeful sports personalities anxious to receive a mention in his column. The majority, he said, are ghost-written rubbish and immediately discarded. For me to be bestowed the honour of headline proportions from such a distinguished writer was the icing on the cake, and made all the sweat and toil of writing the book all the more worthwhile.

Ian offered to send the book to David Beckham, but I doubted he would be interested – raking in his fortune from various ventures and living a fabulous lifestyle would afford him little or no time to read a book which to him was ancient history! Nevertheless, over the following two or three weeks the *Daily Mail* offices in London were inundated from readers anxious to get a copy of the book.

My phone began working overtime as my wife Norma and I set about sending books to all parts of the UK and beyond, particularly to Western Australia, New Zealand and, surprisingly, the United States. Because I did not have the benefit of a publishing company, the *Daily Mail* was not allowed to include my postal address, otherwise I am almost certain the majority of the books I had had printed would have gone to *Daily Mail* readers. It was music to my ears when readers rang me to say how much they enjoyed the book. I also received numerous letters, some of them intimating that they would look out for the next book! Ian Wooldridge also maintained that with the right backing, in other words a publishing company, I'd have sold a million copies!

Of course the *Daily Mail* was not my only publicity outlet. Graham Kelly, the former secretary of the Football Association, wrote a glowing article for the *Independent*, as did John Gibson of the *Newcastle Evening Chronicle* and the newspaper that carried my name during my eight years with Port Vale – the *Sentinel*. Radio BBC Newcastle gave the book excellent coverage, and I was invited on the popular Julia Hankin programme for two half-hour sessions. Other interviews on Radio Newcastle were conducted with Mike Barr on his daily morning show.

To receive such media coverage was heart warming, but the response on the sale of the books was disappointing. I thought my main source of interest in the book would be my local community of Amble and District, where I was a well-known figure, and also in Stoke-on-Trent where I'd made my name as a goalkeeper with Port Vale. Also on the downside was the total disinterest of my former club Newcastle United, where I had begun my career as a 17-year-old, and hailed as a future international.

Stan Seymour, the former England and Newcastle outside left who later became a Newcastle director, paid me a great compliment when he told me I was the best young keeper he'd ever seen. Several years later Jackie Milburn backed up Seymour's assessment but was scathing of the club's apathy and total disregard for my well-being when I was 'written off' and thrown on the scrapheap at the age of 22. The reason for that is, of course, documented in *"Hands, Feet and Balls"*. The final insult was that book being sent back to me with a brief letter explaining that Newcastle United only dealt with products actively involving the club. Nothing could be more blatant than that.

My good friend Colin Askey, Kenny Griffiths and myself – the three remaining members of the 1953-4 team – were instrumental in the sale of the book. Colin received the printed books in boxes of 20. I received 700 at my home in Amble and it was at that moment that the realisation, the enormity of the task facing Colin and myself, became apparent. It was obvious from the start Colin and his wife June could not possibly take on such a daunting assignment – the sheer quantity of books would almost certainly have strained the bond between them. Colin quickly made the decision to send several hundred books to the Port Vale Social Club where one might have expected a reasonable show of interest.

What transpired was a tale of total apathy. Vale were in the doldrums due to bad management and clashes between various individuals striving to take control of a club in debt, and were in danger of becoming insolvent. Once in the hands of a receiver, the club faced the possibility of being thrown out of the league. Under the circumstances my book was the last thing on the minds of Port Vale, it was more of a hindrance, in fact. The situation remained like this for many months before at long last, thankfully, common sense prevailed – a consortium took control with a clear vision that Port Vale FC must come before any individual. Success on the field is paramount of course and it is up to every member of the club – the directors, training staff and players – to pull together to bring about a resurgence of the club and make it worthy of the nickname the Valiants!

Before leaving the subject of *"Hands, Feet and Balls"*, it would be remiss of me to omit an important episode which occurred during my first visit to Thailand. Norma and I were on vacation with our son Gary, in Bangkok. It was here that I met up with Roger Crutchley, the sports editor of the *Bangkok Post*, Thailand's premier English-language newspaper. After reading my book Roger was more than complimentary and responded with almost a full-page spread which covered many highlights from my career and a headline blazing: 'Ray King is not a household name – but he should be'. I'm still working on it, Roger!

Roger in fact has written a book of his own about his experiences of living in Thailand. It is quite hilarious. I'm sure he won't mind me relating one of his stories, all true of course. He and his housekeeper were standing on the pavement hailing a taxi to go on a shopping expedition, or at least that's what they thought. As the taxi pulled up the housekeeper got in and the taxi shot off, leaving Roger stranded – red faced and helpless. Amid Bangkok's traffic chaos it was an eternity before the taxi returned with the housekeeper in hysterics. I too was a victim of taxi-driver syndrome in that city. I took a taxi to the local hospital for a check-up – normally just a 10-minute ride. We eventually arrived after two and a half hours. On the plus side, the views of Bangkok were brilliant! A word of advice to any first-time visitor to Thailand – either learn the language or at least arm yourself with some knowledge of Bangkok because the taxi drivers sure don't seem to have much!

Making money from *"Hands, Feet and Balls"* was a non-starter from the beginning, but writing my memoirs gave me such pleasure as I relived so many memories and images, plus I had the knowledge that a proportion of the proceeds would be given to the wife of a former player who died form the dreaded Alzheimer's phenomenon caused by heading the heavy ball. Many copies have gone astray but providing the recipients enjoyed reading them then all is well and good.

One last little story emanating from the book concerns a good friend of mine living in Amble, Billy Priest. After reading the book Billy chastised me (with tongue in cheek): "What a marvellous book, Raymond," he said. "But you might have given me a mention! Night after night my mate and I took pot shots at you in goal, often when it was pitch dark, there was only the one street light and we went home completely knackered!"

Well...

You did a great job, Billy.

Myself (c) Gary King

My Early Years

From the moment I was thrust into goal as an eight-year-old it seemed destiny was playing its role in my future, and from that first game I knew this was what I wanted to be. I had a natural talent, as all good keepers should. Catching a ball was child's play whatever the weather, and gloves, as far as I was concerned, were merely a hindrance. At an early stage I developed the skill of catching the ball one-handed, practising for hours on end instructing my playing pals to cross the ball from various angles and harass me as I came off my goal line to collect. It was all wonderful training which stood me well in future years.

On the other hand, I had not at that time perfected the art of dealing with one on one situation – diving at the feet of an oncoming attacker. I received several serious injuries in these collisions, being kicked on the head and sustaining a double fracture of the jaw. Serious though they were, the injuries were all part of my learning.

Now, having reached my 80th year, my mind wanders back through all those years, some wonderful memories and others not so wonderful. Ian Wooldridge, the *Daily Mail*'s celebrated sports writer who wrote of my book in such glowing terms, said he didn't know how I survived the age of 11! Even my own doctor is baffled as to how I played any sport at all.

I was born with a spine defect which to all intents and purposes should have prevented me fulfilling the dream of becoming the world's best goalkeeper. My doctor maintained it was a miracle I'd survived a professional career, another reputable sports writer described me as an enigma – with the talent I possessed why had I not gone on to be one of the all time greats? The answer to that question is simple: injuries, from the age of 18, in fact, beginning during my Army days.

My own question is why did I succumb to a catalogue of broken wrists? I doubt I will ever find out. The Army injuries occurred long before the broken wrists syndrome. Playing for a regiment in a 'hospital cup' – very aptly named – I incurred synovitis of the knee. I had to endure nine weeks in splints and was told by the specialist that my playing days were over – at the age of 18!

Having recovered from that, I promptly returned to the same hospital three months later with a broken first metacarpal (my thumb). The doctors and nurses were so pleased to see me – it seemed obvious I'd taken a great liking to the place. Over the years I have tried to analyse life and its mysteries – why are we here, what is the meaning of it all? But of course there is no answer. The great Sir Harry Lauder, a Scottish comedian during the early part of the 20th century, had the right philosophy when he wrote and sang:

Keep right on to the end of the road,
Keep right on to the end.
Though the way be long, let your heart be strong,
Keep right on round the bend.
Though you're tired and weary still journey on
Till you come to your happy abode.

This is how we must all face life if we wish to survive all those trials and tribulations along a sometimes hazardous journey. My son Gary and I do at times have our different opinions, but one thing we do agree upon is that mind over matter is essential in our everyday life – to give in to frailty is the gateway to weakness.

My First Ever Football Match

Memories from far back in my childhood often come to me. For instance, the first time I ever watched a football match was with my aunt and uncle at their Ashington club with my mother, father and brother George, who was then five – a year and seven months older than me. I didn't have a clue who the teams were nor did I really care for that matter, but my memory holds vivid images of certain aspects of that match.

Apparently the game was between two working club teams (there were no pubs in Ashington during that period, only clubs, and there were plenty of those). There were large crowds of spectators around the playing area, many of them my uncle recognised having been drinking in his club prior to the match. I can still smell the stench of beer.

Most of the players were also tanked up. But what caught my eye more than anything else was the purple shirts worn by one of the teams – and almost every player wore a cap back to front except the goalkeeper – he sensibly kept the peak in front! I was fascinated by the antics of this goalkeeper. As he took up his position in goal, puffing a ciggy, he strolled up to each goal post and gave them a hefty kick. I didn't know whether this was to test his boots or to ensure the posts and crossbar were secure.

When the game commenced and his goal was threatened he threw his tab to the back of the net until the danger had gone, before resuming his smoking with his back up against the goal post. I vowed then I'd never want to be a goalkeeper!

On the subject of keepers and pub teams, here in Bangkok the rivalry is intense, with players competing from countries around the world – what better course of action can there be to bring harmony to a troubled world? One season there was one particular team – I won't mention their name to save embarrassment – that had not won a game several weeks into the season. Following a 5-2 defeat, the captain of the team was asked why they were performing so badly. His reply was swift and straight to the point: "Well, it's our keeper, he just stands there signing autographs!"

1914-1942
My Family and Our Lodgers

My father, Harry, was not a very tall man, but he was sturdy. He worked as a miner in his formative years and when war broke out in 1914 he joined the Territorial Army, quickly establishing himself as a first class soldier, rising to the rank of Sergeant Major in a comparatively short time.

His emphasis on discipline remained with him for all of his life. Brothers George, Frank and myself were taught his philosophy at a very early age and I'd like to think we carried on those qualities to the letter.

Apparently dad was an excellent sprinter in his youth, but he never kicked a football, not even in anger! His main interest was singing duets with his younger brother, Joe. They were very popular around the local pubs and clubs, with Joe at the piano. Our son, Gary, has inherited his grandfather's singing talent – he certainly didn't get it from me as I couldn't sing a note to save my life.

It does seem rather strange that a man who never kicked a football in his life produced three sons who all became professional footballers.

My mother, Florrie, with three boisterous boys to bring up, was hard-working for most of her life until, inevitably, old age took its toll. When our father lost his job as a check weighman at the local colliery because of his involvement with the mining union, with no dole money or social security in those days, mother became the bread winner – aptly named as she was renowned for her tea-cakes, which were snapped up by the villagers of Radcliffe where all three of us were born. She baked cakes of every description in her old-fashioned coal oven and Women's Institutes and working men's clubs clamoured for Florrie King's cakes.

When we moved to Amble (population: 5,000) she decided to take in lodgers. Father was now working as a gardener in the historic village of Warkworth, earning the paltry sum of £7 a week – hardly a king's fortune.

My mother's parents left her £300 in their will, with which she at once decided to buy a new two-bedroom house in Lindisfarne Road. It cost exactly £300. We thought we had won the Pools!

To be able to indulge in a full-length bath, a far cry from the tin bath that we all used to share in front of a blazing fire, was luxury itself. And that's not to mention a lavvy *inside* the house with proper toilet paper instead of newspaper cut into strips!

With elder brother Frank having left to take up a career with Everton Football Club, George and I continued to sleep together in the same bed. There were previously three of us together, with yours truly 'piggy in the middle' – it's a wonder I wasn't suffocated!

Mum and Dad occupied the bigger bedroom, rightly so, but the prospect of taking in lodgers meant they had to vacate the comfort of the bedroom and sleep on a 'put-you-up' in the dining/lounge area downstairs. How on earth they suffered such discomfort for several years I will never know.

Our first two lodgers were school teachers. Miss Bevan was a young girl taking on her first teaching role having recently graduated from Newcastle University. Mum and dad treated her like the daughter they never had. Mum's first baby was a girl who was still born and they had hoped that I would be a girl! What a disappointment that must have been.

When Miss Bevan reluctantly left to be relocated at a comprehensive school in another area, she recommended us to all and sundry as she had been so happy sharing with mum and dad. Over the next few days there were several applicants from all walks of life looking for accommodation, but again mum plumped for a school teacher, a Miss Paterson, much more mature than Miss Bevan.

Ida, as she asked us to call her, stayed with us for several years, leading up to the outbreak of the 1939-45 war. She left to get married to a policeman and kept in touch for many years.

One would think at that juncture that mum would call it a day. But no, she was determined to carry on taking in lodgers – albeit a completely new type – RAF personnel stationed at nearby Acklington aerodrome when hostilities began in 1939 with the war against Germany.

At that time, married men in the RAF were allowed to bring their wives with them provided they could find suitable accommodation outside the aerodrome. Although married quarters were available within the base, many preferred to live outside.

Between 1939 and 1945 eight couples shared our house. Every one of them up to 1942 remain vividly in my memory – at the end of '42 I was called up for military service.

Fortunately the bedroom had a coal fire grate which was essential during the winter as no central heating was available at that time. In any case we could not have afforded it. The lodgers were allowed mum's kitchen facilities for cooking, and all in all the situation appeared to be most satisfactory.

The first couple came from London – in fact they were real Cockneys and the most delightful characters one could wish to meet.

Although understanding Cockney rhyming slang was difficult at times, mum was enthralled with them, particularly the young woman, who had us in fits of laughter most the time.

Her name was Monica, and when the moment arrived to say goodbye there were tears all round – needless to say it was a friendship that lasted forever.

Our next couple were newly married. Having been unable to enjoy a honeymoon in the normal sense they had had to settle for the unlikely setting of 16 Lindisfarne Road, a far cry from the comforts of a luxury hotel.

Mum and Dad did however give them a warm welcome and helped in some way by presenting them with a beautiful wedding cake with all the trimmings. The young couple, only in their teens, were thrilled to bits.

It was at this juncture that my rather sheltered upbringing was to be unlocked in the most unexpected fashion. My brother George was working as a counter assistant at the local Co-op, while I was serving my time as an apprentice painter and decorator. I had to start work at 8am and mum ensured we were both out of bed at 7am on the dot. Breakfast was on the table by 7.20 – usually cornflakes and jam and bread – we only got bacon at the weekend!

"Early risers early to bed," mum would drum into us. Dad was out every night for his usual pint of beer (or two) but always made a point to be home before we went off to bed.

On the first night of their residence with us, the young couple were rather embarrassed before going to bed – it was a double bed, of course.

Mum and dad put them at ease, explaining that every new couple were apprehensive on their first night and they would soon adjust.

George and I were already in bed, almost dropping off to sleep, when several weird sounds started coming from the couple's bedroom. Half asleep, my immediate thought was that the bride was crying, but George quickly summed up what was actually taking place. I don't need to elaborate here!

Over the following weeks – or was it months? – we were subjected to regular bouts of animated love-making. We only managed to get to sleep by placing the blankets over our heads.

Neither of us mentioned these episodes to mum and dad – sex was not a subject to be talked about in the home, at least not ours. When the couple eventually left, George sighed with relief. Perhaps now we could look forward to an uninterrupted night's sleep!

The next couple, our fifth RAF lodgers, made the experience of the young married couple seem tame in comparison. Form Yorkshire, they were a dour pair, particularly the man, who resembled a Nazi Commandant – short cropped hair with jowls to match.

Our previous tenants had all been friendly and cooperative, but these two were quite the opposite. Nothing mum did for them was cordially acknowledged.

George had by then been called up to serve in the RAF, and at the age of 16 I had a bed to myself for the first time – sheer bliss! Shortly after my brother left home I was unwittingly involved in an event with our tenants.

It was a day when for some reason I wasn't at work. Mum had gone shopping and I was left in the house on my own – or so I thought. I was taken by surprise when our lady lodger appeared in the doorway of the living room dressed in a dressing gown. She looked slightly the worse for wear and appeared to be intoxicated – every indication that this was a woman bored to tears by the life she had become trapped in, living with a man who personified abject misery. Tears were rolling down her face as she sat down beside me, put her arms around me and cried her eyes out.

I was relieved when there was a knock at the door. A parcel delivery man said he had got a dozen packages in his wagon for our tenants. He asked me to help him carry them into the house, which of course I did. The parcels were large, but not particularly heavy and I wondered where on earth to put them. Having sufficiently recovered, the 'dear' lady suggested we take them upstairs to the bedroom and place them under the bed.

Later, when I told mum and dad about the parcels, they were naturally curious as to their contents, although not half as curious as I was. Our tenants refused to divulge that information, but said one would be taken to the aerodrome every week.

However, curiosity got the better of me and I took advantage when our tenants had gone to the pub while my mum was visiting a friend and dad, of course, was also off to the pub.

Although I felt extremely guilty about my actions, I was determined to satisfy my burning curiosity and solve the mystery contained in those parcels. Going down on my hands and knees I reached out to a parcel that had been opened, placed my hand inside and got the shock of my life at the 'thing' was holding. It was a contraceptive!

My imagination ran riot for a brief moment. "Surely they aren't going to use these?" I said to myself. Then common sense prevailed – he was obviously a contraceptive distributor. No wonder my brother opted to join the RAF!

These days we have drug pushers, but it would appear, judging by what occurred in our house, we were innocently involved in the world of condom pushers!

I never knew whether mum and dad knew what those parcels contained and I was too embarrassed to mention such a taboo subject. Soon after this episode mum gave the couple notice to leave forthwith – not surprising under the circumstances. I did feel sorry for my mum who at all times endeavoured to induce a friendly relationship. Thankfully, those two were the only black spots on what was an otherwise happy period of mum's life.

The Green Field

As I draw inevitably to the end of the road, images of early childhood are as vivid as though I were living my life all over again. The Green Field, as it was aptly named, paved the way for my introduction to the football world. With my brothers Frank and George and Les Young, a lifetime friend, I played on that small patch of green at every opportunity.

Les came from a footballing family and even well into his eighties his enthusiasm for the game never waned. A dedicated Newcastle United supporter, he still remains a fan of Peter Beardsley and reckons he was one of United's greatest players. I totally agree with him. Les's father, Joe, managed Alnwick Town with great success, the highlight being an eagerly awaited fixture between Alnwick and Amble when they both played in the Northern Alliance, a league of semi-professionals. Large crowds, as many as 3,000, thronged around the touchlines – they really were halcyon days!

Les had two other brothers, Jack, the eldest, and younger brother Joe. Jack played for Wolverhampton Wanderers pre-war and Joe, although not reaching professional status, was a fine centre forward who sadly died in his early forties. Regrettably, Peggy has passed away and Les has Alzheimer's so my get togethers with Les are sadly no more but when they were regular, the Green Field was usually our main topic.

There is a verse in that well known hymn 'There is a Green Hill' which goes:

There is a green hill far away,
Outside a city wall,
Where our dear Lord was crucified,

He died to save us all.

This has always been my favourite hymn, but I had the words slightly changed to:

There is a green field not far away,
Within the village walls,
Where we played football everyday
Provided we had a ball!

Silly perhaps, but as one gets older we are prone to say and do silly things: it helps to stimulate the brain!

The images grow slightly stronger as I move on to Low Hall Farm where I lived for four years with my parents Harry and Florrie and my brothers Frank and George. We were as hard up as the proverbial church mice but they were some of the happiest days of my life.

The field, or croft as it was better described, behind the outside lavatories became our own little Wembley thanks to the farmer Jimmy Forsyth who allowed us the freedom to play there to our hearts' content. We walked the mile and a half to school with Jimmy's son Joe every morning, with satchels around our shoulders carrying our lunch, which usually consisted of my mother's homemade bread spread with margarine and meat paste, a most boring combination.

We took good care to keep in with Joe as his sandwiches were spread with best butter and fresh meat of some sort and there were always cakes or biscuits, which he often shared with us. Joe acquired his own farm in another area of north Northumberland, but is of course now well retired, leaving his son to carry on running the farm.

My days on the farm and subsequent move to Amble has been well documented, although there was one important item I missed out, relating to how I became a goalkeeper. I told the story of a school game where I was playing inside right when our keeper Harry Breeze was injured so it was decided to put me in goal. What I didn't say was the reason for putting me in goal was because I'd forgotten which way we were kicking – being in goal there was only one way I could kick! I've often thought how fortunate I was for my loss of memory as it proved to formulate my destiny!

One day I was at school, the next day I was working as an apprentice painter and decorator with the firm N and F Young of Amble. So keen was I to start work I was sacrificing my five weeks' school holiday. But money as always was in short supply as my father's wages as a check weighman at the colliery were extremely low.

Elder brother Frank was at Everton FC and brother George was working as a counter hand at the Amble Co-op, so I suppose I wanted to get in on the act – plus my mother liked the idea of me being a decorator with our own house in mind!

Six shillings and eight pence (75p) certainly wasn't a King's ransom, (excuse the pun). From my wage my mother gave me two shillings (20p) pocket money – a huge difference from my usual 2 or 3p!

An eight-hour working day compared to only five hours at school was hard to bear for the first few weeks. Working with men was a new experience and as well as learning the art of the decorating trade I was also treading new ground in the way of relationships in the adult world. Coarse language was common place, particularly on building sites and very quickly I learnt the meaning of words which were not in the dictionary.

Apparently it was normal for apprentices of all trades to be subjected to some form of initiation, which could be extremely embarrassing. In the case of painters, trousers were pulled down and the unfortunate apprentice had his private parts brushed with knotting liquid, which is used as a sealer for knots in woodwork. Being a naïve 14-year-old the prospect of such barbarism was too awful to contemplate, especially when I became aware that knotting liquid set very quickly and immediate action would be necessary to get it off!

During the ensuing weeks I made doubly sure not to be caught in a compromising situation, and it was with great relief when I left the building site for other work where I knew I'd be safe! N and F Young had a reputation as one of the premier painters and decorators in north Northumberland and working for the firm was considered a privilege. As far I knew they employed 20 to 30 tradesmen across Northumbria, as well as several apprentices. To illustrate pen portraits of all those men would fill another book, so I intend to concentrate on those who played a significant role in my early years as an apprentice.

Jack Young was the boss. He took over from his father and Uncle Neil who founded the firm in the late 19th century. During my lifetime I have met many miserable men but none can compare to this chap. Bobby Charlton doesn't even come close! Every morning on weekdays the workers stood outside the paint shop at 8am waiting for the 'great man' who walked from his house 100 yards up the road. One or two of the men would greet him with "Morning Jack," or "Morning boss," and on every occasion the reply was a pained grunt.

He gave instructions to his workers with unabated joy. There were many occasions when I was on the point of running away, but these weren't schooldays – six and eight pence was too much to lose! Once the boss had got the men off to their respective tasks he went back home to have his breakfast and probably a shave.

Some of the remarks made against him, behind his back of course, were quite hilarious. I recall one in particular: "What the hell does Beulah see in that miserable sod?"

Beulah, his wife, was a lovely looking vivacious lady, but it was the same old story – there is no accounting for taste. Yet apparently Jack was the proverbial Jekyll and Hyde – in the evenings he was to be seen in a club or pub as the life and soul of the party and the following mornings it was back to the same old miserable Jack Young, the sod!

His workforce ranged from the sublime to the ridiculous, and as I attempt to bring some of those characters back to life you will see exactly the point I am making.

The first time I met George Beattie I couldn't believe he was a humble painter and decorator. About 6ft 3in tall with sloping shoulders (much like mine are today) he was dressed like a business man off to the office: stiff collar and tie and a reasonable pressed suit. He had a craggy leathered face, a flattened nose and a walrus moustache – the only blot to spoil the illusion was the flat cap perched perilously on top of his head. Once at the work place, off came his jacket, replaced with his white painter's coat and a white apron which was small enough to fit a schoolboy. He really did look a comical figure and although only in his early sixties he looked far too old to be employed in such a demanding profession. However, I must say he was a delightful man to work with, although he did find me an exasperating apprentice at times – in his wisdom and to his credit he tried to pass on to me the basic rudiments of the trade but more often than enough my mind wasn't on painting and decorating, it was focused either on football or cricket.

On one occasion he was instructed to take me with him on a job and the look on his face was like a wounded walrus. "Jack," he said, "not again. The boy has no brains!"

I must say those remarks did hit home, and it was then I decided to pull my socks up. From that moment George (I always called him Mr Beattie) and I formed a strong relationship which lasted until I was called up into the Army at 18.

There was an episode with George which remains clearly in my memory and never fails to bring a smile to my face whenever I think about it. Working on a new building site on a bitterly cold day, the windows had to be glazed and George was given the unenviable task of putting the glass in. With the weather almost at freezing point the putty in the large container had become so hard it was impossible to layer it on to the window frames. To counteract this I was given the task of lighting a fire in the grate of the bedroom to be glazed, using lumps of wood discarded by the carpenters.

There I was in front of a blazing fire warming the putty, manipulating it with my hands to make it flexible to insert on to the frames. Poor old George was up on the ladder waiting for me to hand him the warm putty, saying: "Crimes, Raymond, it's cold out here."

It reminded me of the song 'Baby it's Cold Outside' and I took a fit of the giggles. It did seem so unfair to see an old man struggling on that ladder on a freezing cold day with his eyes and nose running, desperately trying to insert the putty, using his other hand with the aid of his apron to wipe his eyes and nose.

"Crimes, Raymond I can't damned well see," George complained. That was the nearest I ever heard George come to swearing. I cannot remember exactly if he managed to get all that glazing completed but it was certainly a day never to be forgotten.

My lasting memory Mr George Beattie was meeting him on the High Street dressed like an archetypal English aristocrat with his natty trilby hat, immaculate lounge suit with a rose in the button hole, and a walking stick – one of life's real gentlemen.

As well as learning the art of painting and decorating I was also coming to terms with adult life and all its ramifications – backbiting jealousy, even hate, generated in this world I had been thrust into, a far cry from my innocent schooldays where one felt snug and secure. It was a fascinating experience working with different tradesmen, all with their different views on life. I became a good listener, hearing various aspects of their hopes and fears.

Wilf Park was another of life's mysteries. Any stranger meeting him would never have guessed his occupation – he exuded a touch of class which in no way is a slur on the trade, but a solicitor or bank manager would seem more befitting of his general demeanour. Quietly spoken but with a ready dry wit he did not suffer fools gladly and anyone who crossed him would be subject to the sharp end of his tongue.

He had nicknames for those he disliked – Bob Scott was Scob Rot and Jackie Fenwick was The Little Jap. I was soon to find out these unsavoury characters never had a good word to say about anyone, including me, even though I was only 14. Jealousy, according to Wilf, was their main reason for such hostility and because my brother Frank was a goalkeeper with Everton I became the butt of unabated sarcasm.

Away from the biting and snarling generated by a section of the male fraternity there were so many good things associated with the everyday events in the trade. To watch Wilf Park demonstrate his skills as a paper hanger was an absolute delight, and like the man himself class was written all over him – George Beattie and Wilf Park were in a league of their own.

Albert Mitchell was a larger-than-life character who hailed from north Northumbria, big in stature and extremely outgoing, some would say loudmouth, personality. I did like Albert despite what some of his workmates might say, at least he expressed his opinions without prejudice and he was no hypocrite. Albert rode his motor bike, with me on the pillion, to Stannington Hospital, a distance of 20 miles or so every morning at 6.45am in all kinds of weather, wearing no helmet. This was the time when war was declared on Germany and rumours that we were being invaded necessitated a hasty retreat back to Amble, leaving paint pots and brushes to fend for themselves!

Albert was called up to the Army shortly afterwards. Wounded in action, losing an eye in the process, he never recaptured his happy go lucky attitude to life and died at a comparatively young age.

So many memories and stories to tell but not enough time and space to chronicle it all – suffice to say the decorating trade taught me a great deal but it is the men I worked with in the brief period of my employment with N and F Young that stirs nostalgic moments. Here are a few of those characters:

Ned Nixon was normally a mild mannered man, but when something or someone upset him whatever was in his hand at the time – paint brush, emulsion brush – would be readily brought into action against his protagonist.

Eddy Young, not much older than myself, was an apprentice every firm in the country would gladly employ. He was the complete all rounder, whether it be painting, paper hanging, stain graining or sign writing he could do it all in a short space of time. With his flat cap perched squarely on his head it was obvious he loved his work. Never without a cheery smile and pleasant demeanour, it must have come as a big disappointment to Jack young when Eddy decided to purchase a newsagent's in the town and leave the painting and decorating trade at an early age.

Jack Darling, who spent most of his decorating years with the firm, reminded me recently of that fateful day when as a 14-year-old I fell 40ft or more from two extension ladders strapped together and lived to tell the tale! However as was the case during my football career (there were at least two occasions when Newcastle United and Port Vale should have been sued) I had no one to back me up – but of course that is the story of my life. My problems are miniscule compared to those of Jack and his wife Bridget, who lost their only daughter, newly married and with so much to live for. This is only one of the mysteries in life that will never be solved – why does one person die but another doesn't? Sadly both Jack and Bridget have now passed away also.

Willie Moffatt, at 6ft 2in, was a complex character who kept himself to himself and amused workmates by running up and down the ladder to keep himself fit. He and his butcher brother Andy were keen cyclists and thought nothing of popping up to Edinburgh on a Sunday – there and back only a 180-mile round trip!

Ronnie Craggs, Steven Wardrobe, Jack Snowden and Raymond Hall (who christened me 'Mondy') were among the other young (at heart) decorators with whom I came into contact from time to time.

Two characters who were well past their sell by date were given employment by N and F Young not because of any skills they had but because they were related through marriage – Foster (Foss) Rowell's sister Beaula was of course Jack Young's wife and Bob Pringle was the brother of Florrie Mitchell, Albert's wife.

My main story is focused on Foss Rowell, a man of considerable talent, not I hasten to add in any way connected to the painting and decorating trade, but in the art of thieving. Scob Rot did not even become close! I worked with Foss on several schemes and although he became quite proficient at window glazing his main preoccupation was how much swag he could collect on his daily rounds. Instead of serving my time in painting and decorating I could easily have learned the art of thieving, but I didn't like the idea of serving my time in Borstal!

His most bizarre accomplishment was at an Army camp based on the links near Amble. The base was still in the early stages of becoming operational and the whole concept was extremely basic. There was no cookhouse as such and with tinned foods being delivered by the lorry load there was nowhere to store them. The officer in charge and a handful of squaddies were employed on various assignments, preparing for the arrival of the full battalion, but also had to decide where to store the tinned foods. Finally they decided to bury them under the sand dunes, marking the spot so they could easily be found when required.

Foss watched all this with his eagle eye, contemplating how he would carry out his mission to appropriate the precious tins of food, corned beef, hams and tinned fruits in large canisters. At lunch times the 'skeleton' crew left the base for the nearby battalion headquarters, which was an ideal time for Foss to carry out his unsavoury mission.

As soon as they had left the base he got himself a spade and started digging near where the booty had been stored. To make his task easier there were rabbit warrens all over the links so it didn't take long to created a tunnel that he could crawl through, which he did with comparative ease, making two trips to bring out his ill-gotten gains of corned beef and ham. It was of no concern to him that he was covered in sand from head to feet, he had achieved exactly what he wanted, never giving a thought that I might spill the beans, although that never entered my head either until now!

Foss even offered to crawl through his warren a third time to bring me a tin but thankfully I declined. In any case if I had have gone home with the goods my mother and father would have read me the riot act and sent me packing.

Bob Pringle was a completely different character to Foss. His scruffy appearance created a poor image for the illustrious firm of N and F Young. Several of the workforce were appalled with him being employed and vented their feelings to Albert Mitchell to no avail – Albert was doing this to please his wife who understandably wanted to help her brother. The situation was resolved amicably as he was given menial jobs to do and kept clear of the tradesmen!

When he retired, Bob would walk to his sister's for lunch every day, a quarter of a mile, until his feet gave him such pain that it restricted his movements therefore his daily lunch. Bob never married and lived the best part of his life on his own. He died in his eighties.

When Jack Young died of cancer in his early sixties his son John took the reins and quickly transformed the business with his modern thinking, although the workforce is nowhere near as large as it was in my day, N and F Young's reputation as the premier painting and decorating firm of north Northumberland remains intact.

My memories of my formative years are deep, and although there were many moments of downright misery, it was in later years that I realised the important influence of those men I worked with/. I remain ever grateful to Jack Young for having the fortitude to put up with me!

Football Vs Cricket!

Having to end my footballing days at the relatively early age of 34 was a major blow but I do feel had I been playing today I'd have been able to play on much longer. No more are keepers subject to physical contact, which was the main reason for the decision I took, and today a keeper with reasonable fitness can play into their 40s.

It was an even bigger blow when my cricketing days came to an end. Although professional football provided me with a living, cricket was my great love, and had I received a bit of batting coaching from someone like Geoff Boycott I'd have reached County standard. As it was I did play in several leagues throughout the country, the toughest being the North Staffs where most of the teams employed a top class professional – Sir Frank Worral and Sir Gary Sobers played for Norton the club I signed for and played for when my football commitments allowed.

Other great players such as world class spinners Rhamidin and Valentine, the West Indies' Bill Alley and several Australian greats of the 1950s performed regularly in both the North Staffs and Lancashire leagues. It all started for me at Low Hall Farm, near Radcliffe, when I played until dusk with my brothers Frank and George, using a home made bat and a 'sponger' or tennis ball and stumps marked out with chalk on the outside lavatory wall.

However, it wasn't until 1936, as a 12-year-old, that I played for my school team against a Wallsend team which included Jimmy Mullen, later to become an England football international and Wolves outside left.

Jimmy was my roommate in Yugoslavia when England played them in Belgrade and I was reserve keeper. Jimmy said he never forgave me for scoring 50 and winning that school cricket match – it was the first time his team had lost.

At 14 I played cricket for my local team, Amble, in the Alnwick and District League. Every game was more or less a local derby which added extra spice to the proceedings. In my early cricketing days – the 1930s and 40s – the playing areas weren't as pristine as they are today. Much the same is true of football pitches – many now resemble bowling greens.

To bat first was the order of the day so it was essential to win the toss. Batting second could be a nightmare when the wicket was littered with potholes. Clubs didn't bother rolling the wicket at the tea interval so any team fielding second were on to a winner, especially if they had a bowler who could spin the ball.

Alnwick CC, which now plays in the Northumberland League, generally prepared its wicket quite well, but the ground for which most players had preference was Warkworth CC, with its imposing castle in the background. Unfortunately it was rather on the small side which meant a batsman had to hit the ball over the surrounding rail to register a four, and could only score two if it reached the boundary below the rail. This was particularly galling for a batsman who managed an enormous slog which on any other ground would go for six.

I did clear the boundary once, sending the ball over an adjoining field and a road before landing in someone's garden, narrowly missing a window. The owner of the house was in the garden at the time and gave the young lad who went to collect the ball a flea in his ear and told him in no uncertain manner he would not get the ball back if it happened again! Fat chance of that and wishful thinking on my part!

Warkworth holds many memories, particularly the first game I played there as a 15-year-old. Amble CC, next to Alnwick, had the largest population in the league, but our standard of cricket was not of the highest – village teams such as Warkworth, Broomhill and Stobswood had the edge, although many of their players came from surrounding areas. Warkworth, for example, had an opening bowler called Tommy Pickard, who hailed from Amble. He was a powerfully built chap, weighing about 15 stone, and he was quick. Tommy had been an England schoolboy international goalkeeper but as a professional the only club he played for was Barrow, of the third division. Apparently after every match he stuck his chewing gum under the dressing room bench, retrieving it for the next game. I'm assured this is true!

Earlier in these writings I mentioned the Geordie keepers, who for reasons best known to themselves treat me like a leper! Tom Pickard knew who I was but again I was given the cold shoulder when I tried several times to speak with him. One or two of the old-time cricketers said Tom was a loner and rarely spoke to anyone – he obviously led an exciting life!

The captain of Warkworth was a farmer named Harry Green, whose eminence as a cricketer was synonymous with the club. In all the years I played cricket, almost 50 years, I cannot remember any cricketer, and that includes county and international players, that could match Harry Green for style and panache – he was the quintessence of an English village cricketer. He retired from playing at the age of 62 although his love for the game remained until his death in 2002 at the age of 91.

Whenever England toured Australia or the West Indies, Harry was in the fortunate financial position to undertake such trips, accompanied by his long suffering wife Betty, who once said to me: "If Harry is happy, I'm happy." What a wonderful philosophy.

Harry and I made our acquaintance in inauspicious circumstances during my first game for Amble on the miniscule Warkworth ground. Opening the batting for Warkworth, as he had done for many years as he was recognised as a prolific scorer, Harry must have licked his lips at the prospect of scoring a feast of runs against our mediocre team.

I was fielding at point, which is adjacent to the batsman, and Harry wasn't at all happy when he noticed I was almost standing on the wicket – a matter of a few feet from where was taking guard. Pointing his bat at me, he said: "Move away from there sonny, unless you want to be killed!"

Being brash, with the arrogance of youth, a trait which followed me on to the football field, I stood my ground and waited for our bowler, Donny Hewitt, a schoolteacher, to bowl the first ball. It was a dreadful full toss – the ideal delivery for a batsman – and Harry pounced on it like a tiger, with the added incentive of knocking the head off an arrogant young whipper snapper!

He hit the ball in the middle of the bat with considerable force straight at me, and it was only through quick reflexes and self preservation that my hands shot up to cover my face. Miraculously, the ball stuck! Harry was out first ball! If looks could have killed, I'd have dropped dead on the spot, but now I was faced with the prospect of having made an enemy for life.

Thankfully it did not materialise in that direction as for some reason Harry and I developed a strong relationship which lasted until his final days.

I played many more times against Warkworth, although I can never remember scoring many runs, except for the memorable slog which credited me only four, but I did take wickets every time I bowled against them. Harry was my 'bunny' – a cricketing term meaning I always grabbed his wicket.

How on earth did we remain friends? I'd never considered myself a bowler, although I could deliver an in-swinger if the weather was right – that is the summer sea mists, for which Amble was notorious, which would make the ball swing alarmingly at the batsman. Sheer joy for the bowler!

Warkworth were the opposition again when I took five wickets in one match – including Harry's, of course!

It was many years later when we were living in Poole that I wrote an extensive article for the Northumberland Gazette on the players I'd spent many happy years with in the Alnwick and District League. Harry had been particularly pleased with the article, according to my brother Frank who was on holiday, staying at the Sun Hotel in Warkworth.

My Brothers

Frank and George, my two older brothers, have passed on to the 'other side', having reached the end of the road, hopefully to that happy abode! All I'm left with are the images of a sporting life we shared together, those wonderful days when we played to our hearts content on the Green Field and later at the Low Hall Farm. Little did we know that all three of us would become professional footballers, sharing with each other the highs and the lows of life and all its complexities.

Our careers from the beginning were blighted by serious injuries which jeopardised any chance we may have had of reaching the top at an early age At 16, Frank made his first team debut for Everton against Middlesbrough, then played in the local derby against Liverpool at age 17. Unfortunately his opportunities were limited owing to the first team choice of Ted Sagar, who was also England's keeper. Because of this Frank was transferred to Derby County, also in the top flight, and it was here where he received an injury which certainly brought to an end his career in the top flight.

In a game against Stoke City, when Stanley Matthews was at the height of his fame, Frank sustained a blow to his kidneys as a result of a cross supplied by Matthews. As Frank left his line to deal with the cross Freddy Steele, an England at centre forward, jumped up behind Frank and delivered the fearful blow. Frank was carried off the field and out of the game for a considerable period. On his comeback he continued to receive annoying injuries, which depressed him, and he retired from top class football at the age of 22. He joined the Liverpool Police Force, was later transferred to Southport and when war broke out applied to join the RAF but was turned down because of his police role. He combined those duties with ambulance driving when German bombing was causing havoc.

He played part-time for Southport before he was forced to retire because of injuries. His run on bad luck started with the kidney punch from Freddy Steele, who was the protagonist who put me out of the game for a month when he split the webbing between my thumb and forefinger in a practice match – nice chap that Freddy Steele!

In *"Hands, Feet and Balls"* I wrote an extensive piece on Frank's subsequent career, as Leicester City physio and Luton Town physio when they got to the FA Cup Final in 1959. Retiring in his late sixties he developed hip problems, had three unsuccessful operations and spent 10 years in a wheelchair before he died at the age of 86.

Frank played 30 games in the first team for Everton and 32 for Derby County.

Brother George was still in the RAF when I recommended him to Newcastle United in 1945/46. His prowess as a free-scoring centre forward was becoming well documented. He had also run at London's White City, the headquarters of British Athletics, coming second to McDonald Bailey, who was the British Empire champion.

Several English clubs tried to sign George, including Leeds United and Burnley, but when Stan Seymour of Newcastle United heard about him he signed him on the spot without having seen him play.

After several Central League games an SOS was sent out on a Friday night when United's first team were in London for their game against Spurs on the Saturday. Jackie Milburn had failed a fitness test and George, who was due to play for the reserves against Sheffield United at St James' Park, had to catch the first available train to London. Coincidentally I'd come home on an unexpected weekend pass from the Army and had been selected to play in the reserves game. Although I was disappointed we would not be performing together, the opportunity to play at White Hart Lane against one of the country's top clubs was a dream come true.

The result was 1-1 and George received rave reports in the Sunday newspapers. Former Arsenal and Scotland star Alex James, writing in the *News of the World*, awarded him man of the match and rated him quicker than Jackie Milburn.

United went on to Coventry the following Wednesday and George retained his place even though Jackie was reported fit. Joe Harvey told me some time later that Jackie didn't relish the prospect of playing against George Pryde, a centre half who had a reputation for committing his opposition centre forward to hospital!

It was obvious from the start that Pryde had read the Sunday reports on George, and after only a matter of minutes when George went up for a head on goal, Pryde thumped him in the back with his knee. George was carried off the pitch and took no further part in the match. 'Wor' Jackie certainly knew the games to miss!

George never really recovered from that experience and was later transferred to Hull City, where the great Raich Carter, a former Sunderland star, was player-manager. From then on George became a journeyman. He went to Port Vale, which was fortuitous for me as he recommended me to the club that gave me the opportunity to resurrect my career, culminating in an all-time defensive record and selection as one of England's keepers for the 1954 World Cup in Switzerland.

It was at Barrow that George really came into his own again, becoming the league's highest goal scorer. Bradford City then came in with an offer of around £5,000 which Barrow readily accepted – to them in those days it was a fortune.

George continued his travels after two seasons with Bradford, moving to Gillingham and subsequently to non league Kings Lynn, finally ending his football career as player-coach with Ely City, a minor team playing in the Cambridgeshire League.

After more than a decade of swings and roundabouts it was at Ely that he fulfilled his ultimate destiny. The team enjoyed a great deal of success under his leadership and reaching the first round of the FA Cup against Torquay United was the icing on the cake.

When he decided to retire from the game George continued to live in Ely with his family, wife Brenda, son Bruce who was a fine cricketer for Cambridgeshire, and daughter Jackie. George built up a successful chiropody practice and made himself a reputation as a snooker player, being chosen to play against Steve Davis, at the time world champion, in an exhibition match.

During the war his ship was torpedoed by the Germans and he survived several hours in the water before being rescued. He never talked about the ordeal. Two years ago he died, suffering from the dreaded Alzheimer's disease resulting from his prowess for heading the heavy ball. George, like all of us, was an all-round sportsman. Frank and George have paid the price, but if they were asked to do it all again, they would.

1942
My Army Years

I would be sorely disappointed if I failed to relate two very special happenings which occurred during my army term in 1942. To many readers, especially those who don't hail from the North East of England, my first recollection may be of total insignificance - but to me it remains a special, momentous occasion.

It was my very first 48-hour pass, having served a year which seemed the longest period of my life. A year which was crammed with many incidents, but I remember them as though they were recent events. Three months of sheer torture, crammed into Nissan hut together with 30 other unfortunates, which I described in ""Hands, Feet and Balls"".

In appalling weather conditions, I experienced freezing cold winds which almost cut you in two – it couldn't have been any colder in the upper regions of Siberia!

Once the initial 6 weeks training had been completed, I was assigned to the 3 inch mortar section, which I hated from the start. Transported to the desolate Shap Fell, which must be the coldest providence in the country, with hands frozen stiff we had to insert 'shells' into the mortar barrel, sliding our hands down the sides very quickly otherwise they'd be "blown off". Can you imagine my feelings at the thoughts of such an event happening? There would have been no career, and no book called "Hands Feet & Balls"!

My immediate thoughts centred on that one issue – how was I going to get out of this mess? As events unfolded, I did get out of it in the most unexpected circumstances.

My footballing exploits with Newcastle Utd. had been noted by the battalion's sporting fraternity, and I was installed almost immediately into the battalion team – not as goalkeeper, but inside right! Their current keeper was Bill Shortt, who later became Wales' regular keeper – I played against him much later when I was with Plymouth Argyle.

After only a few games at inside right, the opportunity to resume my goalkeeping position came when Bill left to join another unit. Back in familiar territory, I did my part in helping the team through to the final of the 'Hospital' Cup final, which was to be held at Carlisle Utd's ground, Brunton Park. "Hospital" was the operative word, because it was where I ended up having received a horrific kick to my left knee – this was my first indication that playing for Newcastle Utd was not to my advantage! Nine weeks in hospital, encased in splints, with a knee filled with fluid, then just to sweeten the blow I was then immediately cast as a B2 category (down from an A1) and at the age of 18, my short career was ended before it even began!

As I lay in the bed of Carlisle Infirmary, looking down at my left leg swathed in heavy bandages and splints from thigh to foot, the words coming from the mouth of the hospital surgeon filled me with trepidation.

"King, I regret to say this to you, but you will never play football again. You are diagnosed as a synovitis victim, which means your knee is very badly swollen with synovial fluid and the condition will continue to deteriorate throughout you lifetime."

He went on: "You will now be categorised from being an A1 soldier to a lower grade of B2."

He didn't say I was no good for the Army, just that I should forget any sporting dreams! But this leg was not going to stop me! Here I was, 18 years of age, being told my sporting life, which had only just begun, was to all intents and purposes at an end. This footballing injury was the first serious mishap I sustained, but within a matter of weeks I was back with my unit at Durranhill Camp Carlisle taking part in a 10-mile forced march with full pack, rifle and helmet. I came in first out of 30 and received a fresh egg from the physical training officer who offered me a place on his gymnasium staff – and I was AB2.

Before sustaining the knee injury, caused by a direct kick during a Hospital Cup game, taking goal kicks with either foot had never been a problem. Afterwards it was never quite the same again, even though my mobility wasn't impaired and kicking out my hands was adequate, although lacking power. It is remarkable when one considers the diagnosis of the Carlisle surgeon, and here I am writing in my eighties having fulfilled a lifetime of sporting memories, it is only now that my knee is beginning to trouble me – thankfully now I no longer have the problem of hoping I can get fit for Saturday's match!

I know I have said the same things over and over again, but I ask the question – why on earth can't present day professional players enjoy the thrill of participating in a wonderful game when they are so highly paid for it? In every game I watch on television the players only have to touch each other and they fall over as though pole-axed, feigning serious injuries in an effort to get an opponent sent off.

An Arsenal–Manchester United game one February not so long ago was an x-rated affair with players' faces filled with hatred for their opponents. The worst example was Wayne Rooney, a talented player without doubt, but the word 'thug' comes readily to mind – in my view he should have been sent off – I'm sure this will happen regularly unless Alex Ferguson calms him down and fines him heavily. Rooney wants to be a man before he is a boy!

At that point in my life, I suppose 'throwing in the towel' would be the easier option, but I had no intention of allowing such a situation to happen.

Once back at base camp, I worked like a beaver to get my leg into reasonable shape, and this I achieved in record time. Within a matter of just 2 months I was back playing in goal, although there was a weakness in my knee and I was unable to take goal kicks with the left leg, which was most frustrating. One might assume my troubles were over as far as injuries were concerned, but I was soon to learn life has its own mysterious pattern, in which we as mortals have no control. Within a very short time I was back in the same hospital bed, this time with a fracture of my right metacarpal (thumb), injured when an opposing player viciously kicked me as I was snatching the ball from his toes. I did wonder, "When will this nightmare end?"

Returning to base camp, I was given the pleasing news I'd been granted my first 48 hr pass – my luck was changing! As my train was pulling into Newcastle Central station, what a wonderful feeling it was to know I was back in the homeland – a place I thought I'd never see again! If that wasn't enough, as I strode out of the station a tram car (yes, tram cars were still in vogue at that time) was moving away, bound for the Haymarket where I'd catch the No. 28 bus for the 30 mile journey to my home in Amble.

Running after the tram, the most wonderful sound penetrated my ear drums; "Howay hinney, Jump on!" It was the voice of the conductress –one of my most memorable memories.

48 hours was, however, gone in a flash and I was back at Durranhill camp to resume what was to be another 3 ½ years of army life!

On the bright side, I did have many friends (as well as the occasional enemy) and I was intent on making the most of the situation we were thrust in to. Ron Suart was a member of the gymnasium staff, and a pro player with Blackpool. It was he who pulled some strings to get me on to the PT staff, a position I'd hoped to acquire as some point. Ron became a very good friend, and invited me to his home on Walney Island situated near Barrow-in-Furness. His mother was a lovely lady, and I still remember her delicious teas – she had so much in common with my own mother.

I was really enjoying myself as a trainee PT instructor; although I had not as yet got my first stripe (Lance Corporals were usually referred to as the lowest form of the human race).

There was, however, a much worse member on the PT staff, and he was the 'self styled black bastard' who ruled the gymnasium staff with a rod of iron – even the officers were afraid of him!

With his black wavy hair, black tracksuit and plimsolls, and even a thin black moustache, he fitted the role admirably! The Gestapo had nothing on him.

I was probably shaking in my shoes on my first confrontation with him! His bark was equally as compelling as his bite, and he warned me in no uncertain manner that I had to attain a high degree of efficiency before I'd be 'awarded' with my 1st stripe.

As I look back to those dark days when the country was embroiled in a World War, thousands of our young lads were blown away, and those that survived came home tattered and torn! A platoon of about 20 of those who came back were allocated at Durranhill, and I was given the daunting task of helping them to begin a reasonable standard of fitness. When the platoon arrived in the gym, it was at that point I realized the horrendous ordeal these war torn lads had experienced. With haggard faces and sunken eyes, they cast their eyes on me as nothing more than this young 19 yr old 'whipper snapper' who had never seen any 'front line' action. I was about to put them through an ordeal which none of them wanted. In my opinion, they needed gentle rehabilitation, but the 'Black Bastard' who watched the procedure from a distance was obviously intent on assessing my performance. He expected strict discipline without any show of 'sympathy'.

The hate in those lads' eyes was plain to see as I was putting them through their paces, but I'd no option but carry out the BB's instructions. My wish to establish myself as a permanent member of the PT staff depended on my exhibition. Thankfully, after 20 minutes he left the scene, and it was then when I relaxed my demeanour and became the real Ray King. The lads responded quickly to my obvious unwinding attitude, and within minutes they were eagerly enjoying animated conversation. Some told me of the dreadful conditions in the Middle East – apart from the threat of death at any time, they had contended with blazing sun, sand storms and inadequate food. I also learned they were attached to the famous 'Desert Rats' and to this day I feel privileged to have met them! However, it wasn't until I took part in a 10 mile forced march with full pack, helmet and rifle together with 30 others in which I came in first, that I was offered my 1st stripe.

No sooner had I joined the elite clique than I was confronted with a situation I hadn't bargained for. As I have already written about this in "Hand Feet and Balls", on that issue I shall not enter too much detail.

The battalion I was attached to were hosting a boxing tournament in our gymnasium, which was an enormous building.

The battalion heavyweight boxer was scheduled to meet the champion of North Western command over 3 rounds. When our man had his first glimpse of his proposed opponent, he immediately backed out! His reason was clear to see – 6ft 5ins in height, built like an ox, a face like granite – his opponent really was a frightening figure.

It was now panic stations – not one of the other contestants would volunteer, and I couldn't blame them!

To this day 66 years on, what transpired later is just a blur in my memory. My 'good friend" Ron Suart somehow cajoled me to take on the formidable task of entering the ring, against an opponent who just looking at you scared the living daylights out of you!

6'2" but resembling an over grown leek, I had never been in a boxing ring before - although my brother George and I had donned the gloves as kids. I don't think that was much preparation for such a contest as this.

The gymnasium was packed to overflowing with spectators who must have been astonished when taking in the spectacle that unfolded before them. Their immediate thoughts must have been they were going to witness a massacre of gigantic proportions. On the other hand, my turn of thoughts centred around one word – survival! It was imperative I not allow this giant of a man to hit me first, otherwise there were only two possible words – 'Contest Over!'

From that very first bell, I tore into him like a maniac with arms which seemed to sprout from every direction – perhaps this was the reason comedian actor Terry Thomas labelled me with 'octopus' arms, following a FA cup match.

I continued in the same vein for two rounds, never 'letting up' for a second, until my arms felt like lead. Thankfully, my opponent only succeeded in catching me with an occasional glancing blow on the top of my head. As the bell rang for the 3rd and final round, his second threw in the towel – I'd won on a technical knockout! What a relief that was – I was champion of North Western command after only one fight: I retired on the spot!!

Never in my wildest dreams did I think I'd rise to the dizzy heights of becoming a boxing champion, when my main object in life was to become the world's best goalkeeper!

So much was crammed into my first years of army life – a year which seemed to go on forever. Two lengthy stays in hospital, becoming a physical training instructor, winning the 10 mile forced march, winning an army cup final medal and becoming a boxing champion!

It was all too much!

Deliberate Acts of Violence

I am often asked if I am bitter at the way my life has been subject to such a series of misdemeanours appropriated by individuals who were intent on causing me serious injury. In my younger days my answer would have been a definite no – but now in my dotage my views have altered considerably to such an extent that the answer to that question would be a positive yes. In my youth, life was full of expectation, the challenge of something new and exciting just around the corner. Even if it didn't happen right away, there was always the prospect that it would. I never sat around and moped, thinking about what might have been. I was still young enough and full of energy, ready to take on the world even if I was continually knocked off the top of the ladder – at least I still retained my enthusiasm and a talent no one was going to take away from me.

Now I have all the time in the world to ponder on the actions perpetrated against me they are as clear as though they happened yesterday.

The first two serious injuries I sustained were deliberate acts of violence during my early Army days when still a teenager – my football career was threatened barely before it had begun. The broken wrists syndrome over a three-year period is a mystery no one seems capable of explaining to me to this day. I worked as a painter from the age of 14 until call up into the Army at 18, and the work involved – painting, washing ceilings caked with old whitewash, stripping off wallpaper six or seven layers think – gave me the strength to punch the heavy ball as far as the half way line. I also drank gallons of milk which is full of calcium – but the mystery remains unsolved.

The perpetrators who were responsible for breaking my jaw and my nose were amateurs, but at least they have apologised, even if it did take several decades to do so. On the other hand, Freddy Steele, Arthur Rowley and Jock Gardner, professional international footballers, were intent on causing me serious injury.

Steele in particular, my own club manager, was responsible for the most vicious act of all when he deliberately kicked me on the hand during a club practice game, splitting it wide open and putting me out of the game for a month – all because my brother George scored the only goal of a match for Bradford City!

In today's football climate any player subject to such an act would have no hesitation in suing the perpetrator but in those days we had no one to represent us. Taking the broad view however, what happened to me was only a slight aberration compared to the horrendous events which happened in New York and Thailand and all those other countries around the world where the killings and violence go on and on. However, human nature being what it is we are all guilty of self preservation and I am no different to anyone else. There is a popular saying: "Life is survival of the fittest." I don't know about the fitness part but I'm still aiming to hang on in there!

Image (c) Smith Davis Press

1941-1947
Not a Real Geordie

I was regarded in some quarters as a Mr Nice Guy but once on that field my image was in complete contrast to my normal demeanour. One had to adopt an aggressive attitude, otherwise there was no chance of survival. Timid goalkeepers were doomed. In my opinion, the only centre forward in recent time who would have relished a confrontation with the keeper in my day would be Alan Shearer. Alan was not afraid to go in where it hurts, which has been proved when one considers the number of serious injuries he sustained during his long career.

A national Sunday newspaper writer said in his column some time ago that Alan was a miserable character, lacking in charm and considered a loner by general consent. Not having met Alan I am in no position to question that judgment, but having seen him interviewed several times on television, he comes over as someone who speaks with a lot of common sense. He is a rarity in that respect.

Alan's alleged surly disposition reminds me of something said by Harry Haslam, the Luton Town manager when I was the youth manager. Whether he addressed his remarks to me or not I wasn't quite sure, but he regarded all Geordies as miserable moaning bastards and claimed to have never met a congenial one.

I asked him: "In that case, why did you appoint me?"

"Well, you're not a real Geordie, are you?" he replied, and walked away! He was of course right in that respect as I come from Northumbria but I am still tarred with the same brush as Alan.

Reg Drury, the former chief sports editor of the *News of the World* who sadly died in a road accident in 2003, also considered many

Geordies uncommunicative, including my brother Frank, who I must admit wasn't easy to respond when confronted with strangers. Reg was a good friend of mine for many years and both he and his wife Cepta spent a short vacation at my home in Poole, Dorset. Talking to Reg took me back to when I was a 17-year-old keeper making my mark in the football world.

I had the experience of playing against three Geordie keepers, all top class. But the memories are not ones I cherish. Sam Bartram, the former Charlton Athletic keeper, was by repute the best uncapped player of the war years. It was the early part of the World War Two when I was in goal for Newcastle United playing at Bootham Crescent against York City, for whom Bartram signed as a guest keeper (permissible during those war years).

In that same game Tom Finney, the great Preston North End outside right, guested for United. Tom and I formed a great friendship, which happily remains today. On the other hand Bartram declined the handshake, which is normal procedure before the game starts, and was equally lacking in affability at the end of the match.

On another occasion Ray Middleton of Chesterfield (and later Derby County) was my opposite number in a game at St James' Park, and once again I was given the cold shoulder. Many years later our paths crossed again when I succeeded him as manager of Boston United, who were at that time playing in the Midland League. During my three seasons there I occasionally arranged benefit matches for Boston players who had contributed sterling service to the club. On one particular occasion the player in question asked me if he could invite Middleton to play in goal, to which I agreed. I also extended invitations to great players of the past including Wilf Mannion of Middlesbrough and England, Len Shackleton of Newcastle United, Sunderland and England, Jimmie Mullen of Wolves and England and Eddy Baily of Spurs and England – a formidable range of celebrity.

It was quite a surprise when Middleton arrived with Brian Clough on his arm, metaphorically speaking. Before and after the match I cannot remember one instance when those two communicated with any other members of this star-studded line up. It was particularly noticeable during the customary social get together – normally an enjoyable event for ex-players to relive some of their memorable experiences. Middleton and Clough sat huddled together the whole evening, deep in conversation. Len Shackleton – not one to mince his words – voiced his disapproval with stinging criticism in a familiar verbal onslaught. I shall offer more on Brian Clough later.

Jim Strong, formerly of Burnley, hails from Morpeth, 14 miles from my home town of Amble. Jim was another goalkeeper of repute who gave me no welcoming handshake before or after a fourth round FA Cup game at Turf Moor when I played for Port Vale. One other keeper from the north-east, Tommy Swinburn, a regular for Newcastle United pre-war and still first choice when I signed for United in 1941, sticks in my mind for his less than welcoming demeanour. Following my initial two reserve games I was selected to play in the first team where I remained until called up at the age of 18 for Army service, which put a temporary end to my United career. Not once did Swinburn make his presence known to me even though he visited the dressing room and talked with other United players.

In 1945/46, with the end of the hostilities with Germany and Japan, football was returning to normal, although still on a regional scale, north and south providing their own competitions. The war was over but I still served a further two years before being demobbed in May 1947. On the bright side I was allowed to continue my association with Newcastle United – they recalled me when they learned I was once again available, taking over once again from Tommy Swinburn. Obviously Tommy was upset to be superseded by this young upstart for the second time and his attitude remained the same – I was given the cold shoulder.

Now that I think about it Tommy Swinburn should have been thankful he regained his place in the team when I was called up – and then again when my whole Newcastle United career came to an end because of the broken wrists syndrome. Like the rest of my United team mates during the war I could have taken the easy way out and got myself a job like Jackie Milburn and some of the other lads at a colliery and continue playing for United on the Saturday. But that is all very well in hindsight – I have no regrets on the long and eventful journey that I have taken through life's highway.

My experiences with those Geordie goalkeepers was my first realisation of the amount of jealousy and envy connected not only to football, but to life in general. What a complete contrast then when I was selected as one of the goalkeepers to take part in the 1954 World Cup in Sweden. To play for England must be every Englishman's ambition and at the age of 29 I felt at long last my impossible dream had become reality. The first two footballers to congratulate me were Bert

Williams of Wolves and Ted Ditchburn of Spurs, two of England's finest keepers. It had been expected they would be automatic choices to take part but to be left out to accommodate a third division keeper must have been galling for them. If it was, they didn't show it. Every one of the keepers I've mentioned would have cost a fortune had they played today, particularly Williams and Ditchburn.

1946
Playing Under Stress

It is ironic that the two finest saves I ever made were accomplished when I was playing under severe stress. The first was at Barnsley in the second round of the FA Cup in 1946 when I was still playing for Newcastle United. It had not at that time been confirmed that I was playing with a broken wrist, even though the pain was becoming increasingly unbearable.

In the pouring rain, with a ball as heavy as lead and a crowd of 30,000 roaring them on, Barnsley were awarded a penalty. There have been many conflicting opinions in books as to who actually took the penalty, whether it was George Robledo (later transferred to Newcastle) or George Milburn, cousin of Jackie. Whoever it was does not concern me, what I did know was he could really whack a ball, as I can verify to my cost. In diving to my right I punched the ball with the broken wrist over the main stand into the car park beyond. Jackie Milburn said it was the finest penalty save he'd ever seen and later paid me the compliment of being the best keeper in the country at the age of 22. He also condemned Newcastle United with regard to their shabby treatment of me when it became apparent I could not carry on playing with the condition I was in.

To play 15 games with a broken wrist against hardened professionals does seem highly improbable, but the facts speak for themselves. My last match for United was against Bolton Wanderers at St James' when Nat Lofthouse was making a name for himself at centre forward. Apart from being my last game for United the match was of special significance because the previous week Bolton had played Stoke City at Burnden Park when a stand collapsed, killing 30 people.

Before our game both teams stood in the centre circle as a token of respect for one minute and 63,000 spectators stood in absolute silence – probably a fitting moment for me to say farewell to the United fans who had been so supportive.

When I view the game as it is today I feel saddened to think a top club like Newcastle United never wrote to me offering condolence or financial inducement of any kind, yet they can afford to pay enormous fees for players who in turn become millionaires.

Eight years after that penalty save, the stop I made against Leyton Orient in the sixth round of the FA Cup was hailed by newspapers as the save of the season, but *Daily Express* sports writer Bob Pennington went one further, describing it as the save of the century! I was like a twirling leaf floating through the air! The remarkable thing about this save was, again, my physical circumstances – I was playing with a poisoned foot which had been bathed the whole of the previous night by Ken Fish, the club trainer and physio. To enable me to get on the pitch Ken borrowed a boot from the opposing team. It was so old it must have been discarded from World War One – it was also two sizes too big!

Winning 1-0 with only minutes to go a snap header from George Poulton was destined for the top left hand corner of the net. From a standing position I performed my ballet twirl to flick the ball over the bar. My brother George, who was watching the match, closed his eyes. He couldn't believe I'd made the save. My team mate Colin Askey described it a better save than Gordon Banks' effort against Brazil's Pele.

Most managers and coaches will tell you they couldn't care less how his team scores a goal providing the ball hits the back of the net – any part of the anatomy except the hand will do. It is the same procedure with keepers and I certainly had my share of saves made with my head, face and backside. The most bizarre was during a game against Cardiff City in the fourth round of the FA Cup at Ninian Park on a frozen pitch. As I took off to make a routine save my foot slipped on the ice causing me to go arse over tit. I lost the ball in flight, but as my legs stuck up in the air I kicked the ball away with my heel. We won the game 2-0.

"There's 'Kingy' showing off again!" came my team mates' typical response.

I have mentioned the occasion during my early days with Newcastle United when I saved a penalty between my legs, which was a bit too close for comfort. But in a match against Millwall at The Den I actually did prevent a goal with the most delicate part of my anatomy. Millwall had a player called Frank Neary, a formidable character with the most incredible crab toes I've ever seen. When he kicked the ball it would swerve in all directions – and that was with the leather ball – heaven knows what he would achieve with the toy ball they play with today!

He took all free kicks, corners and penalties, causing goalkeepers all kinds of problems. It was one of his corners that almost caught me out. As the ball flew in like a boomerang it swerved into the near post and all I could do was jam the ball between my body and the post, bringing tears to my eyes and excruciating pain. The pain would have been much worse had the ball gone in the net.

Albert Stubbins is a name no Newcastle supporter will ever forget. With his ginger hair and flattened nose he was instantly recognised wherever he went in the city of Newcastle. He even resorted to wearing a cap, which he hated, but it didn't seem to make any difference. Albert was a star and he paid the price of fame. From the beginning of my career with United, Albert and I developed a friendly relationship which lasted more than six decades until his death at the age of 84.

Opinion has it that Albert was more than 6ft tall but in actual fact he was only 5ft 10in. The illusion was no doubt due to his enormous shoulders which gave the impression that he was a much bigger man.

The game I remember most vividly was against Blackburn Rovers at St James' Park when Albert scored a remarkable goal, with me playing a minor role in its execution. I raced out of my area, and not being allowed to handle the ball I caught it on the volley, sending it to the heavens with the crowd shouting: "There's 'snair' (snow) on it!"

As it dropped out of the sky Albert nonchalantly caught the ball on his left instep, did a little shimmy to send the opposing centre half the wrong way, then on the half turn volleyed a tremendous shot from fully 35 yards into the back of the net. The keeper never moved.

We beat Blackburn 9-0, Albert scoring five and Jackie Milburn and Charlie Wayman sharing the others. Those really were halcyon days! If only there had been TV in those days, that goal would have been replayed time after time!

Recently *Newcastle Journal* sports writer Simon Rushworth arranged a reunion at a Newcastle hotel for Albert and myself, not having seen each other for 57 years! It was a wonderful occasion and the nostalgia generated from memories of bygone days were discussed with animated enthusiasm. Before lunch we decided to visit the loo, which normally would only take two or three minutes were it not for a middle aged chap, having done what he had to do, shouting excitedly: "Albert Stubbins, I haven't seen you for ages!"

Without pausing for breath he documented Albert's career with incredible accuracy for at least 20 minutes. Poor Albert stood there transfixed, not even getting a word in until I finally grabbed his arm and said our lunch would be getting cold, or something along those lines. As we walked back to the dining room Albert turned to me and said: "Who was that chap, Ray? I've never seen him before in my life."

I replied: "Albert, you must remember, even if your football career did end many years ago people still consider you a legend and think they know you personally."

As we sat down at the table it dawned on us that we hadn't accomplished what we'd set off to do in the first place! As we both got up to go back to the loo, I quickly sat down again and whispered: "You go first Albert, otherwise it may be interpreted that there's something funny going on between us!" Albert's face was a picture to behold!

After lunch we settled down and resumed our reminiscing of days gone by, recalling names of players and grounds we had played on, certain incidents, some amusing and others unsavoury. As we talked I noticed Albert's face take on a blank look. He began to appear rather uncomfortable and our conversation became stilted. He leaned toward me and said: "Excuse me, would you mind telling me who I am talking to?"

This rather threw me off balance and when I gave him my name he still remained rather vague. I knew Albert was in the early throes of Alzheimer's. It came as a relief when he continued the conversation we'd just been having before his memory loss, as though nothing had happened. He even rattled off the 1932 players' names from a game between Newcastle United and Arsenal, which was quite remarkable when only moments before he couldn't remember where he was and who he was talking to – that is a sure sign of the dreaded Alzheimer's. Although Albert was a top class player, like Jackie Milburn he was never a good header of the ball, but I suppose at the age of 84 the problem was simply a case of old age. What horrible words they are!

Albert and I shared a wonderful three or four hours together and when I dropped him off in my car near the shopping centre, where he was still instantly recognised, there were tears in my eyes. Albert

Stubbins was unique both as a talented footballer and a gentleman on and off the field of play. In a touch and demanding game he more than held his own against opponents who asked no quarter and gave no quarter. Albert's powerful build and broad shoulders made him a match for anyone and I can never remember one occasion when he lost his temper.

When he scored, which was often, just like Jackie Milburn he'd run straight back to the centre circle to await the restart. I see players of today going berserk, doing handstands, cartwheels, whipping their shirts off – even Alan Shearer, who ought to have known better, held his arm aloft as though he'd just been pronounced the winner of a boxing contest!

The next thing to happen will be goalkeepers swinging on the cross bar every time they make a brilliant save!

It would be a complete waste of time explaining to young lads of today the contrast in behaviour of those of yesteryear when players of calibre such as Albert Stubbins, Jackie Milburn, Stanley Matthews and Tom Finney played the game with dignity. I was proud to call every one of those great players a friend and I cherish the memories of those days.

The last words Albert Stubbins said to me as we said goodbye were: "Ray, you were a keeper who kept them out the net and I was the one who banged them in!" A fitting comment from a great man!

Third Division Call-up

When I set out on the long and winding road I never realised the many obstacles, events and people I'd encounter along the way – a sometimes hazardous and other times most enjoyable journey.

Throughout the whole of these writings I have endeavoured to portray the events as they happened, and as I occasionally sit back and ponder I'm completely mystified as to how on earth I have stayed the course. After reading *"Hands, Feet and Balls"*, celebrated sports writer Ian Wooldridge of the *Daily Mail* said he was amazed how I'd survived to the age of 11. This comment portrays my life in its true perspective. On reflection I should be grateful to have got so far in the sporting world, but it still bugs me to have been denied, together with my Port Vale team mates, the opportunity to play at Wembley in the FA Cup Final. To be beaten by a fluke goal, a penalty that never was and a legitimate goal ruled out by the referee's decisions was almost too much too bear!

Being selected as the first third division player to be honoured by an England call up, particularly as it was for a World Cup, seemed too good to be true. Before the World Cup I was chosen as reserve to Gil Merrick of Birmingham for a game against Yugoslavia in Belgrade. Just to be taking part in that red hot atmosphere was an experience never to be forgotten. Then to play my first England B game against Switzerland in Basel was, I thought, the beginning of my international career at the age of 29! The playing surface was the best I'd played on since my early days with Newcastle United at Aberdeen's Pittodrie Park – just like a bowling green and the same conditions as Premier League teams play on today.

The game itself was so relaxed and lacking in passion with no challenges on the keeper from high crosses, which seemed strange after the hurly burly of the third division. I said afterwards: "If that is a sample of international football, please give me more!"

To play in the same team as the great Duncan Edwards (later killed in the Manchester United air disaster), Denis Wilshaw of Wolves, and my former team mates at Port Vale, Ronnie Allen and Bill McGarry, who have all passed away suffering from Alzheimer's, was a great experience.

For the following three years I was voted top keeper in the second division by the football writers, but a full England cap eluded me. It wasn't until I received a letter from England manager Walter Winterbottom to apologise and gave me the real reason the selectors left me out in the cold (the manager did not pick the team in those days): because Port Vale wasn't considered a fashionable club it would be demeaning to the England team!

Everyone in this life thrives on a bit of praise, however small, and I am no exception. I have certainly had plenty of criticism along the way, raw dealings and more than my share of injuries so when that bit of praise does materialise I soak it up with great pleasure.

Dickie Cunliffe, the diminutive outside left at Port Vale nicknamed The Pocket Battleship by myself, was the first person who made me realise my full potential. In his broad Lancashire dialect he said to me: "Ray, thee's the best keeper in t'world, tha's nee one to touch thee."

It was said with that lovely cherubic face and a smile so disarming I knew he meant every word. Dickie died in his early forties, a legacy of his heavy smoking, but I still remember him with great affection.

Image (c) Smith Davis Press

Soldier King!

In my days with United, Stan Seymour, a former player who became its managing director, controlled the club in every aspect with quiet efficiency. I had the utmost respect for him. Stan did not forget about me when, at the age of 18, I received the dreaded call-up letter from the Army requesting the pleasure of my company. That 'pleasure' was to last four and a half long years. During that period I received a letter from Stan Seymour which was in effect a glowing testament to my goalkeeping ability. His words are as clear to me today as they were more than 60 years ago. As soon as I became available my place as first choice keeper was secure, he said.

When I eventually informed him of my availability, even though I had another 18 months of Army service, he selected me in the team to play against Bury at Gigg Lane. We won 3-0 and I was labelled Soldier King because of my marching up and down the 18-yard line. It was great to be back! I am still rather unsure why my life turned out the way it did, and one sports commentator probably put it in perspective when he described me an enigma.

It continues to bug me when I think back to those games with United, playing with complete confidence, enjoying every moment and suddenly, as so often in life, the unexpected happens. Punching the crossbar instead of the ball from a Len Shackleton lob at Bradford was a legacy thrust upon me and the primary cause of my last days with Newcastle United. I played 15 games with an undiagnosed broken wrist. Even the RVI Hospital x-rays did not detect the break first time.

The scaphoid bone in the wrist is one of the smallest in the body, but it is difficult to detect and takes nine months to heal. Having these bones broken in both my wrists over the space of three years, and then to receive a double fracture of the jaw was more than I could bear.

To compound matters the player who broke my jaw came to see me years after to tell me he was given orders by the manager to put Kingy out of the game. It was my first game back in goal after three years. Quite recently a man rang me up to say he had read my book and cried all the way through it. He told me it was he who had given those instructions to his player. He wanted my forgiveness before he met his maker. I had no answer to that.

There was never any doubt Stan Seymour had been a star outside left with United. The fact he played many games for England was proof enough. That is not to say his ability and knowledge of the game constituted and ability to coach and manage a team. Stan never gave team talks or worked on any particular strategy, but his mere dressing room presence was such that every player had the utmost respect for him and woe betide anyone not giving of their best.

Stan's only words of wisdom before the players went down the tunnel on to the pitch were: "Go out and enjoy yourselves, boys, but don't come back here if you lose."

Those words, and a tot of whisky from the trainer Norman Smith standing at the door of the dressing room with the bottle in his hand, were sufficient. Since those days football has become a completely different ball game, in my view not for the better. Coaching has become the order of the day, with playing formations frequently being introduced in place of the familiar 2-3-5 line-up which players and spectators could understand with ease. We now employ complicated patterns varying from 4-3-3 to 3-4-3 to 4-2-4. And we hear of the 'diamond' formation! Whatever next?

Football was always regarded as a simple game but today's coaches, with their weird tactics, are strangling what was once the beautiful game. I am in favour of working on set pieces – free kicks, throw-ins and corner kicks – but the general game should remain uncomplicated. In the whole of my goalkeeping career only once was I given advice, when I played for the Football Association at Bristol City's Ashton Road ground. The manager in charge of our team, which included several full internationals, was Bill Nicholson, the former Spurs wing half and later that club's manager. Bill died at the age of 86 in 2004, but he will be fondly remembered as one of football's true gentlemen. His quiet demeanour was in contrast to so many managers and coaches who consider effing and blinding a formula to success – it is little wonder young players are quickly caught up in these ignorant clichés.

Before our game at Bristol, Bill talked to every player individually, stressing particular points about their respective roles. He then talked most impressively to the whole team together. This was the first time a manager had spoken to me about how I should organise a defensive line-up when a free-kick was awarded against my team just outside the box. Bill was never renowned as a genial character, but I made him smile when I told him truthfully I wanted a clear view of the ball and that at all times instructed my team mates to keep well clear.

Only once was I beaten by a free-kick outside the box. It was during my Newcastle days at Everton's Goodison Park, on a pitch that was frozen at one end of the ground and ankle-deep in mud at the other, where the sun had penetrated between the stands. As the kick was taken both my feet were entrenched fully in the quagmire with the ball floating into the back of the net!

I did follow Bill's advice, organising my line-up of four, five or six players, depending on the angle of the kick, but I still insisted on seeing the ball leaving the foot of the striker. Keepers today are continually beaten from these free kicks. David Beckham in particular built his reputation on curling the ball from free-kicks just outside the penalty area.

With so much emphasis being concentrated on keepers organising their defensive line up, referees are favouring the attacking player. Thierry Henry took advantage of this on at least two occasions while playing for Arsenal, scoring a goal when the opposing defence was in disarray – within the rules of course but a bit tough on the keeper.

Image (c) Smith Davis Press

1946-1956
From Quagmire to Quintessential

In a column on Saturday, April 17th 2010 Nobby Piles wrote on the dreadful condition of the present Wembley playing field. It certainly is a far cry from the days when the same pitch on Cup Final Day, the highlight of the football season, resembled a bowling green. In my opinion, to play the semi-final games at Wembley takes away so much of the glamour and prestige that have long been associated with the actual final cup. Now the Wembley pitch is little more than a playing field in a public park. What used to be Cup Final Day at Wembley has lost its magical appeal.

The beautiful, pristine pitches at Eastlands, Old Trafford, White Hart Lane, Villa Park and the Emirates are still immaculate, as we encroach upon the end of a nine month season. I have to wonder why can't the premier football stadium in the country have a pitch of similar grandeur and quality?

As Nobby rightly says, players of today are extremely lucky. For one thing, they are millionaires, and have the good fortune of playing on magnificent playing surfaces throughout the season. Nobby mentions the playing days of George Best and Bobby Moore, but even they both had it better than I did in the 40s and 50s.

I vividly recall playing for Newcastle United in 1946 at Everton's Goodison Park, before a capacity crowd of 70,000. It was there that I experienced playing conditions that were a nightmare, by any stretch of the imagination. Following what had been a heavy frost, one goalmouth was still frozen hard, but the other one was a quagmire in which players were ankle deep in thick mud. This had occurred because there was no grandstand behind that goal, and the sun had penetrated directly through to the pitch.

I only had one pair of boots, and one set of studs which were extremely long. Trying to combat the icy conditions at one end of the pitch was reminiscent of someone taking to the ice rink for the first time. As if that experience wasn't bad enough, worse was to follow. At the other goalmouth, my feet and boots sank into the mud which came above my ankles. Trying to constantly extricate my feet as I dealt with a rampant Everton team remains a clear memory to this day.

It was obvious that the goalmouths had been left untreated, in order to place me in an uncompromising situation. The Everton keeper had two pair of boots, one pair with long studs and another with much shorter studs. My boots had been bought for me by my parents, as I couldn't expect Newcastle United to provide those as well!

During my days at Port Vale, the pitches I played on were often quagmires, particularly during January and February. The playing field at Port Vale was labeled "The New Wembley" when it opened in 1951, but soon became a mud heap extraordinaire. During a game against Fulham in 1956, Fulham was awarded a free kick just outside of our 18 yard area. One of our players stood on the ball and it completely disappeared beneath the mud. I'll never forget the face of the great Johnny Haynes trying to extricate the ball – a picture to behold!

Also during this game, just as the diminutive Fulham left winger Tosh Chamberlain was about to take a corner kick, I was hit squarely in the eye by a clump of mud thrown by a player. Thankfully, the referee spotted my distress. He then proceeded to shock everyone, especially myself, when he walked up to me and licked, yes licked, the mud out of my eye. I have to say that the treatment was most effective. Tosh Chamberlain laughed so much he completely missed the ball, kicked the corner flag, and almost broke his toe in the process! None of the Fulham players would admit who threw the mud but it was a regular occurrence in those days, with the keepers the obvious targets.

There are many stories to tell of mud-laden, icy and bone-hard pitches. In addition, we played with the old leather ball, that would become heavier and heavier as it soaked up moisture throughout the game. It is little wonder that so many players have died from Alzheimer's disease, perhaps as a result of heading that heavy ball. The Newcastle United team I played for have all gone. Charlie Crowe, my very good friend, was the last to go from Alzheimer's just a short time ago. Colin Askey and I are the only two surviving members of the

1953-54 Port Vale team. Sadly, most of them died as a result of Alzheimer's.

1953-4 lineup image (c) Smith Davis Press

1954
Stanley Matthews

I played twice against the great Stanley Matthews – the first time guesting for Chester during the war years when Stanley was in his prime, then later in 1954 when Vale beat Blackpool in the fifth round of the FA Cup. The previous season Blackpool had beaten Bolton Wanderers at Wembley in what was labelled the Stanley Matthews Final.

Football supporters today talk about the merits of George Best and many of the star foreign players, but not one of them could match the skills of Matthews and Tom Finney – remember, they played with heavy boots and a heavy ball!

The Blackpool game at Vale Park was of special significance, particularly as Stan was born within a stone's throw of the old Vale ground in Hanley, so this was a game he desperately wanted to win. To beat them 2-0 was perhaps the most satisfying result of a successful season for us and my personal duel with Stan in the latter half of the game was a truly memorable occasion.

Although playing in his customary position at outside right, he developed a roaming role in the second half, took corner kicks on both sides of the pitch, causing me most problems from the left side as I was looking into a blazing sun which was sinking low and shining directly into my eyes. Stan did not want to miss an opportunity like this. Even though I pulled the peak of my cap well over my eyes, it was impossible to follow the flight of the ball once he had delivered his in-swinging corner. It was by sheer instinct and timing I was able to cover the near post as the ball and gather the ball as it was about to enter the net.

I also challenged him in two one-on-ones, blocking his shots both times. On the second occasion I head Stan mutter an expletive not usually in his vocabulary. As we walked off the pitch at the end, he was clearly disappointed but shook my hand and grudgingly said: "King, you're unbeatable!"

Praise like that from someone of his calibre is praise indeed. I have repeated many times over the years the importance of a reliable keeper and making brilliant saves is an essential part of the job. To remember every save of importance one makes in a long career is well nigh impossible, but there are those that stand out, never to be forgotten.

1955/56
Not Only Boxers Have Head Injuries...

What finer example is there of sheer physical and mental perfection than that of Max Schmeling, the former heavyweight boxer from Germany, who recently died at the age of 99? In an age when sportsmen are dying at a relatively early stage in their lives, it is quite remarkable that Max at times suffered heavy punishment to his body and head, yet survived to ripe old age. We often read in the press of boxers succumbing to chronic dementia – even the great Cassius Clay (or Mohammed Ali, as he prefers to be named) is in the deep throes of Parkinson's Disease, which affects the central nervous system.

Footballers of the 1940s and 50s have died and are dying in their hundreds as a result of the dreaded Alzheimer's phenomenon, caused in part by heading the heavy ball. I have written comprehensively on that particular subject and have been interviewed on radio, but for the time being it is stalemate. Although I cannot comment fully on this controversial subject, behind the scenes activity is being exercised as I write. Information I have received from a coroner who is involved in this issue is most heartening so we trust a breakthrough is not far away.

Physical injuries are bad enough, but when the brain becomes affected life has no real meaning. My own brother George was a victim and I do know what a heartbreaking disease Alzheimer's is. One of the pleasing rules in football today is the substitution system. Not only does it give more opportunities to players who otherwise are confined to reserve team football, but any player who may be struck down with an injury can be readily replaced. It also gives managers an option to take a player off at any time in the game if that player is struggling through lack of form, or not giving of his best.

Goalkeepers appear to be an exception to the rule, even though standby keepers are stripped ready for action, especially in the Premier League. Unless the goalie on the pitch is injured, his deputy merely sits it out, which is most frustrating.

I talk from experience on this issue, which takes me back to the war years when I was in the Army, stationed near Wrexham. The Wrexham FC manager at that time was a wonderful man called Tom Williams – I still remember him with great affection. Although he already had a very good keeper named Whitelaw, Tom wanted me to be at every match as a standby and paid me the same wages as those playing. It was a marvellous gesture on his part which I very much appreciated, but I was desperate to play, and when Chester came along to offer me regular games I could not refuse.

Nevertheless, Tom wished me well, and intimated he'd have me back if it didn't work out for me at Chester where I enjoyed every moment until my wrist was broken saving the Lawton penalty.

I was involved in an important penalty issue in 1955/56 season when Port Vale were facing relegation back to the third division if we lost a crucial game against Rotherham United, who needed at least a draw for promotion to the first division. Port Vale were leading with only minutes to go, when Rotherham were awarded a penalty. I saved it. Vale stayed up and Rotherham stayed down.

There was a sinister undercurrent connected to this story as the night before the game I'd been offered a £2,000 bribe to throw the game – that was big money in those days. This burden placed tremendous pressure on me. Had I informed the manager about the bribe he may have been reluctant to play me, but this was a match I did not want to miss and thankfully I kept that important clean sheet.

Ironically a Jewish Vale director awarded each player with £50 and gave me an extra £50 for saving the penalty. Unfortunately one of the Vale players saw this and complained about it so I handed it back to the director, who couldn't quite believe what I was doing! Stupidly, I banked the money – five years later the taxman took it from me and I paid an accountant £200 for his work!

Had I for some reason accepted that bribe and lost the game, I cannot imagine living with myself knowing I had committed such an act of treachery, but the practice still goes on.

Notable Players

Goalkeepers have been the butt of comedians' jokes throughout the ages, which necessitates the skin of a rhinoceros. Being the last line of defence, any mistake is vividly highlighted, especially in the game today, when television replays the incident over and over again. No goalkeeper is infallible – even those at the top of the profession will commit the odd bloomer.

One of my five C's – control – applies not only to the body but also to the mind, of one's emotions when the going gets tough. For me this was particularly important in the Newcastle United jersey during those early days, when the country was embroiled in a fearsome war with Germany.

As I mentioned earlier many clubs took the opportunity to field guest players and United were no exception. The most notable were Tom Finney (Preston North End), Eddy Carr, a Geordie on Arsenal's books, and George Stobbart, another Geordie who played for Middlesbrough, who at that time, if memory serves, weren't fielding a team. The rest of the team varied from week to week, although the veteran Joe Richardson was a regular at right full back with up-and-coming Dougie Graham at left back.

Many other names are indelible in my memory: the wonderful Scot Jimmy Gordon, another Scot Jim Woodburn, Ronnie Sales, Steve Howdon, Tommy Walker, who played in United's cup final in 1952, at outside right, another Scot Tommy Pearson, at outside left. He was one of the best left-footed players I ever saw.

So many names keep coming back to me – left back Bobby Ancell, Johnny Dixon, who later went to Aston Villa and became their captain, and last but certainly not least the diminutive Ernie Taylor, the smallest player I ever played with or against. To achieve what he did was quite incredible for someone so small in such a physical sport. Not only did he play a large part in United's glory years, the two cup finals in 1952 and 1955, but he also played for Blackpool in their victory over Bolton Wanderers in what was named the Stanley Matthews Final of 1953. He also gained international honours with England, and it is to my ever-lasting shame that I did not select him as one of United's best ever players in the 50 years from 1950 to 2000. Instead I plumped for Len Shackleton, who was of course a wonderful player, but on reflection Ernie should have got the vote.

A lady who read *"Hands, Feet and Balls"* said how much she enjoyed reading it but also chastised me for overlooking Ernie – I hope she is well and notes my change of thought. These were times even before Jackie Milburn came into the picture. It was a great learning process for me, what with players of vast experience and young lads striving to make a name for themselves. Joe Richardson, a wily old bird, was scathing in his attitude towards me because of my dislike to the wearing of gloves, even with a wet and greasy ball, which it was on my debut against Sunderland at St James' Park.

As I mentioned in *"Hands, Feet and Balls"*, without warning he would turn in possession of the ball and unleash a shot at me with considerable force, and in his jocular manner say: "That was just to give you a feel of the ball Ray!"

To recall some of the incidents in those baptism games fills me with pride. Monetary considerations never entered my mind. In any case, the 30 shillings (£1.50) we received for each match wasn't going to change my life! Apart from the Sunderland game, which was played in pouring rain, plus the horrendous ordeal I was forced to endure prior to the match (documented in *"Hands, Feet and Balls"*) there were particular games and incidents I shall never forget.

Following the Sunderland match the team, accompanied by several directors (what a charmed life they led), were off to Central Station where we boarded the midnight train en route to Aberdeen, which at the time seemed a million miles away, for a friendly which had been arranged to celebrate an occasion that I cannot remember. The match was on the Monday so on Sunday we were free to explore the impressive Granite City. After an extremely long journey, during which sleep had been at a premium, none of us felt exactly thrilled at the prospect of a day's sightseeing, but our hosts, who had organised and laid on various attractions, would have been most offended had we shown any resentment.

As events unfolded, the hospitality afforded us was something I've never forgotten. It is a myth that all Scots are stingy – nothing could be further from the truth. At 17 years of age this was a whole new world to me, to play on the beautiful turf at Pittodrie in contrast to St James' Park which had resembled a boating lake on the Saturday. Against an opposition which included several Scottish internationals, it was at this point that the significance and realisation of playing professional football at the highest possible level hit me. I had achieved a dream that few will accomplish.

We drew 0-0. To keep a clean sheet, to be paid £1.50 and a box of Aberdeen kippers – what more could anyone ask for?!

There are other games which come readily to mind, two in particular against Yorkshire teams – Leeds United and Bradford City. Matches were played on a home and away basis – home one Saturday and away the following week. All the teams in the war years were an unknown quantity – it all depended on the players available on the day. Leeds dominated throughout the whole match at St James' Road, which gave me the opportunity to display the talent I was fortunate to possess. The game ended in a 5-1 defeat but from my own point of view it was this game that really endeared me to Newcastle supporters. What a wonderful feeling!

The return match at Elland Road the following Saturday was, to Leeds supporters, a foregone conclusion – if they could wallop us 5-1 at St James' Park just imagine the havoc we would endure at Elland Road.

As events unfolded no one in their right mind could have forecast the end result – we won by a staggering nine goals to one. One would have expected the manager to be 'over the moon' (a familiar cliché!). But strolling towards me he whispered: "Do you realise Ray, if we hadn't scored nine goals we would have lost 1-0." I've never forgotten those words.

As I remember it, one player made all the difference. Ernie Taylor, on leave from the Navy, gave one of the finest exhibitions of inside forward play I've ever seen. For such a small chap his skill in beating an opponent and his supreme passing ability were a joy to behold – he simply tore the Leeds defence apart. How on earth I could leave him out of my best United team for those 50 years is beyond me.

Thirteen years later Ernie and I met again, but this time playing against each other in the fifth round of the FA Cup when he was playing for Blackpool and I was with Port Vale. That game has been well documented, and from the Vale's point of view it was probably the most glorious victory in the club's history.

As one never knew until kick-off which players were turning out for the opposition, many of the teams from lower divisions were stronger than the likes of Newcastle United on several occasions. Bradford City, for instance, were particularly formidable during that period. They had the services of a centre forward named Dougie Reid, on loan from Portsmouth. Without wishing to be disparaging to Dougie he had the most frightening presence of any player ever seen on a football pitch. Anyone who has seen Boris Karloff in the role of Frankenstein will know what I mean. At least 6 foot 4 inches tall, with an enormous build, the prospect of facing up to him filled me with apprehension – and there was not an air raid shelter in sight! Those were early years in my physical development, and to players like Dougie Reid I must have resembled an overgrown leek, which must have whetted his appetite.

Apart from one significant incident I cannot remember too much about the game. I do know we won 2-1. At one stage Bradford were awarded a penalty, and who should take it but the redoubtable Doug Reid. From the beginning of my goalkeeping days it has always been my philosophy never to move until the kick has been delivered. It certainly paid dividends judging by the number of spot kicks I saved during my career. Keepers today are often made to look silly anticipating the striker's delivery and diving the wrong way. Occasionally a striker chips the ball straight down the middle, knowing the goalkeeper will have dived out of the way. Perhaps it may have been a better option had I dived out of the way when Reid delivered his spot kick.

Dougie shot straight at me with such force that the ball stuck between my legs. This infuriated him and he followed up in an attempt to knock me into the back of the net with the ball tightly wedged and causing me agonising pain. Thankfully I avoided his challenge, extracted the ball and threw it round the post for a corner. It was never going to be remembered as one of my more elegant saves but I shall never forget the excruciating pain.

I faced numerous penalties over the years from renowned players such as Tommy Lawson, who broke my wrists, and I always maintain John Charles possessed the most lethal strike – Dougie Reid came a close second.

As I entered the dressing room after the game Joe Richardson, in his inimitable jocular fashion, exclaimed: "Three Balls King!" The title has clung to me for a long time – perhaps it inspired the title of *"Hands, Feet and Balls"*.

Every one of those players is etched in my memory box. They were men who demonstrated their skills on the big stage to an adoring public and to someone like myself, a country bumpkin, the incredible roar from a Geordie crowd was an experience of a lifetime. Sadly, that popular war cry, "Howay the lads", has no place at St James Park these days. I no longer even recognise the stadium.

Again and again, I make the point, referees can win or lose you matches on their decisions. Make him your friend however good he is, because mistakes will be made – after all he is only human!

1956
Black And White

In the mid-nineties I predicted that in 10 years every club in the country would have more black players than white. The percentage hasn't quite materialised as far as that but there are a fair number in every team. It's a far cry from the days when fans threw banana skins on to the pitch when any visiting team included a black player.

Football is now experiencing an increasing surge in racism, which I and all fair-minded spectators simply deplore. The majority of these lads were born in this country, but whether that is the case or not it is beneath contempt to resort to the vile behaviour of this minority of half-wits. Many of these players are well educated and adept at the spoken word, as is portrayed on talk shows and radio and television interviews.

It reminds me of my days in South Africa, touring with the Football Association in 1956. Apartheid was at its height, the white rulers forbade black people to mix or socialise with the whites – no sitting on the same park benches, banned from the beaches if whites were present, segregation was present in all walks of life. We were warned to obey their ruling but none of us did. As far as we were concerned black and white were perfectly compatible. We are all as one.

There was much publicity when Ron Atkinson former Oxford United player and manager of several top clubs in England, including Manchester United, became embroiled in a vile racist outburst on live television. Having known Ron since his playing days with Oxford, where I held the position of trainer-physio, he was the last person in the world one would associate with such an outrageous remark, but because of it he will never regain his position as a TV pundit, although I expect he will continue to pop up from time to time in some chat show or other. Ron isn't the type of individual who will be out of the spotlight for long, you can bet your life on that!

Bobby Robson also played a part in that South Africa tour. Bobby was sacked by Newcastle United early in the 2004/05 season, and only had himself to blame for allowing the a situation to develop the way it did. The team's performances were being hailed such a success two years previously, when Bobby was 70 years old. That was the time to call it a day. He would then have left the club with dignity instead of being ridiculed by his chairman and spectators, who had lost faith.

Whatever my views, no one can dispute his high standing in the game as a player, coach and manager. I played against him during my days with Port Vale when he was a 23-year-old making his name with Fulham in the days of the great Johnny Haynes (the best passer of a ball I ever saw), Jimmy Hill, who later became more famous as a TV pundit, Tosh Chamberlain, the chirpy outside left who broke the corner flag when taking a corner and almost broke a bone in his foot!

Bedford Jezzard, a centre forward, also toured South Africa with Robson and myself. Back in England he received a serious injury which prevented him ever playing again. It was during a game at Vale Park against Fulham, a match which stands out in my mind for more personal reasons: at some stage a lump of mud was thrown at me, hitting me in the eye. The referee stopped the game and kindly licked the mud out of my eye! The *Daily Express* headline read: 'The ref and Ray King must be muddy good friends'. The players had another name which I won't repeat here – and we never found out who threw the mud.

My co-Keeper on the South African tour was a droll Yorkshire man named Ted Burgin, of Sheffield Utd. Ted wasn't originally selected among the 28 players, but Reg Matthews of Chelsea pulled out at the last moment, which was a great opportunity for Ted to join up with us on this prestigious journey.

Initially I was disappointed for Reg, particularly as we'd forged a close relationship when paired together for an England 'B' fixture against Switzerland, played at The Dell, Southampton ground. However on reflection, I remembered only too well that Reg was a 'chain smoker', and memories of the night we spent together in the hotel bedroom prior to the game came flooding back to me. He was an absolutely nervous wreck, pacing up and down and smoking incessantly throughout the night. In the morning I too was a wreck, not having a wink of sleep. On reflection, the thought of sharing a bedroom with Reg for a period of 3 whole months would have been unbearable!

As events unfolded, Ted had an excellent tour but like me, he was denied a full England Cap – surely he wasn't a victim also of prejudice? Ted and I were enjoying what I thought was a quiet drink in a small club, discussing the issues of the day. Ted went over to the bar to buy his round of drinks and was away less than 5 mins, when he returned to our table with not only drinks in his hand but also two 'Ladies' hanging onto his arms! Sidling up to me he whispered, "I don't like the look of yours, Ray!" How right he was!

One of the girls was a Marilyn Munroe lookalike which he'd obviously 'bagged' for himself, but not only was her friend a real 'plain Jane', she smelled strongly of carbolic soap. What had been a relaxing evening up to that point now became an absolute nightmare (for me, that was) whilst Ted was enjoying a canoodle with his glamorous blonde. I quickly 'downed' my drink and shot off to the bar, where I ordered the drinks for Ted and his guest then said to the bar tender, "Would you please deliver the drinks to our table, them inform them I'm not very well and am returning to the Hotel!"

The following morning, Ted and I went off as usual to the training ground, and not one word was mentioned of the night before – it was as though it never happened! We carried on with our usual workout, 'drop kicking' the ball to each other from a distance then gradually closing in, all the time increasing the power of delivery.

As my left shoulder was still causing me considerable pain, I asked Ted to concentrate on my right side, where I performed my 'party piece' catching the ball with my right hand. Interested bystanders gathered round to watch us performing, continuing to bang the ball at each other with considerable force. My initial training as a young lad catching a ball with one hand was now very much in evidence, enthralling our audience, which was now gathering in large numbers – little did they know the reason for my performing act, but we did enjoy the applause when our double exhibition ended!

For those 3 months together, Ted and I worked in close proximity and I can't remember a word out of place during that time – as I said earlier, Ted was a droll Yorkshire man, but as far as I was concerned he was a delightful and engaging personality.

1956
England's Tour of South Africa

The World Cup that is due to be held in South Africa in 2010 evokes wonderful memories for me, tinged with a certain sadness. In 1956 the Football Association selected 28 players from the football leagues to represent England – a mixture of full internationals and others on the fringe.

The tour lasted three months, from May to July, and a fixture list of 18 games were played in towns stretching throughout the whole of South Africa. The huge distances involved meant we had to travel by air – not a popular choice among several players who hated flying, particularly as all internal flights were on small aircraft easily buffeted about by frequent small storms. Seeing those players on their hands and knees kissing *terra firma* once the plane had landed was quite hilarious!

Apart from the occasional hairy moment when the plane hit an air pocket, plunging the light aircraft into a downward spiral at breakneck speed, the flights were usually uneventful. Mind you, those lads who were allergic to flying probably wouldn't agree.

In "Hands, Feet and Balls" I covered many aspects of this beautiful country, including Apartheid, which was at its height at that time. Thankfully for the black residents the pendulum has swung in a different direction, enabling them to enjoy complete freedom from white domination. Sadly, crime is on the increase and the murder rate is quite alarming – problems we never encountered during our long, exhausting, but wonderful tour.

We were feted wherever we went – we were invited to the mansions of millionaires, the cream of society dressed in all their finery, particularly the ladies, who were fascinated to hear the various dialects of players who hailed from almost every county in England. Food was in abundance, vegetables and exotic fruits we had never heard of before, all of it fit for a King (excuse the pun).

A banquet was held after each of the 18 games – seven courses was the norm – and explained why South Africans were simply enormous, something that was also in evidence when it came to facing them on the football pitch. Goalkeepers were especially vulnerable as charging the keeper was allowed in those days. Normally I thrived on such confrontations but my left shoulder was still giving me considerable pain, I thought from having been subjected to injections before leaving England. It later turned out that I'd torn ligaments during a game against Leicester City (my bogey team) and it wasn't until I arrived in South Africa that the diagnosis was made.

I was unable to play in the first few games and I feared I would be sent back to England – this was the last thing I wanted and although my shoulder continued to trouble me there was only one thing to do: I had to play.

I've played through the pain barrier many times in my career, but a goalkeeper's shoulders are such an important part of the anatomy for charging and taking high crosses under pressure.

As events unfolded I played each game with one arm. Thankfully my right shoulder was in working order and being able to catch or punch the pull with one hand I managed to struggle though. The fact that we did not lose a single game was a testimony to the fitness and dedication of every player who featured in those gruelling 18 matches.

South Africa has to be one of the most fabulous countries on this planet. There were countless problems then that still exist today, nevertheless, the sheer beauty that surrounds this wondrous land shields those problems when travelling around on sight-seeing tours such as Table Mountain, the Valley of a Thousand Hills and beautiful beaches. Cape Town has the cold waters of the Atlantic Ocean on one side and the warm waters of the Indian Ocean on the other – an amazing contrast.

We also flew off to Zambia to see Victoria Falls – an incredible sight not to be missed. Then there was the frightening experience of travelling in a small boat down the Zambezi, said to be infested with crocodiles. Fortunately we didn't see any, nor did we want to! Later, monkeys entertained us on a small island but the guides advised us not to hang around as there were predators all around us. Several of the players never even got off the boat!

We were soon to find out that the principal predator was the human female. From the moment we stepped on to South African soil the female species forced their presence upon us. They seemed to appear from everywhere, their minds totally focused on bagging a super fit English footballer! How could 28 virile men resist the attention and charm of these ladies, many of them extremely beautiful? This is the sort of reception the players participating in the 2010 World Cup can expect!

On odd occasions we were transported by bus to locations not too distant. One such trip was to the Valley of a Thousand Hills. On the journey we were overtaken by an open top lorry loaded with a group of young black girls. They screamed in delight when they saw us and lifted their dresses, displaying their womanly charms as we sat there transfixed on no apparent sign of underwear.

A pretty young lady came up to me at one of the many functions we attended. She said her father would like to meet an Englishman as he'd never met one before. She warned me he was a dour Afrikaner who still hated the English because he blamed us for starting the Boer War! Nonetheless I agreed to meet him, although it was with a certain fear an trepidation, not knowing what sort of reception I'd be greeted with.

The family lived way out in the bush on a ranch which reminded me of all the cowboy films I'd seen as a boy. The young woman drove me in her rickety old car on roads that must have been built before the Boer War, holes and deep ruts all along the 10-mile route. I wondered what I was letting myself in for.

At our destination a grizzled character came out to greet me (for want of a better word). His face, especially his eyes, seemed to bore right through me in a way that could only be described as hostile.

Thankfully his wife was a complete contrast to her husband, warm and friendly. She had prepared a lovely meal of springbok – equivalent to our deer – a tasty, rather salty meat.

After the meal my host offered me a drink of 'real' South African wine, which almost sent me through the roof! One sip was enough – my face must have spoken volumes and for the first time my host burst in to fits of laughter. This certainly broke the ice between us and for the rest of the evening our conversation centred mainly around sport.

It was only when his wife and daughter reminded us of the hour that I thought I had better be off – after all their daughter had to drive me back to Durban in the dark, and having to negotiate those dreadful roads again in tricky conditions was not to be relished.

On the bright side, my host and I parted as the best of friends and his final words to me were: "You come back, marry my daughter!" I hadn't the courage to tell him I was married with a six-year-old son.

Bill Perry, the outside left on that tour, was born in South Africa, but for some reason was eligible to play for England. Bill played for Blackpool in the 1953 FA Cup final against Bolton Wanderers in which he scored the winning goal from a cross by Stanley Matthews, who also provided the goals for Stan Mortensen's hat-trick.

To be selected to represent England on the South African tour must have given Bill great satisfaction, particularly as it allowed us all to live a life of luxury for three months, all for free.

He knew all the night clubs, some of them on the seedy side, which of course was just what some players were looking for. To be fair, not one player stepped out of line – it was always a possibility considering the many temptations available – after all these were 28 young men at the height of their physical fitness having sex practically offered to them on a plate! There was only one player as far as we knew who got himself into a bit of a tangle with a young air hostess whom he met on our 36-hour journey to South Africa, which included five stops.

The romance continued until we left for England. Unfortunately for him his wife wrote to say she would meet him at the airport on his return and his air hostess girlfriend was on the plane – she didn't know that he was married, of course. I didn't stick around to see how he got out of that one.

It was a wonderful tour, except for the fact that it ended the careers of my good friend Jackie Teasdale of Doncaster Rovers and Bedford Jezzard of Fulham. Both sustained knee injuries which became infected.

I met Jackie several years later when I was player-manager of Boston United in 1958. He came to see me in the dressing room after our game at Doncaster and showed me his leg. It was swollen to twice its normal size and as hard as a rock. He was only 25.

I played against Bedford Jezzard several times. Bedford got one full cap for England until that injury put an end to a promising career. Yes, South Africa hold many happy memories for me, but for Jackie and Bedford it was just the reverse. Sadly, Bedford died recently, joining his great friend Johnny Haynes on the celestial playing field.

A final word on South Africa, and a warning to those players who visit the country for the first time: beware of those lady predators, the biggest threat of all being the lesbian fraternity. They assemble in packs, as we found out when we were chased back to our hotel in Durban by these butch white women for having the audacity to dance with their girlfriends. We feared for our lives!

1957
Footballers' Injuries

When I wrote *"Hands, Feet and Balls"* I intended to cram in as much as possible relevant to the topsy turvey adventures of my lifetime. It is impossible to detail every single episode appertaining to such a project but there are some important issues which I will endeavour to clarify now.

Boston United, the club which signed me as their player-manager in 1957 from Port Vale, received little informative gossip in the book and I wish to redress my impractical interpretation now.

In my opinion a player-manager, coach or captain should be in a central position of the field – an ideal spot to direct his team in defence and attack. A goalkeeper's main concern is to command his own territory – the 18-yard area. A BBC Radio 5 Live broadcast on goalkeepers recently featured a section from *"Hands, Feet and Balls"*, focusing on my dreams that featured football. These dreams occurred on a regular basis and there were times when I sustained a injury which was, of course, self-inflicted.

These injuries happened not only when I was in the sticks, but I also often found myself playing up front, shooting for goal, although instead of the ball I kicked the bedroom wall almost breaking my big toe and seized with violent cramps. On one occasion, on holiday with my son in New York, his two Siamese cats got the same treatment when I sent them flying with a full blooded kick – they kept well away from me for months afterwards!

Back in goal was an absolute nightmare – often the ball slipped between my legs and a number of times when taking a goal kick I couldn't place the ball because of deep ruts on the ground, or the ball became a block of wood. I would wake up completely worn out!

The programme also depicted real incidents, such as the referee licking mud out of my eye in the Fulham game and an incident in a match against Leicester City when I ran out of goal to take the throw-ins, feeling the after-effects of an injection prior to the South Africa tour with the Football Association.

A serious injury was sustained by Arsenal's Ramsey in their game against Stoke City. An injury such as this can take a considerable amount of time to heal, and the rehabilitation period that follows takes even longer. Initially, there is the shock of the injury itself, followed by the long and tedious wait for the healing process to begin. Finally, there are the many arduous hours spent in rehabilitation. This entails not only the physical side of the recovery but also the mental aspect, which can be most difficult of all.

Having been subjected to many serious injuries during my own playing career, I can talk from experience. To give a comprehensive account of these would fill a book.

Perhaps the most serious injury I received was blow to my knee as an eighteen year old. This caused a condition known as synovitis. Synovitis is the medical term for an inflammation of the synovial membrane which lines the joints. As a result of this, I was told by the army medical specialist that I would never play competitive football again. Later in my career, I lost three years of actual playing time when I had both of my wrists broken, followed by a double facture of the jaw!

I wrote an article for the Bangkok Post a while ago about serious injuries that affect the lives of professional footballers. One year ago, I predicted that David Beckham's career would come to an abrupt end because of the extreme pressure he has habitually placed on his left ankle and Achilles tendon. This has occurred particularly during the execution of "set pieces". This type of procedure has been David's forte since his schoolboy days. He has one object in mind, and that is to create the perfect crossing of the ball. He directs it towards his teammates, culminating in exciting goal scoring opportunities on a repeated basis.

During his distinguished career, David has perfected this art. The "set pieces" to which I refer involve him directing the ball away from any point within the attacking zone, or from a corner kick on either side of the field. With his exaggerated style of delivery, it was inevitable that the intense pressure that he placed on his tendons would eventually produce a disastrous result.

Sadly, David's long career could now be over. At the age of 34 the healing process involved with an Achilles tendon injury is one of the most difficult from which to recover. Let's all hope for the best!

Ray King, Boston United Manager

Managing a football club at any level is a daunting experience, as I proved during my three years with Boston United and later at Poole Town where I also served almost three years. Boston were renowned as one of the top non league clubs in the country and at 33 I was the youngest manager in professional football at that time. As I stated earlier a goalkeeper is not in the best position to manage or captain a team – his main concern is the domination of those 18 yards marked out in white lines. Any other distraction is fatal for the keeper, who as the last line of defence cannot afford to make a mistake which may result in giving a goal away.

From a personal point of view the manager's main concern is the performance of his team and he can only judge that by standing or sitting in a position where he can see every movement and make changes where necessary. This was the main reason I became manager only after one season, adding an extra dimension to my managerial career, which proved to be a success as Boston finished in the top three during my three seasons and reached the first round of the FA Cup.

Although Boston attracted crowds of 3,000 and 4,000 regularly, I missed the atmosphere of the big crowds. It was only when we played against Peterborough United, our main rivals, in front of a crowd approaching 10,000 that I really displayed my best form.

Another big crowd turned out when we played against my former club Port Vale in the benefit match which was to pay part of the fee for my move to Boston – I of course got nothing! We won the game, which prompted the Vale directors to ask me why I'd left League football. I wondered myself too after giving one of my best ever displays, but I'd made my bed and had to lie on it.

The Vale manager informed me later that Blackburn Rovers came in with a late offer. This did not concern me too much but had the opportunity happened in today's football climate I would be, in that well worn cliché, 'gutted'. Nevertheless I was proud of my achievements during those three years, particularly on the playing side. The players, all with League experience, are indelible in my memory: Williams (Rotherham), Withers (Spurs), Snade (local lad), Hazeldene (Derby County), Miller (Doncaster Rovers), Lowder (Nottingham Forest), Hukin (Sheffield Wednesday), Garvie (Lincoln City), Graver (Newcastle United and Stoke City), Lewis (Cardiff), Lister (Notts County).

We played the system that was so successful at Port Vale, although as often happens there were underlying problems, which I can now reveal.

Boston United had for many years been under the control of a millionaire named Ernest Malkensen – like most football chairmen his decisions were implemented, rightly or wrongly. For reasons which were never made clear to me, Malkensen was deposed shortly before I arrived at the club to be replaced by Horace Luesby, a cherubic figure in his early sixties, and it was he who instigated my employment as Boston's player-manager.

My first two years with Horace were most enjoyable – we shared a good relationship which applied also to the other six directors, mostly wealthy farmers, a butcher and an accountant.

It wasn't until my third year that dark clouds began to appear where before it was sunshine every day. Ernest Malkensen had been keeping a low profile during those two years out of office but one had the feeling he continued to lurk in the background. This became more apparent owing to his frequent visits to the ground – Malkensen was creeping back into the limelight and Horace Luesby was slowly fading into the shadows!

As everyone expected, an extraordinary meeting was called and Malkensen was reinstated back on the board, resuming his position as chairman. This turn of events was no surprise to me and I knew my contract would not be renewed at the season's end even though the team was still performing well.

It was also well known that Malkensen had kept in touch with Ray Middleton, the Boston manager previous to me and there were signs that he'd be reinstated at the first opportunity. Before the death sentence was delivered, certain incidents within the club were making the job untenable for me – worst of all Malkensen instructed me to sack the trainer, Freddy Tunstall, because he wasn't proficient in the treatment of players' injuries. That was the last straw! Freddy was long time servant at the club, in his sixties and naturally hoping the club would offer him a benefit match in recognition of his services. As a former Sheffield United and England left winger he scored the winning goal in a cup final at Wembley and at Boston he demonstrated on occasions he still had an ability with the ball.

Obviously he was distraught when I broke the bad news to him, even though it was with the assurance that he would be staying as groundsman, at least while I was there!

Another unsavoury incident occurred in the social club following a match at Shodfriars (Boston's home ground) in which I unwittingly took part. As the directors, wives and friends (hangers on) were leaving to go home I noticed the bag containing the match takings had been left lying on the floor under a table. I called out to the last group which included two directors, their wives and friends about the bag containing the cash. One of the ladies, whose husband was the managing director of Massey Ferguson, worldwide producers of farm machinery, came running back and said: "Okay, Ray, I'll see to it. We can't leave all that money lying around can we?"

The secretary of the club, Charles Hodson, a lovely man prone to be a bit of a scatterbrain, had left the premises earlier, forgetting to take the cash home with him. When I mentioned this to the lady (to all intents and purposes a respectable person) she said her husband would keep it in their safe until morning, then return it to Mr Hodson.

I thought no more about it until I received a phone call from Charles the following day asking if I'd seen the bag with last night's takings. When I explained what happened he rang the lady in question, who in turn said she knew nothing about it I couldn't believe my ears! I intimated to Charles that we were obliged to make an issue of it, even though I realised it was a case of her word against mine – but Charles really put the kibosh on it when in his own inimitable voice shocked me even further when he said: "Better to just forget it, Ray. That lady is having an affair with one of our directors. If the missing money became an issue the balloon would go up and many other discrepancies could rise to the surface."

At first introduction, Charles Hodson gave an impression of a somewhat vague individual. During my three years with Boston I never saw him without his beloved bicycle, clips around his ankles, on his rounds as an insurance agent combining the duties with BUFC. Although I got on well enough with most of the directors, Charles was the only club official I really trusted – he would often inform me of clandestine meetings I had not been invited to.

One of these meetings concerned two of my youth players, Gordon Bolland and Alan Ashbury, both kids with an abundance of talent. As a safeguard I signed Gordon straight from school and together with another budding talent, Michael Robinson, took them on as ground staff.

Before long, big name clubs were ringing me to inquire about the lads, particularly Gordon and Alan. Two of those clubs were Arsenal – managed by George Swindin, a former goalkeeper with the club – and Chelsea, under the leadership of Ted Drake, who made his name with Arsenal as one of the all time great centre forwards.

Ted was first on the scene with a substantial offer for Gordon Bolland, which I placed before the board at an emergency meeting. The offer was readily accepted so I made arrangements to take Gordon down to London where we'd meet up with Ted Drake at Stamford Bridge.

One of the nicest men I've ever met in football, Ted explained to me the terms of the transaction, assuring me I would receive a percentage from the fee being paid to Boston. I discussed this issue with Horace Luesby, who was still chairman at the time, and he confirmed exactly the terms agreed with Chelsea, the matter to be placed before the board at the next meeting.

At around the same time George Swindin made an offer of £1,000 for Alan Ashbury and once again the directors readily accepted – the chairman assured me I'd receive a percentage subject to tax.

Days, weeks and months came and went but no remuneration was offered, and when Mallkensen was reinstated as chairman any hopes I had before were reduced to nil. I knew it wouldn't be too long before the 'new' chairman came to see me with his doom-laden message: "I'm afraid we won't be renewing your contract, Ray, but not to worry – you won't have a problem getting another club."

That statement was quite a hoot as I'd never seen any contract. According to Charles Hodson none had been finalised and any details that did exist were locked up in the boardroom! At least the chairman was right when he said I'd not have any difficulty being offered another management post – within days of the announcement in the Press that I was leaving the club I received three offers – Poole Town, Gravesend and Kettering.

1960
Ray King, Poole Manager

The Poppies wanted to acquire my services as player-manager, which I rejected at once – at 36 my playing days were over. With the game as it is today I'd probably play on into my forties or longer, but of course that is pure speculation.

The Gravesend chairman, who was also in that capacity with the Southern League, pulled no punches. He invited Norma and I to a well-known beauty spot well away from Gravesend to meet the other directors and their wives. It was a lavish occasion coupled with a financial offer far exceeding my salary at Boston.

I realised it would be difficult to turn down, but when the chairman drove us to the town of Gravesend, it wasn't difficult to work out where it got its name from – what an utterly depressing place. The look on Norma's face said it all! The house we were shown would have been ideal in a more picturesque setting, but with the docks in the background this wasn't exactly the environment we were hoping for.

Although our minds has already been made up I though it better to leave the final decision until our visit to Poole, situated on the south coast adjoining Bournemouth. I had been there once before with Boston when we played against Poole FC at what was then their new stadium, complete with a speedway and greyhound track. Not the best setting to create an atmosphere from a football point of view.

The game itself was one I remembered with enormous pride having displayed a classic exhibition of football. The Poole directors remembered the game too, not only for my team's display, but because the defeat relegated Poole from the Southern Premier League, hence offering me the manager's post.

The interview with Poole's directors was a beautiful summer's day – and anyone who has been to that area will understand why we accepted the offer of a three-year contract. The financial offer wasn't as lucrative as Gravesend's but having the opportunity to live in an environment such as this was worth more than any cash inducement. Granted I wasn't particularly thrilled with the stadium, impressive as it was, but crowds of no more than 900 from a population of 90,000 would create a horrible atmosphere. Nevertheless I viewed it as a tremendous challenge and was determined to make a success of it.

There was one little matter to be taken care of – finalising my links with Boston United. Norma and I had enjoyed most of our time there – she particularly the fresh country air and the open market where fruit and vegetables were sold in abundance. On reflection it did seem unfair that we were forced to leave because of one man whose sole object was to reinstate Ray Middleton on the back of their previous friendship.

If certain revelations within the club had been brought to the surface, revealed to me by Charles Hodson, it would not have been only me who left the club. The crowning moment for me came when the subject of our house became a major issue. As I was so naïve in terms of contracts, with no agents to advise me, Boston conned me out of that house. Charles Hodson told me it was rightfully mine. When the house was purchased for me I unwittingly signed for it and by doing so saved the club three years of tax payments, which *I* had to repay several years later. The whole thing required me to bring in an accountant – and I also had to pay him!

Weeks before moving out of the house, a director named Platt, a local butcher, continually harassed me into signing the property back to the club. Although Charles Hodson assured me by law the house was mine I was so fed up with the constant harassment I eventually gave my signature. In retrospect I should have sought a solicitor's advice, but the thought of ending up in court was too much to bear. Little did I know then that 35 years later I'd be faced with an even bigger momentous court case in Newcastle Crown Court!

That Boston house, which we named Jesmond Dene, must now be worth about £300,000! No doubt many readers will be sceptical about my version of events at Boston and Poole. Compared to the Manchester Uniteds and Arsenals of the football world they have a point. However, corruption rears its ugly head in one form or another whatever the status of a club. Back biting, jealousy, power-seeking individuals who know little or nothing about football in their quest to establish themselves as sporting personalities – that is your average director!

While Boston had only six directors there were almost double that at Poole. They loved to call a meeting at every opportunity. I was expected to attend on each occasion to listen to 10 or 12 of them determined to say their piece. One can imagine the exciting evenings I spent.

To start with they released every first team player but one, which meant I had no more than six weeks to sign a whole new team plus another 11 to form a reserve squad. Signing players is a headache at any time, but to recruit so many in such a short space of time made my task doubly difficult. I knew quite well that some would be a risk.

Letters from cast-off players littered my office desk, some well-known, others I'd never heard of. The underlying problem was their age – many of them were well past their sell-by date!

I was fortunate to be given the opportunity to sign a full youth team which had the unusual name of Police – nothing to do with the law enforcers! A Poole director by the name of Frank Turner (who became a good friend) introduced me to an 18-year-old lad called Peter Dooker, who captained the Police team. This was the beginning of a great friendship. Although Peter did not graduate into one of my first team players he captained my reserve team with great success in the Western League, the highlight being a 7-0 win against Bristol City reserves.

Having signed my full quota of players the season got off to a disastrous start when we lost the first eight games. We drew the ninth away from home at Dartford and in a remarkable turnaround finished the season in tenth position.

My second season flourished – the system adopted from my Port Vale days, carried on at Boston, was now a successful formula at Poole. It earned us promotion back to the Southern Premier League. The crowds, previously hovering around 1,500, were now reaching 2,000 and increasing all the time.

My third season, 1963/64, started even better considering we were playing against a higher class of opposition. The team was in the top three and we fought our way to the first round of the FA Cup, in which we were drawn to play Watford, who were top of the Football League's third division.

To reach that stage we had to dispose of Weymouth, formidable opposition managed by Frank O'Farrell, a big name formerly of West Ham United and Ireland and later to become manager of Manchester United.

There was extra interest in the tie because it was a local derby, with a bitter rivalry between the two clubs. Even though we were drawn to play at home, experience from my many FA Cup exploits guarded against being over-confident. Cup ties are one-off affairs and home advantage counts for nothing. This was proved conclusively as two games were needed to bring about a result.

Apart from the financial aspect, which benefited both clubs, the FA Cup creates a special aura, and it was a joy to see 7,000 spectators packed into the Poole Stadium, extra seating around the touchlines. This was the atmosphere we were all craving.

The match itself was an anti climax. We were fortunate to draw 0-0. I made the prediction, because the team performed so poorly, that we would win the replay at Weymouth – probably a bit rash, but there are occasions when confidence runs high!

Another crowd of 7,000 squeezed into the small Weymouth ground and once again the atmosphere was electric – there is no more wonderful feeling than being involved in games such as this, even if I wasn't taking an active part. Thankfully my prediction was spot on – we won the game 2-0 and the words of a disappointed Frank O'Farrell capped it when he said: "You played us off the park!"

There was much speculation at that time that several league clubs were inquiring about me, but that was as far as it got – it wasn't until much later that I learned why. I'll deal with the issue later.

We were now through to the first round of the FA Cup, away at a Watford side managed by Ron Burgess, formerly with Spurs and a Wales international.

As a seaside resort Poole was second to none, with its beautiful beaches the second biggest harbour in the world next to Sydney, Australia. Famous film stars, stage actors and TV performers lived in the luxurious setting of Sandbanks. Football was way down the list in the interests of a town boasting 90,000 residents, but the magic of the FA Cup caught the imagination of those who had never seen a football match in their lives.

Thousands packed special trains for the trip to Watford, whose supporters were pleasantly surprised by the behaviour of the Poole contingent (I couldn't really label them fans, knowing these occasions were one-off affairs).

We enjoyed every moment – especially as the lads gave a wonderful display. We were losing 2-1 with minutes to go when Colin Osmond, a tremendous competitor with a never-say-die spirit, scored the equaliser which earned us a replay at Poole Stadium. I enjoyed many memorable moments during my career but none gave me more pleasure than watching my team. All but one player – Peter Bellett, a local lad – were my signings, which was indeed of special significance on a day I shall never forget.

Preparation for the replay was immediately put into action and with a record crowd expected even though the match was to be played on an afternoon mid-week as there were no floodlights. Extra seating was provided from every available source; volunteers, many taking time off work, were there to assist in any capacity – it was a period which makes one's whole life seem worthwhile.

There is a saying, however: "It never rains but it pours." And my goodness that rain did come with a vengeance on the day we were so much looking forward to. From early morning it never ceased and when it rains in the West Country there can be no other place in the Universe quite like it. The expected 10,000 gate was drastically reduced to 6,000 which under the circumstances was extremely good, but it was a bitter disappointment for all concerned, except for Watford, who won 2-1. Their goalkeeper had an inspired game, saving them time, time, time again – as a keeper myself I realised even more the importance of the man between the sticks!

Whatever the result of that match we proved to be a force to be reckoned with. Ron Burgess paid us a compliment by saying his team were given their toughest test of the season and were fortunate to survive. My name was being mentioned freely in the press concerning several league clubs and their interest in obtaining my services, and I will now explain why.

Charles Hodson, the secretary of Boston United, proved to be a very good friend, supportive in everything I attempted and always available when I needed advice. In complete contrast the secretary of Poole Town, a man named Dan Clarke, undermined me at every opportunity. Football club secretaries, as in most businesses, rule the roost – they have their finger on everything pertaining to their employer!

Previous to his association with Poole Dan Clarke gained quite a reputation as secretary of Portsmouth FC and became involved as the principal character in one of football's biggest financial scandals. Dealings within the club, according to Clarke, were not being transacted to his satisfaction and he promptly reported the Portsmouth chairman and fellow directors to the Football Association. I cannot comment on the fate of those directors but I know Clarke was given the boot, which in the long term did not auger well for me.

With the glamour of the FA Cup behind us it was time to concentrate on the domestic scene of Southern League competition – the bread and butter of football. The expression about pouring rain that I used on the day of the Watford match was about to continue literally and figuratively over the following few months – the weather changed to ice and snow, culminating into one of the coldest winters on record. All football was suspended for seven weeks and with it came the beginning of a rapid decline in both our performances and my prospects as the manager.

My version of events is well documented in *"Hands, Feet and Balls"*, but I had other reasons for leaving the club in such haste. Looking back, it does seem incredible how one's fortunes can change so quickly although in my case I blame myself for allowing my departure to happen.

Our cup displays and league successes were highly acclaimed by the media, and my name was once again associated with Football League clubs. The chairman of Poole Town, Stan Pauley, came to see me at the club office with a message from fellow directors saying how delighted they were at the team's success. He also offered me a substantial rise in my salary and another three-year contract. This was of course before the big freeze and when play resumed after those six or seven weeks my team floundered on the mud heap pitches, an aftermath of melting ice and snow.

We were purely a footballing outfit, and teams we would play off the park in normal conditions were in their element in the mud, using hit long and chase tactics which completely put us off our stride.

Our position in the league was now causing concern and when Stan Pauley came to see me again it was with regret that the directors had withdrawn their initial offer. I was to receive no raise in salary and only a one-year contract. I was so furious I went straight home, informed Norma I had no intention of accepting their offer and informed the chairman of my decision.

The same evening I received a phone call from the chairman of Sittingbourne FC, offering me the manager's position, a three-year contract and almost double my Poole salary.

In ordinary circumstances it was doubtful, even considering the financial inducement, that I would have accepted their offer. But Frank Turner, my director friend, confided to me that Dan Clarke was the fly in the ointment – not only did he denigrate me to the directors but he was the main reason I never heard from clubs who expressed interest in my managerial future.

When Basil Hayward, a former playing colleague of mine at Port Vale, brought his Yeovil team to Poole Stadium, he also warned me of Clarke's stab in the back reputation at Portsmouth, where Basil had played following his Port Vale days.

It is inconceivable, just as was the case at Boston, that one man can destroy someone's life, whether it be through jealously, envy or sheer mindless behaviour. Call it what you will, but I appear to have a strange habit in my working relationships!

In hindsight I should have hung in there for that one season, not because I had anything to prove, but in leaving I let down myself and my family. We loved living in Poole, our son Gary was doing well at the Grammar School and moving to a nondescript town like Sittingbourne was sheer stupidity – not only from a football point of view, where it became apparent they couldn't afford to pay my wages, but Gary's schooling suffered too. To achieve what he did was quite remarkable especially as our subsequent move to Oxford was also a disaster.

My three years with Poole Town had largely been successful save the odd blip or two (Dan Clarke being one of them). Besides, any manager from any club, large or small, would be lying if he said there were never an problems.

Apart from leaving the town of Poole I was saddened to end my association with the players so suddenly, it all seemed so unnecessary. As at Boston my Poole team remains firmly in my memory (their experiences with professional teams are in brackets): Fred Brown (Portsmouth), Tommy McGee (Portsmouth and Reading), Tom Graham (Dundee United), Billy Elliott (captain of Ayr United), John Wembridge (Bournemouth and Dundee), Peter Bellett, Middleton, Denis Pring (Southampton), Dave McGuinness.

Any successful team must play a system which fits in with the players at the manager's disposal. An excellent team spirit is also essential and I'm proud to say we had at both Boston and Poole. I prefer to think back to the good memories rather than the negative ones – I've had plenty of those in my lifetime.

To meet people like Frank O'Farrell and Ronnie Burgess – Weymouth and Watford managers respectively – was an added highlight during our FA Cup run. Frank went on to become manager of Manchester United, which at the time seemed ironic as he had said to me, when we beat Weymouth in the cup, that I would soon be in the big time! I met Frank several years later when we both played in a benefit match somewhere in Devon. He told me his tenure with Manchester United had been an absolute nightmare because of a man named Sir Matt Busby! Frank said he was always lurking in the background (where have I heard that before?), undermining Frank's decisions and criticising team selection, which made Frank's position untenable. Yet people like Busby are placed on a pedestal by the media – there are many more in the game I could mention but no doubt I'd be accused of sour grapes, not to mention being sued!

Ronnie Burgess, like Frank, was a wing half (midfield) with the great push-and-run Spurs team of the 1950s. I saw a first division fixture at the Victoria Ground in the 1951/52 season between Spurs and Stoke City on a Monday afternoon. Alan Martin, another wing half, had been signed that day by Stoke from my team, Port Vale, and he was to make his debut against Spurs.

Alan said after the game: "I've never run so much in a game without touching the ball!"

This was football at its best – without being biased, the Chelseas, Arsenals and Manchester Uniteds of today wouldn't even come close to that Spurs team. They beat Stoke 6-0 that day.

Sadly, Ronnie Burgess died at the age of 87 and Alan Martin died of Alzheimer's aged 78.

Basil Hayward, at the comparatively young age of 62, died of a heart attack leaving the Stoke City ground after a game he'd been watching. Basil was a whole-hearted player who converted to centre forward from his centre half during our successful run in 1953/54. I'm convinced Basil's health problem was a legacy of his prolific heading prowess – the heavy ball has so much to answer for.

Ray King, Sport Master

Homefield School, situated between Bournemouth and Christchurch, is where I spent six of the happiest years of my life as a sports master. So it came as a shock when I heard that the school has closed after 80 years of existence. The kids were given letters to pass on to their parents, telling them not to send them to the ever again. Apparently the headmaster and chairman of the governors overreached themselves.

Not so long ago they bought an extra 20 acres of sports fields. They set out to build a national and international school of excellence for sports. Mr Taggart, the headmaster who founded this school in 1924, the year I was born, would turn in his grave if he knew his lifetime pride and joy had all been in vain.

I have wonderful memories of my time there, spent with kids varying from four to eighteen years of age and teaching staff who will mostly have passed away by now.

Quite a lot of those students are now in their late 40s but still keep in touch with me, especially since reading my book depicting several incidents which occurred in my time there.

One of those students was Mark Austin, a sports broadcaster who has worked for the BBC and ITV. As I wrote in my book, Mark was an excellent sportsman, especially in cricket and football – I'd hoped he would graduate as a county cricketer. Proficient in both batting and bowling, he was a supreme left-handed batsman and bowled left arm medium pace, with the ability to spin the ball both ways.

A memory I shall never forget at Homefield was the day when a Methodist Priest named Norman Hallam came to see me to ask if he could come and give the boys a talk. I knew Norman as a former footballer with me at Port Vale, so I was delighted to make his acquaintance again, and said the headmaster would be most agreeable to his request. We arranged a convenient time and date and informed the boys over the tannoy system that the Rev Hallam would be giving a talk at lunch time in one of the larger classrooms.

Come the appointed time I made my way to the venue, only to be met at the door by a crestfallen Norman.

"I've only got two or three boys here, Ray!" he groaned.

"Leave it to me Norman, wait five minutes," I replied.

I quickly collared Mark Austin, telling him to get round the school as quickly as possible and tell the boys that the talk is about football! Before five minutes was up the classroom was jammed full, with others lining up desperate to get in.

"How on earth did you manage that, Ray?" Norman said with a beaming face.

"No bother at all, Norman," I said, "but remember your talk is on football!"

"But I've nothing prepared," said Norman, to which I replied: "Give them a few anecdotes – make them up as you go along."

Thankfully it was a great success.

1963-4
Ray King, Cricketer!

There are many, many memories of my life on the sporting scene, some of which remain vivid as though it were yesterday, especially the happy or funny times. Cricket probably evokes more memories than any other sport, especially club cricket, which is played in a more light-hearted spirit than the cut and thrust of league and county cricket. Having played in eight different counties and mixed with hundreds of cricketers, I can say there is no better way to make friends.

It didn't take me long to associate myself with a local cricket club, however, during my brief association with Sittingbourne Football Club as manager. Before the football season of 1963-4 commenced most of my time was spent on the cricket field, and the fact that the cricket ground was situated next to my house was especially pleasing. Perhaps the standard wasn't as high as I'd been used to, but even so to reach 1,000 runs before leaving to concentrate on job for which I was being paid, I was selected to play for a select XI against one of the top village cricket teams in Kent.

Apparently they had a very fast opening bowler named 'Windy' Thompson, which we all thought was rather a strange nickname, but we soon found out why he was such a prolific wicket taker. As he ran in to bowl, every now and again at the point of delivery he would break wind – most disconcerting for the batsmen, especially as they did not know when it was going to happen. Thankfully he had been taken off when I went in to bat: no doubt he'd run out of wind!

When we all got together after the game we inquired as to how he managed to fulfil such an obligation every match. It transpired he was rarely seen without chewing gum, and got himself well stocked up on the days he played cricket. I suppose at some time in their lives most people have sampled chewing gum – one only has to glance at the pavements in any city or town to see them littered with discarded gum, with many walkers being unlucky enough to have it sticking to the sole of their footwear.

To a young lady of our acquaintance working at a shop in Amble, chewing away at her gum, I once said: "Do you know eating chewing gum helps to stimulate the brain?"

Quick as flash she retorted: "Ugh, it's done nowt for my brain, all it does is fill me full of wind!"

This reminded me of the seven-year-old boy I was treating for a leg problem when I was living in Poole. As I mentioned in *"Hands, Feet and Balls"*, I went to his house to carry out his daily treatment and just happened to mention the weather – how windy it was outside.

"Windy?" he said. "You should've been here during the night and heard Auntie Mary!"

Auntie Mary, incidentally, was only in her early 20s. I have changed her name to save embarrassment. She was a compulsive gum addict in her efforts to quit smoking.

Footballers in my day were offered gum from the trainer, which was supposed to help soothe the nerves, but I thought it could be dangerous if swallowed during a game and so the practice being brought to a halt.

However, managers of football clubs appear to thrive on the stuff, with Sir Alex Ferguson, of Manchester United, one of its main protagonists. I wouldn't be at all surprised if he was sponsoring the product! Mind you, if gum was responsible for creating the gastronomic effect on those persons I have mentioned (and I'm convinced that it was) those standing next to Alex Ferguson during the game, especially in an exciting moment, must be continually looking for cover! If Sir Alex is sponsoring chewing gum I'll bet his payoff is a bit more than I got for sponsoring Sugar cigarettes the princely sum of £6!

A true story that has been told many times over the years is that of Alf Gover, fast bowler for Surrey, playing for England in a test match against India in Delhi, in front of 90,000 spectators. As Alf came in to bowl the first ball of the innings, he ran straight down the wicket, across the outfield and into the pavilion with the ball still in his hand – he vowed never to eat curry again! Had he known at the time the explosive powers chewing gum had on the digestive system he might have got himself many more wickets. Perhaps it's stretching things a bit too much, but I ponder at the popularity of the book *Wind in the Willows*.

Writing by the pool in the 90 degree temperatures of Bangkok, it is difficult to contemplate the cold, damp and miserable weather back home in England. And yet just a few weeks before I wrote this, Thailand experienced one of the greatest catastrophes the world has ever seen – indeed the whole of South East Asia suffered the loss of many thousands of people from all parts of the world. Tsunami – a word most of us had never heard of before unleashed its fury on the beaches and the mainland without, it seemed, prior warning. The world stood still and watched the drama unfolding on television.

Several days before the tsunami struck, Bangkok was bathed in dark heavy clouds, in sharp contrast to the normally bright sunshine at this time of year. Large animals such as the elephant (a symbol of Thailand) and the tame working buffalo became restless, a sure sign something out of the ordinary was happening. The elephant was seen to be shedding tears – most unusual – and the buffalo ran off into the hills surrounding the city, yet these warnings went unheeded.

Incredibly, residents of Bangkok appeared quite unconcerned at impending disaster. They carried on their normal lives with customary smiling faces, despite the surrounding gloom.

1972
Luton Town FC

After writing *"Hands, Feet and Balls"* I received many letters from readers congratulating me, not only because they enjoyed the book, but also for the fact that I wrote it myself instead of employing a ghost writer. Ian Wooldridge, the excellent *Daily Mail* sports columnist, who died in 2007, told me ghost-written books were a load of rubbish and he just binned them.

One reader's letter read: "Ray, I enjoyed your book but I was disappointed that you did not give enough credit to your wife."

That gentleman was absolutely right and I intend to address that oversight now, not that she will thank me for doing so!

In our 60 years of marriage the pendulum of happiness has swung back and forth many times – we have tasted the good times and experienced the direct opposite; the same is true of everyone's lives – a little rain will fall, and at times it will become torrential.

In 1972 I was working as youth manager at Luton Town FC. Norma was still living in Poole and I travelled back every weekend after Saturday games. Out on the training field one morning I received a message to ring Norma immediately. Our poodle, Snowy, was very poorly at that time and my first thoughts were that he must have died.

I picked up the phone with a heavy heart, and heard Norma's devastating words: "Raymond, it's not the dog, I've got to have an operation for cancer immediately. Tomorrow will be too late."

The shock to my system almost brought me to my knees. It was imperative I returned home at once. The manager was sympathetic and offered to drive me to Poole but I said I'd be okay to drive myself. This transpired to be a foolish decision as my concentration was not as good as it should have been. Images of every conceivable outcome flashed through my mind. The journey was an absolute nightmare.

As I was about to pull into the driveway of our home, Norma was just returning from a walk with Snowy! I'd fully expected to find her stretched out on the bed, deep in abject misery. Yet here she was exactly the same as she always was when I returned home, with a smile and a hug – and the prospect of a life or death operation the next day.

Thankfully our son Gary was still at London University so he came to offer me support during his mother's prolonged stay in hospital. It was indeed a major operation, even her ovaries and appendix were removed, before she was required to lie on a bed in small room on her own for a week while she was treated with doses of radium.

Only doctors and nurses wearing special protection were allowed in the room. It was a most frightening experience for Gary and me, but Norma took it all in her stride. I heaved a great sigh of relief when the surgeon said the treatment had been a complete success and would add 20 years to her life. In fact, she has accomplished 15 years on top of that surgeon's forecast, at a cost.

The Move to Amble

Having lived in Poole for 26 years, Norma and I made the difficult decision to return to our roots, knowing that now in our sixties it wasn't going to be an easy transition having been away from the area for almost 40 years. Most of our generation, old like ourselves, would now be leading their own lives.

Wherever my footballing commitments lay, one of my first points of contact was an appropriate cricket club, a sure way to establish new friends. Initially our fears were fully realised back in Amble, and there are many unsavoury incidents described in *"Hands, Feet and Balls"*, but having lived almost 19 years back in our native community and becoming involved in various activities we now feel part of the scene.

Another of my early ventures on our return was to visit the local welfare field where I'd spent many long hours during my youth indulging a passion for football and cricket.

A cricket match was in progress when I arrived and one of the locals informed me it was Amble's second XI, which apparently included several youngsters little more than schoolboy age. This was of special interest to me and I sat down on the grass outside the boundary perimeter with avid anticipation, memories of my youth flooding back.

Amble were fielding (the captain must have lost the toss!) and instead of the usual banter that I had expected between the players every other word these lads uttered was the F-word. I had only been watching for a few minutes. This kind of language I never heard in a lifetime of cricket – that was my first and last visit to the Amble Cricket Ground.

Three years ago, because of a lack of interest, the club ceased to exist. Now, with a brand new sports arena in the pipeline, cricket can be restored if supervised by responsible disciplinarians. Cricket is a great game to be enjoyed by all, even if I do say that with tongue in cheek.

After my disappointment at Amble CC I decided to visit Warkworth Cricket Club and renew my acquaintance with Harry Green, who was now President of the club, and Derek Pringle, another Warkworth CC stalwart who played in my day but continues to work for the club in several capacities, including sweeping and rolling the wicket at tea.

Derek was an excellent swing bowler and I'm confident that with his relaxed style of action he could have carried on into his sixties. His argument, of course, was that he packed it in to give the kids an opportunity to play, which is sound policy in some respects but for someone of his quality and experience it would have been more beneficial to take an active role on the field.

On the plus side Derek has a son called Billy, who at 6 foot 5 has developed in stature and in skill, having become one of Warkworth's finest all-rounders, if not *the* finest. Having watched Billy in action on numerous occasions, I always got the impression he never played to his full potential in both his batting and bowling technique. A top notch coach would have been ideal during his early development, and with the essential slice of luck he may have graduated on to county cricket.

The welcome I received from Harry, Derek ad several other Warkworth Club members was heart warming. They invited me to visit the clubhouse at any time for plus a cup or two of tea, sandwiches and cakes – what more could anyone ask for?

Once we got ourselves back into the swing of things at Amble I decided to keep myself busy on what I thought would be on a moderate scale with shiatsu – an alternative form of therapy devised by the Japanese. To cut a long story short, before many weeks lapsed I was inundated with clients from all over the country. I will elaborate later in these writings on the episode in my life when it almost came to an end – and the people who caused it.

Harry Green was having problems with his back during that period, as was his wife Betty, and he called me to his house in Warkworth with a view to receiving treatment. Harry intimated that they would like several treatments but stipulated it had to be on a Monday at 9.30am – Harry, having sold his farm to the government, was now a millionaire, but he still hated Mondays!

On my first visit, Betty greeted me in her charming manner, pointed to the staircase and said: "Harry's upstairs waiting for you, Raymond."

As I got to the foot of the stairs, he was standing at the top, resplendent in a beautiful silk dressing gown, his hair and indeed his whole demeanour an exact replica of the Warkworth cricket captain leading his team on to the field. The image reminded of a Noel Coward production, all that was missing was the cigarette in its holder.

The illusion was somewhat shattered when I greeted him with the usual: "Good morning Harry, how are you?"

"Oh, it's Monday," came his droll reply – and that was his retort every Monday.

For a man nearing the 90 mark Harry was in remarkably good shape – a sound body with very little fat around the midriff. I'm quite certain he would have reached his century (as we say in cricket) had it not been for an road accident in which he was involved with another car. I happened to be out of the country when it happened, and it was only when he rang me on my return did I learn all the details and its ramifications. Harry said it was 'a mere scratch' but other sources told a far graver story.

He had been hospitalised and kept under observation for quite a while in the event of any after-shock or delayed physical problems. Being extremely resilient Harry was back on his feet quickly, but his back was giving him quite a bit of pain and I did notice a lack of general mobility.

When I treated him before the accident we would focus on the cricketing scene, both local and national. Now it was not quite the same. After five or ten minutes of treatment Harry would drop off to sleep and emit a gentle snore while I carried on with my soothing massage until he regained his composure as though nothing had happened. I had no intention of embarrassing him, as after all he was only off for a few minutes at various intervals. The procedure took place until he felt well enough to move around without pain.

Sadly, I'm convinced the car accident took its toll and Harry was never quite the same man again. Although he was not everyone's cup of tea, to me Harry Green was a true gentleman. I never heard him curse, swear or belittle anyone and the only time in his life when he might have contemplated murder was the memorable day I caught him out for a 'duck', and who could blame him for that?

Harry played a significant role in my life when together with Arthur Lamb and Ian Murray they guaranteed surety of £1,000 each pending my court case in 1995. I'd already booked my holiday to Florida at that particular time which meant I had to receive special permission from the Police Authority to make the trip with the proviso that I returned, hence the £3,000 surety. I shall be dealing with this issue later, but on a lighter and more humorous note, Harry, not known for throwing his money around, said to me: "You will be coming back, won't you, Raymond?"

Of course I had every intention coming back – my conscience was clear – but the 19 months of waiting until the day of my trial proved to be the blackest episode in my life. Arthur Lamb, former deputy governor at Acklington Prison, and Ian Murray, a retired professional yachtsman, were clients of mine, like Harry Green, and we became very good friends. I shall never forget the wonderful support they gave me when I was at my lowest ebb – Ian drove me to Newcastle Crown Court from Amble for the trial, which lasted four days, and Arthur was truly tremendous when called upon to speak on my defence. Arthur's wife Audrey, daughter Barbara, also my clients, testified for me as well, as did four other ladies.

To stand up in court as they did takes a great amount of courage and when I remember their testimonies I am filled with admiration for each and every one. I could never repay the debt I owe them. As for the four women (certainly not ladies) who were responsible for the horrendous ordeal I was forced to endure, well, they were beyond contempt – the lowest form of humanity.

Some years ago in Poole I visited an old lady to administer treatment. She warned me then to beware of a certain type of woman.

"Remember," she said, "a bad man is a bad man, but a bad woman is a *bad, bad* woman!"

Well, several years later, I met four of them. They were set to destroy me, one even said as much, and they almost did. I was rushed to hospital, struck down with an embolism in my lungs and left leg, barely able to breathe. There I was, incarcerated for a month, followed by three more at regular intervals. It is quite incredible to think I am kept alive by taking rat poison in tablet form – warfarin, to give it its proper name.

Even though that episode happened a long time ago I still cannot fathom why certain individuals go out of their way to ruin someone's life. The older I get the more cynical I've become. Of the many hundreds of ladies I treated over the years it was inevitable that one or two dodgy characters would slip through the net.

One such character appeared in New York when Norma and I were on holiday, staying with our son Gary. Another was in Poole.

I hadn't intended to offer my services in New York but one only has to mention something of interest and word gets around very quickly, as it did in this instance.

Norma and I were in Central Park watching the New York marathon, which was nearing completion when a French lady whom we had met began to shout at a British competitor: "C'mon you Engleesh!"

Her ears pricked up when she learned of my Shiatsu treatment, and she wanted to know all about it. She then asked me for an appointment. I explained I hadn't planned to carry out any treatments and in any case I did not have suitable premises. Not to be outdone she invited Norma and I to her apartment adjoining Central Park. How could we refuse?

She explained how much she enjoyed running in Central Park, but now her back was starting to give her trouble and needed attention – these French are certainly adept with their persuasive tongues, which of course culminated in my agreeing to administer some treatment in her bedroom while Norma waited in an adjoining room.

She asked me what the procedures were, to which my stock reply was: "Whatever makes you comfortable."

She went behind a screen and in no more than a few seconds came back completely naked! How does one react to such a situation? My reaction was one of panic – there was Norma only a matter of metres away in another room and here I was faced with a nude woman!

After I got my breath back I explained it wasn't possible to treat her without some clothing on. She almost exploded.

"Oh, you Engleesh, so prim and proper, in F-r-a-n-c-e ve 'ave ze treatment, then we make l-o-v-e!"

I quickly replied: "If we did that in England we'd both be locked up!"

Thankfully she understood the difference in cultures and after I'd worked on her back and neck we parted company the best of friends.

Although it wasn't quite the same scenario with the lady in Poole I was again faced with an embarrassing situation, especially as her husband was a friend of mine.

After the treatment she said: "That was wonderful, what's for afters?" The implication was clear!

In the run-up to the trial many lady clients I had treated over the years wrote to me with offers of support which brought tears to my eyes. Two in particular were very special.

Joyce Earnshaw, Harry Green's sister, wrote the most wonderful letter to me. A young American lady who travelled regularly from the south of England for treatment wrote to me and to my defence lawyer intimating that she would be willing to fly over from the United States to testify on my behalf at her own expense. At moments such as those, it gladdens one's heart to know there are people in the world who know the difference between right and wrong – I shall forever remember them.

Ian Murray, the yacht expert and ex Army officer with whom I became great friends, died recently of a cancer-related illness. Ian had suffered for many years with severe arthritis in his spine, for which I was treating him – a legacy of the arduous years of sea sailing. Months before he died Ian implored me to write another book, as he knew I had so much more to offer, but whether this materialises into a book I cannot forecast at this juncture.

My Norma

Those who knew Norma most of the lives will remember her as a smart young woman who could kick to her own height with ease and perform a credible tap dance. Since the operation her back began to cause he considerable pain. No amount of massage would help and it was then that I realised her spine was causing the problem. Pain killers were her only relief. This was the beginning of osteoporosis, a bone degeneration which attacks the whole body. I have always maintained it was the removal of Norma's ovaries that caused this devastating disease. Without them there is no control.

As if this condition was not enough to contend with, Norma recently began to experience dizzy turns which developed into a continuing need to sleep during the day. The hospital carried out various tests to determine the cause of this latest medical problem, but doctors remained puzzled for some time.

Finally, they decided to probe inside her body with a scientific machine in the hope of finding this mysterious enigma. The probe made extremely slow progress – the whole process took two hours – while Norma watched the whole procedure on a monitor.

At long last the offending problem was solved. Incredibly it was a piece of radium, the size of a strawberry, that had been left in her lower abdomen since the operation all those years ago. The doctors told Norma the object had to be removed otherwise it would quickly spread to other vital parts, and may even have already been spreading.

We faced the daunting prospect of another operation, but one that was unavoidable as Norma's life would otherwise be in peril. The procedure was performed by keyhole surgery and was successful – but that is not the end of the story. After a week in Wansbeck Hospital, to give her time to recuperate, she was transferred to Alnwick Hospital for further recuperation. It was therefore a tremendous shock when she developed thrombosis in her legs, which swelled to an enormous size. Water leaked from her pores. It was most distressing.

Having survived another tricky operation this was a burden she could have done without – and her problems did not stop there. Having returned home it transpired she had a heart complication which required urgent attention. So once again off we went to Wansbeck Hospital to see a heart specialist.

We were beginning to think that surely nothing else could go wrong, could it? Well, yes, it could. When we told the heart specialist Norma had been struggling to keep food and drink down for some time he was most concerned and said she should stay in hospital for investigation. We weren't prepared for this and I said we would rather go home and think about it, then have a word with our own doctor. The thought of going into hospital again was abhorrent.

Norma's condition worsened over the next few days so hospital was the only option. Off she went again to the Wansbeck where tests were performed to establish the cause of her continuing sickness. For several weeks – it seemed an eternity – we drove the 14 miles to the hospital every day. It took its toll on me. I was even caught for speeding once. Apparently I was barely exceeding the 30mph limit as I was leaving Amble, where for years I had been campaigning against motorists who thought nothing of racing their vehicles at up to 90mph in and around Amble. This of cause does not excuse the fact that myself and other careful drivers have still broken the law, yet it does seem so unfair. I was handed a £60 fine and three points on my licence, which I said they ought to have given to Newcastle United!

On the bright side the doctors at the hospital could find no cause for Norma's sickness and the usual medication was prescribed. These days the mystery illness persists and the osteoporosis continues to plague her. She cannot walk without her walking frame and although she is very resilient, she finds it hard not being able to carry on with a normal lifestyle.

Our doctors and nurses in Amble provided a wonderful service, as did Social Services, who even gave Norma a special bed and chair. I now know the meaning of 'cook, slush and butler' – I'm an expert!

Our neighbours have been most helpful. Way back in my young days neighbours would enter each other's houses without knocking, just shouting: "It's me!" That friendly attitude does not exist today –

most people lock their doors and won't answer a knock unless they know who the visitor is, and who can blame them in today's violent society?

We are very fortunate that we had true friends in Edie, Alec and Anita, who catered for our every need. There are also my friends from Stoke-on-Trent, Pat and John Poole, as well as Elaine and Geoff, who rang on a regular basis to ask about Norma and to support me through one of the worst periods of my life. As they so rightly said: "What are friends for?"

2004-5
The Ambler

Writing my column in the *Ambler* magazine early in the 2004/05 season I offered my opinion as to why Newcastle United were struggling in the Premier League. Bobby Robson had signed three or four players with chequered histories and because of that he lost control of the dressing room, he lost the support of the chairman, and worst of all the supporters lost faith. Make no mistake about it, being sacked as Newcastle United manager was a most humiliating experience for him, even more so than losing the England job – he fully expected to end his long career with the club he idolised as a youngster.

I also wrote two years previously, when the team was on a high. That would have been a good time to retire – he was 70 years old and his status would have remained unsullied. Sadly his stubborn attitude was his downfall.

When I watch Newcastle on television I find it difficult to feel any sort of nostalgia or allegiance towards them. The players may still wear the black and white shirts, but that is the only semblance of identity. The ground is unrecognisable, as are the players themselves. Alan Shearer was the exception, in my eyes the nearest approach to the great Geordie heroes of the past – 'Wor' Jackie, Bobby Stokoe, Albert Stubbins, Ernie Taylor, Charlie Wayman, Bobby Cowell, Bobby Corbett, 'Tot' Smith, Charlie Crowe, Tommy Walker, Georgie Hair – the images brings tears to my eyes! Those lads were the real Magpies.

How Times Change!

When most old codgers are content to sit back and cogitate, my philosophy is always to engage in some form of activity, even if one is confined to a wheelchair or bedridden there is no such word as can't! To be physically incapable is horrendous but when the mind ceases to function there are no words that can ease the plight of the person who has been struck down in such cruel fashion, nor of their dependants. This situation has befallen hundreds of ex-professional footballers.

Many have died or are dying from the dreaded Alzheimer's disease, which in my opinion was caused by heading the heavy leather ball that we used in the 1940s and 50s. I have campaigned many months on the behalf of these players with a view to receiving some form of remuneration for the benefit of their dependants. Some of the proceeds from *"Hands, Feet and Balls"* have been donated to the wife of a former Port Vale player, but of course that is a mere drop in the ocean. Perhaps one day soon there will be a breakthrough on this distressing situation instead of the 10-year study that is being undertaken by the FA: young players are being monitored in this period but that is no consolation for those old timers – action is needed now.

I consider myself extremely fortunate. As I wrote sections of this book from my son's apartment in Bangkok, Thailand, where the sun shines most of the day and the temperature rarely drops below 90 degrees Fahrenheit. With a beautiful cooling breeze, what more could anyone ask for? One might think, being 6,000 miles away from England, my mind would be focused on anything but football. Not a chance! Thailand, like the rest of the Far East, is football daft. English,

Spanish, Italian, as well as their own domestic scene, games are on television 24 hours a day. It is absolute football saturation.

I have watched several games featuring my old team, Newcastle United, but I find it difficult to believe those famous black and white shirts are currently worn by players who 50 years ago would have stood little or no chance of playing for Newcastle United. How on earth can spectators shout out that famous chant, "Howay the lads"?

With every team in the Premier League obsessed with foreign players, the competition should be renamed the Foreign Legion Football League! A similar situation exists at Port Vale, the club that resurrected my career, when to all intents and purposes I had been placed on the scrapheap by Newcastle. Fifty years ago the name of Port Vale was heralded by football lovers around the country after they reached the semi-final of the FA Cup. The team consisted of nine local lads and two 'foreigners', Dickie Cunliffe from Bolton and myself from the north-east. We had a wonderful team spirit and played with a simple game plan which I named the butterfly system. When we defended, the wings closed in; when we attacked, the wings opened up to a display of beautiful football which was sustained week after week.

When I played for Newcastle United in 1946 every player was from the local area except for Joe Harvey, a Yorkshireman who became a cult figure with United as player, manager, chief scout. A loyal servant to the club.

Today we see enormous transfer fees and salaries, often paid to players with limited ability. This state of affairs surely cannot go on much longer? The bubble is about to burst. For the game's sake sanity must return and young local talent must come back into the reckoning. Sadly at the moment, they will play for peanuts and the love of the game.

My mind drifts back to those early years at Newcastle as a raw 17-year-old, blessed with a unique talent. Little did I know then the vagaries of life and the complex route it would take. Images flash constantly into my memory box, halcyon days when all those local lads wearing the famous black and white shirts exerted their energies across the turf of St James' Park, roared on by crowds regularly reaching 65,000. King, Cowell, Corbett, Harvey (captain), Smith, Crowe, Milburn, Taylor, Stubbins, Wayman, Hair – that team will live in my memory forever. Apart from Charlie Crowe and myself all those wonderful lads have passed over to the 'other side'.

A similar situation exists at Port Vale, the club that resurrected my career following three years in the wilderness. I make no apologies for naming those local lads who created a historical record I doubt will ever be beaten: King, Turner, Potts, Mullard, Cheadle (captain), Askey, Leake, Hayward, Griffiths, Cunliffe.

In 46 league matches we conceded 21 goals. In the FA Cup the goals against column read four in eight matches – a total of 25 goals conceded over 54 matches.

Myself, Colin Askey and Kenny Griffiths are the surviving members of that great team, plus Derek Tomkinson who played in the FA Cup semi-final in place of the injured Ken Crout.

Off-Pitch Antics

Managers continually come under the spotlight and in today's high profile extravaganza the pressures are greater than ever before. One has only to watch matches on television to see the cameras conveniently situated to pick up every twitch, grimace, furious gum-chewing, clock-watching and general agonies every manager endures for those 90 minutes.

Some managers are more composed than others, in particular the foreign contingent, who rarely show emotion. The money they earn is enormous but their health is bound to suffer from the continual tension their bodies are exposed to. Jock Stein and Bill Shankly, two of the most accomplished Scottish managers, both succumbed to the pressures at a relatively early age. In fact, one needs look no further than Port Vale's Freddy Steele, who couldn't bear to watch a game – he spent the entire 90 minutes in the shower room with the jets fully on so he couldn't hear the roar of the crowd – when it gets to you like that, get out quick!

I only managed clubs at a lower level, Boston United and Poole Town, but it was still done in a professional manner – there was no allowance for failure. Sir Alex Ferguson, one has to admit, comes top of the list where durability is concerned – he would never win a popularity contest but he has all the ingredients necessary to sustain the continued success of Manchester United. No doubt many of the tabloids and commentators would argue he has the good fortune to manage a club that has the financial clout to buy the world's best players. Maybe so, but at the same time the club have a wealth of young talent emerging from the assembly line – it seems never ending. Of course it could be argued United can command the best youngsters, enticed by the juicy carrot!

The Glory Days Are Gone...

John Poole was an up and coming goalkeeper who, during my concluding days with the Vale, was being groomed to take my place. But for his lack of height – 5ft 8in – John would have been up there with the best of them. Had he been playing today, with physical contact so restricted, I've no doubt he'd achieve top billing.

Both John and his wife Pat have been instrumental in their efforts to support the Vale through good and bad times, giving up much of their spare time in the process. Their help has never been fully appreciated by the club, which is sinking further and further into the mire.

Geoff Wakefield, a former Vale director, and his wife Eileen also directed their energies into the club, but all to no avail.

All the glory days of the 1950s have long since gone. Will they ever return? Certainly not in my time. The same could be said about Newcastle United – sheer bad management brought about its recent downfall.

I'm delighted to say I remain great friends with John, Pat, Geoff and Eileen. They regularly send me oatcakes from the Potteries. I am also grateful to Brian Herbert, another Potteries friend, John Palmer, who keeps me supplied with Vale videos, and fans who write letters to Ray, King of Keepers!

Pop star Robbie Williams is the biggest shareholder (whatever that is) as I write, but apparently the club continues to be deeply in debt. His emergence as a prominent Vale fan is just one illustration of the inextricable link between sport and show business. Another example of a more light-hearted nature concerns the great comedian Tommy Cooper. Although not known for his sporting prowess, he once allegedly asked Des O'Connor if he could play in one of Des's charity cricket matches.

Des, well aware that Tommy liked a pint or six, was rather reluctant to play him, but Tommy said the exercise would do him good, so Des relented, realising that Tommy would be a popular choice with the public.

On the appointed day Tommy looked resplendent in immaculate cricket whites and size 13 boots.

"Do you think I should wear my fez?" he asked Des.

"I wouldn't advise it, Tommy," replied Des. "It would fall off when you run for the ball, and might drop on your wicket when you're batting."

Tommy laughed. "I was only kidding!" he said.

Des won the toss and decided to field first. As he was leading the team on to the field someone shouted: "Where's Tommy?"

"Probably in the bar having a quick pint," said Des. "I'll go and fetch him."

Sure enough there was Tommy with a pint in his hand. "Just finishing this pint, Des," he called. "I'll be out in a minute."

The game commenced with no sign of Tommy. When the first wicket fell the incoming batsman shouted: "Tommy says he'll be out in a minute, Des."

As wickets continued to fall, each incoming batsmen gave the same message. As the last wicket fell, Des rushed to the club bar where Tommy Cooper, still with a pint glass in his hand and a silly grin on his face, spluttered: "Jush finishing thish pint, Desh. I'll be out more than a minute."

With those mangled words, Tommy slid to the floor, out cold.

Bobby Robson – And Other So-Called Football Personalities

As manager of Ipswich Bobby Robson built a successful first division team and his youth policy was hailed as best in the country. When I was youth manager of Luton Town we arranged several friendly games against Ipswich, which culminated in a good relationship between the clubs. It therefore continues to remain a mystery why the friendship between Bobby and myself soured the way it did.

Let me make it perfectly clear there were no harsh words uttered from either of us at any time, which confuses the issue even further.

Readers of *"Hands, Feet and Balls"* may remember a story regarding two 15-year-old black kids who I was led to believe were being sought by all the top London football clubs. At the time I was living in Poole, Dorset, when my son, deputy head at an Acton comprehensive school, rang me urgently to the effect that his sports master was ecstatic about the two lads. Knowing my football connections he asked my son if I could recommend any top team, providing they were well away from the London area – where they would be subject to unsavoury influences.

It didn't need much thought to work that one out. Bobby Robson's Ipswich was the obvious choice. I knew the lads would get a fair deal, especially from Bobby, for whom I had a great amount of respect. I rang Bobby immediately at his Ipswich office and gave him the information I had been given by the sports master, who played for a top London amateur team. I emphasised to Bobby I had not seen the lads play myself so could only rely on the sports master's integrity and knowledge of the game.

Bobby was delighted and asked me if I'd go up to London to make arrangements for the lads to get to Ipswich as quickly as possible. He also added an invitation to me to see his Ipswich team play at Southampton. I would be his guest. In my battered old car (the Mercedes and the Rolls weren't available on the day) I drove the 100 miles up to London where I met the sports master and his two excited schoolboys. Although only 15 they were both six-footers, which gave me an optimistic feeling. So my hope now was if they can play as well as they look, Bobby has two potential stars on the way.

From that day, more than 20 years ago, I am still completely in the dark as to what transpired at Ipswich. During the few days the lads were to spend there, my son left his London school to take up an appointment in Bermuda, which left me in a totally untenable position. It was many years later, when Robson was appointed manager of Newcastle, that our paths crossed again, albeit somewhat distantly. I was interviewed by several newspaper and radio reporters, asking my views on his appointment. I answered quite truthfully, saying that even at the age of 68 his experience at the top level and comparative success, plus the fact he was a Geordie, made him an ideal candidate for the post.

Once he was installed at St James' Park I wrote to congratulate him and offer my best wishes – my letter was never answered. For some obscure reason I wrote to him again, at the same time asking why he hadn't answered my letter. A week or so later his secretary rang me to say Bobby had not received my letter, then went on to tell me he was a very busy man and had no time for writing letters! Then why the hell didn't he pick up the phone himself?

It has baffled me over the years. If someone is good enough to put pen to paper, place it in an envelope and pay for the postage, then surely the person receiving it should have the common courtesy to answer. It also happens quite frequently when ringing someone on the phone, a recorded message will claim that they will ring you back, but they rarely do – unless of course it is to their benefit!

I wrote to Robson on two more occasions. He must have thought I had nothing else to do. My fourth letter requested an invitation to the United-Sunderland 'derby' on behalf of Albert Stubbins, Charlie Crowe and myself. Albert had been in poor health for quite some time and I knew Charlie was having problems. Not wishing to be left out I too was struggling with a chronic back problem which has plagued me most of my adult life (no, it wasn't caused by picking the ball out of the back of the net – my full backs did that!) Still I received no reply from Robson, even though I mentioned the fact it was probably our last chance to visit St James' Park.

A few days before the game I received a phone call from the club historian, to inform me that myself and several other former United players had been invited to the game. After thanking him, I asked if it would possible for me to use the club's car park because of my back condition. He said it was doubtful, but would do what he could. Needless to say I didn't hear any more.

On the morning of the match I knew the only way I was going to get anywhere near St James' Park was to travel on the supporters' bus, which even then was quite a distance from my house. After walking no more than 25 yards, there was no way I could make it so I reluctantly crept back to the house. I wrote to the chairman and directors at the club, thanking them for the invitation and apologising for my absence, explaining the circumstances – as expected there was no reply.

There are four other football personalities (for want of a better word) who have fallen into this trap: Bob Wilson, ex-Arsenal goalkeeper and TV pundit; Jackie Charlton, former Leeds United player, World Cup winner and manager of several league clubs as well as the Republic of Ireland's national side; Bryan Robson, former Manchester United and England midfielder and now an experienced Premier League manager; and Paul Gascoigne, a former world class player who succumbed to a lavish lifestyle which now threatens his life.

Bob Wilson and I had corresponded on several occasions with regard to the goalkeeping situation, especially from England's point of view. At that time David Seaman, the Arsenal keeper, was never in danger of losing his place – there simply was no one with the necessary attributes, even though I felt David's career was in decline, which was confirmed during the 1998 World Cup. I also spoke to Bob on the telephone when he told me the tragic news that his daughter was suffering from an incurable disease. Obviously I didn't think it was the right moment to discuss my book, but once Bob knew I had completed the manuscript he asked me to send him part of the script so he could give me his approval or otherwise.

If my memory serves me right I sent him 67 pages on various issues I'd written. After reading the shortened script, which apparently impressed him, he requested the full manuscript of 360 pages. At no little expense I duly sent the bulky package to Bob. To this day it has never been acknowledged.

I did take into consideration the sad circumstances surrounding both Bob and his wife, which must have been devastating for them, and when his daughter died I did write a sympathy letter, as I'm quite sure did hundreds of others. However, I did feel after a reasonable passing of time that he would have responded in some way. After all, apart from the expense involved I'd worked damned hard on a very demanding project. Perhaps Bob had resented my criticism of David Seaman, who in my opinion was fortunate to retain his England place for as long as he did. No doubt his resentment had to be because he was David's coach at Arsenal and my criticisms reflected on him also.

I combine the names of Bryan Robson and Paul Gascoigne for the simple reason they were together at Middlesbrough, Robson as manager and Gazza as player. It was a period when both were enduring a torrid time in their respective capacities, the press particularly showing no mercy whoever their pens were directed at – past reputations counting for nothing.

Knowing the turmoil both men would be experiencing I decided to send my book to Gazza, care of Bryan Robson, accompanied by a letter stating my reasons for doing so. The book itself should have been sufficient evidence for the mind over matter theory – in plainer language there is no such word as failure, and to remind you of the Sir Harry Lauder ditty – 'Keep right on to the end of the road'.

Whether or not they received my book, I don't know. Suffice to say even if they did I doubt very much if it will ever be acknowledged. In Gazza's case did he even read the book or my letter? The advice I gave obviously failed to inspire him.

When I heard that Jack Charlton was living back in Northumberland I decided to get in touch with him about my proposed book. He was still a big name in the football world and his autobiography was currently on the book shelves. With this in mind I thought he might like to see part of the manuscript and maybe have some advice about contacting publishers.

I put the question to him on the phone. He readily agreed to read part of the script but was rather vague on the question of publishers. He admitted his own book was entirely ghost written – he was asked various questions on his career and lo and behold the book was on shop shelves in no time at all!

Nevertheless I did send him 67 pages of script, which cost time, effort and postage just like the others, but once again I received no reply. I should have taken the hint when Jack told me on the phone he was merely asked a few questions for his proposed book. Jack was not in the habit of writing or indeed picking up the phone unless someone rang him.

It beggars beyond belief how so-called high-profile individuals can treat a fellow professional in such a callous fashion – or indeed treat anyone in that way. Maybe I did not reach the height of celebrity in their capacity, although in 1954 when the Vale captured the imagination of the whole country, reaching the semi-final of the FA Cup and creating a defensive record, becoming household names in the process. That I suppose in relative terms was our 15 minutes of fame, which supposedly everyone at some time in their lives will experience if you believe Andy Warhol!

In my younger days I was never one for shouting my mouth off until I got on the pitch, when my whole demeanour changed. My problem was being afraid of upsetting anyone, at all times the nice guy – how boring!

Many years ago some friends of mine, Major Bob Broach and his wife Joan, said to me: "Ray, why do you hide your light under a bushel? Let the world know who you are and what you have achieved."

Even at that stage I was reluctant to let rip, but now I've reached my twilight years it is time I spoke out, after all I have nothing to lose, especially when telling the truth.

Bob Wilson, Bobby Robson, Bryan Robson, Jack Charlton and Paul Gascoigne were born with a talent that has brought them undoubted fame. Without fear of contradiction, I too was fortunate to be blessed with a talent which in terms of quality was at least equal to any of them. That I didn't reach the pinnacle could be construed in two four-letter words - fate and luck. I lost seven and a half years of my footballing life to four and a half years of Army service, and three years to my broken wrists syndrome, followed by a double fracture of the jaw.

During the whole of my eight seasons with Port Vale my wrists were heavily strapped before every match and my back massaged in order to get me out on the pitch. It wasn't until two years ago that my doctor informed me I was born with a serious spinal problem. He was astounded that I'd played any sport at all, never mind professional football! To accomplish what I did, he said was little short of a miracle.

To put it in perspective, Graham Kelly, the former secretary of the Football Association now writing for the Independent newspaper, gave a glowing account of *"Hands, Feet and Balls"* and described me with a quote from Marlon Brando in the film *Waterfront*, in which he refers to his chances of being heavyweight champion of the world with the phrase: "I could have been a contender." That's right, the dream never fades!

My Strong Opinions on Goalkeeping

One subject I do know something about is goalkeeping, and I have strong opinions on goalkeeping today. As I have said so many times before, the goalkeeper is the most important member of any team that wishes to be successful. No club can afford to have a bad keeper and this is why all the top clubs are prepared to pay enormous fees to acquire the very best. Centre forwards, or strikers as they are now called, have always been held in higher esteem because of their ability to score goals. That's all very well, but to my way of thinking a striker may score one, two or three goals in a game but that does not ensure his team will win the match. On the other hand if a goalkeeper consistently keeps a clean sheet his team cannot lose, even though they may not always win. One point is better than none!

This is why so much emphasis is targeted on the man between the sticks. It has saddened me for some considerable time to note the decline in British keepers. During my early years England were heralded as having the best goalkeepers in the world – almost every club in the country had a good one. Today, most Premier League clubs field a foreign keeper. Is it any wonder that England haven't got one of real international standard?

Why is there such a dearth of upcoming keepers? My theory is over-coaching. Every keeper I see throughout the professional and minor leagues employs the same technique, particularly in one on one situations. Nine times out of ten the attacker scores simply because the keeper, instead of using his own initiative to combat the threat, follows the coach's advice. Never having been coached at any level I am convinced much of the natural ability a young keeper may possess will be destroyed from negative coaching.

Every keeper, whatever his strengths, professional or amateur, will make brilliant saves from time to time. But there is much more to goalkeeping than that. Containing the 18-yard area is paramount – this is the keeper's domain and he must make the whole of this area is his responsibility – be vigilant, poised to move at lightning speed when his goal is threatened. Advancing off one's line to intercept high crosses has always been a keeper's nightmare, especially if there is a strong wind, which can play havoc at times, but I have not seen one goalkeeper in the Premier League who dominates with confidence. This skill is so essential in safeguarding his territory.

As a young, inexperienced keeper myself I would sometimes come out for crosses in crowded situations when my own defenders were going for the same ball. On a couple of occasions I knocked out two of my team mates by punching them on the head! On their recovery I was 'educated' with language I'd never heard before!

From these incidents, however, my whole attitude to the goalmouth melee taught me the art of dealing with these situations in the future, culminating in an agreement with my co-defender on how to deal with aerial threats. As I move off my line, both full backs would drop back on the goal line and other defenders would take up positions in areas that would not to impede my challenge for the ball against the attacker. This is illustrated on the front cover of *"Hands, Feet and Balls"*. It was a very successful operation.

Watching today's keepers struggling to reach the ball over a ruck of players is painful to see – on many occasions the ball runs loose which is to the advantage of the attacker. Punching the ball appears to be a lost art but I think the ridiculous gloves worn by keepers today may have a lot to do with that – they are like huge frying pans!

Another failing is their inability to successfully gather the ball safely when faced with a one on one. At this point I must emphasise the importance of lightning reflex reactions by the keeper – speed is essential, they have to be as quick as any outfield player, particularly over five, ten or fifteen yards. My strategy was to fling myself across the attacker, spread my arms in front of my body while reaching for the ball and curl up into the foetus position once the ball had been safely gathered. With this method there is no way I could have fouled the attacker.

I sometimes ponder how today's keepers would cope with the robust challenges we had to contend with in the 1940s and 50s. Formidable characters such as Nat Lofthouse of Bolton Wanderers and

England, Trevor Ford of Sunderland, Aston Villa, Cardiff City and Wales, Dave Hickson, a Huddersfield and Everton player, Blackburn Rovers' Tommy Briggs, and England B international Arthur Rowley of Leicester City. All these lads were a keeper's nightmare, hassling away as soon as the keeper held the ball. Shoulder charging was all part of the game and an enjoyable pursuit – I loved every moment, except on one occasion against Leicester City (my bogey team) when I became the target for Rowley and Gardiner, a 6ft 3in Scottish international with the boniest knees I'd ever seen. He played a major part in inflicting me with a thigh injury (dead leg) – a legacy which sidelined me for a month.

Up to that point we had played 14 games in our first season in the old second division. I had only conceded four goals and Port Vale were riding high in the top five while I was receiving newspaper headlines advocating my selection for the England team. As fate would have it (a familiar pattern in my life) my brother Frank, a former Everton and Derby County keeper, was a physio with Leicester at that time. Rowley, 14 stone himself, and the gangling Gardiner arranged to harass me at every opportunity, especially as they knew my fondness for coming out to deal with crosses. Their opportunity came almost on half-time with the score at 0-0 when in mid-air Rowley banged me from the back and Gardiner jabbed his bony knee into my thigh. It felt as though I'd been shot. I was completely pole-axed – it was one of the most excruciating injuries I sustained throughout my football career – the pain was almost unbearable.

There weren't any substitutes allowed at that time so I was forced to play out the full game even though I could barely stand, never mind keep goal. Of course this did not deter Rowley and Gardiner and the continued their vicious assault whenever the ball was in my possession. Ironically, Rowley and I had been nominated by the Football Writers as Footballers of the Year in 1954. It is never easy to castigate other players, whether they are one's own team mates or from other clubs, but I did rate Arthur Rowley as a rather unpleasant, sarcastic and bombastic individual, even though he was a prolific goal scorer and has been listed as one of the all time greats!

I suppose I have become cynical in my twilight years – where before I would keep a low profile I can now offer my opinions on certain characters, whether they belong to the past or the present.

Every one of the players I have mentioned, apart from the treacherous Gardiner and Rowley, played the game physically but fairly – they could take it as well as dish it out and at the end of the game it was handshake time. However, there was a particular centre forward who gave keepers more harassment than any other player in the game. His name was Billy Roost, of Bristol Rovers. He is probably not remembered by the footballing public today, but I shall never forget him. Only 5ft 8in, but built like a barn door, his constant marauding against the goalkeeper was an absolute pain and I found it very hard to counteract his aggressive challenges. Despite being six inches taller than him it was a hopeless task attempting to match him shoulder to shoulder so my only solution was to clonk him on top of the noddle with the ball – discreetly but effectively. He would emit a little grunt, a slight grimace, shake his head, then continue his campaign to rough me up – thankfully the game only lasted 90 minutes but on the day it seemed a lifetime!

I cannot help but smile when I see today's keepers straying out of the area with the ball at their feet and not one opposition player comes anywhere near. I'd love to hear what players like Nat Lofthouse would have to say about that. A few years ago he told me he wouldn't know what to do with himself in today's game.

Brian Clough and My Youngsters

When one of the game's great characters died he left a void which will not be easily replaced. I refer to Brian Clough, whom I wrote briefly about earlier, on his association with Ray Middleton. Brian was still playing for Middlesbrough in the second division when I was with the newly promoted Port Vale.

His talent as a goal scorer was making headlines during that time with the expectation he would beat the goal-scoring record of the great George Camsell, a pre-war centre forward. I played several games against Brian and at the age of 22 his skill on the ball was much in evidence. He did score one goal against me and it was one I shall never forget – neither did he – he described it to a national newspaper as the best goal he never saw! I didn't either!

Facing his own goal as the ball was played to him, he turned quickly and with little back lift (Jackie Milburn style) it was in the back of the net before I could move. Falling over as he completed the shot, in Brian's eloquent phrase, "I went arse over tit". Even the cameras behind the goal failed to capture his golden goal.

Much has been written about Brian, particularly regarding his great success as a manager, and quite rightly so. However, there was a downside which is rarely mentioned. For instance, when he was installed at Leeds United, where Don Revie had previously achieved enormous success, it was widely expected Brian would carry on where Don had left off. Unfortunately, like many things in life, it did not work out the way most people thought it would. After just a few days Brian was unceremoniously booted out, collecting £30,000 as a going away present, not bad for a few days' work. It transpired some of the

Leeds players, hardy pros, were not prepared to put up with Brian's abrasive style of management.

It wasn't until much later that I met him again in the most unusual circumstances. I had been appointed youth manager at Luton Town and Brian was managing Brighton and Hove Albion – neither of them the most glamorous club in the world!

When I took over the team, all under 18s, they were struggling near the bottom of the league which embraced top teams such as Arsenal, Spurs, Chelsea and West Ham. In a short space of time we were climbing up the league, arousing the interest of the London's football fraternity as well as Brian Clough.

His Brighton team were performing badly, which necessitated the need for new players. He came to Luton with that in mind, hoping to sign an inside forward. However, unbeknown to the Luton manager, Harry Haslam, Brian's was also interested in two of my youth players, Andy King (no relation) and Alan Biley.

Having managed to sign the inside forward in question, he cornered me in the social club, where there was much activity, and proceeded to question me about the two lads. His aim was for me to talk to Haslam, making the point that it would great experience for the lads to go to Brighton, especially as Brian's intention was to play them in his first team.

I told Brian it was a complete non starter as I was only the youth manager and I held no real authority. In typical Clough fashion he replied: "Come on, bonny lad, you and I can make ourselves a couple of 'thou' – think it over and I'll be in touch next week."

I had no intention of talking to Haslam on any account and I doubted whether the kids themselves would be interested as they had their sights on bigger clubs than Brighton.

The mysteries of life on earth continue to intrigue me – events can change a person's future at any given second. Brian Clough was no exception to the rule as his future was determined in a matter of days. On the following Saturday his Brighton team were thrashed 8-0 so it wasn't surprising to hear he had left the club on the Monday, whether on his own volition or sacked, no one but the club knew the answer.

It was obvious Brian's interest in my two lads had fallen by the wayside, which was a relief to me, as I wasn't looking forward to his phone call! As for the futures of Andy King and Alan Biley, they too were determined in a positive direction. Both lads were quickly signed up by Everton shortly after they had finished their apprenticeship at Luton.

Andy, in particular, became a regular at Goodison Park, making quite a name for himself before moving on to Queens Park Rangers. Alan meanwhile really came into his own when he moved to Portsmouth, becoming a big favourite with Pompey fans, who still remember his outrageous hairstyles and the tremendous enthusiasm which remained during his whole career.

Following his playing career Andy managed Swindon Town, was sacked, then reinstated for an obscure financial issue. In between appointments with the Robins he was chief scout at Sunderland under the management of Peter Reid and it was at this juncture that I rang Andy at the Stadium of Light in connection with a young keeper demonstrating distinct promise at my coaching school in my native Amble.

From the start of our conversation it was obvious this was not the chirpy Andy King I had known as a talented youngster. His whole demeanour suggested he carried the whole world on his shoulders – I seemed to remember he once had a sense of humour which is sadly lacking in the world of football today.

Needless to say, his interest in my young keeper was nil, although he did make the comment one hears on a regular basis from those in authority – I'll see what I can do and ring you back. Unless it is for their benefit, they never do – end of story.

What a delight it was talking to Alan Biley, though. In complete contrast to Andy King, Alan sounded exactly the same as he did a decade or two ago. His personality on the field was portrayed in his general lifestyle, a perfect example as to the way young professionals should behave both on and off the field.

Another of my youth team, 'Lil' Fuccillo (Italian heritage), also made it into the professional ranks for Luton and several other league teams, eventually becoming player-manager at Peterborough United followed by several scouting positions, a brief period as Luton Town manager, then a return to scouting after coaching non-league clubs.

Lil was the most unlikely footballer I ever saw. I'm sure he will forgive me for saying that, but his body was like a large beer barrel – something he managed to defy once out on the football pitch. He was exceptionally skilled on the ball and his speed belied his outside appearance, and to hear his shout of "Lil's ball" whenever he demanded possession was the key to much of his success.

David Carr was another apprentice who made it into the professional ranks with Lincoln City, but I lost touch with his subsequent career. To see four apprentices graduate as full professionals is a rare achievement for any club. These days I have to ask what chance any aspiring youngster has with so many foreign players taking over our game?

My tenure as Luton's youth manager came to an end when my photograph appeared along with the youth team in the local newspaper. Harry Haslam was furious because he wasn't included, heralding the beginning of my disenchantment with Luton Town football club.

Having written extensively on my two years at Luton in *"Hands, Feet and Balls"* I have no wish to make any further comments on the subject, except to say that apart from my brief association with the youth team it was the unhappiest period in my 30 years in the professional game.

My last connection with a club was scouting for Coventry City, at the time a formidable top-flight side with Noel Cantwell, the former West Ham player, as their manager. The chief scout was Bob Dennison, who hailed from my home town, Amble, in Northumberland. Bob had played for Newcastle United before moving on to other league clubs – including a spell as manager of Middlesbrough in the Clough era.

When he became chief scout at Coventry City he asked me if I'd be interested in scouting for him, to which I was agreeable. Bournemouth had a centre forward called Ted McDougal, who was attracting many league clubs with his goal scoring exploits, and this was my first assignment, assessing this player in the company of managers and scouts from various clubs.

Sitting well away from the assembled group, and with the game having been in progress for 15 or 20 minutes, the two unoccupied seats with reserved stickers next to me were approached out of the gloom by two figures – a man with an overcoat, collar turned up, wearing a cap and a scarf covering most of his face, and a lady who on closer scrutiny looked more like a 'dolly bird'. Although they only spoke, or should I say whispered, very occasionally, it was obvious to me that the mystery man was none other than Brian Clough!

During the half time break they stayed huddled together, then 20 minutes before the end of the game, got up and squeezed past me. I couldn't resist whispering: "Goodnight, Brian."

He froze on the spot, turned to me and, on a night of whispers, said: "For God's sake don't say anything or the press will crucify me!"

His secret was indeed safe with me – this is the first time I have mentioned this episode, which happened 25 or 30 years ago. Whatever Brian Cough's frailties, and there were many, no one on this earth can claim to be holier than thou – everyone at some time will succumb to temptation, hiding the proverbial skeleton in the cupboard. Except from his own family no one knew Brian Clough, and although I was labelled an enigma by a sports columnist a short time ago I think Brian was way ahead of me in that department.

It would be interesting to hear his comments on the football world as it is now. One thing is certain: he may have been self-opinionated but his knowledge and bold assessments were qualities no manager today can match.

Health

Whenever I give talks to kids or sportsmen still actively involved in their chosen sport I stress the importance of enjoying every second, every minute, every hour and every day. Youth is fleeting, gone in the blink of an eye. In a normal life span we spend a large part of our lives as senior citizens, which can lead to sheer and utter boredom. This is why it is necessary as we grow older to keep both body and mind active – even the gentlest of exercises, including deep breathing, can contribute to sustaining a reasonable lifestyle. Taking up a hobby will help even more.

Some years ago I devised a health programme for the benefit of those with physical and mental problems. My leaflet, which carries the label 'Dynamic Tension', is distributed throughout the country and even interested Prince Charles, who suffers from chronic back problems. His secretary wrote to me on behalf of the Prince thanking me for the advice and wishing me good health, which disproves the theory that he thinks only of himself.

As I emphasise time and time again, our health is the most important concept during our lifetime – enjoy it while you can!

To my way of thinking, bullying is one of the most evil forms of torture. Having endured these odious practices as a child, I have endeavoured to protect those who are vulnerable to thugs, who are themselves little more than cowards.

It is not only boys who are on the receiving end as there is evidence that girls being bullied by their own sex is on the increase. My wife Norma and I sat in our car on the main street of Amble and witnessed a girl of no more than 15 being kicked viciously and jumped on by two or three other girls of the same age. As I got out of my car these thugs ran away screaming out obscenities. The attacked girl was rushed off to hospital where thankfully she recovered, but I ask: "What sort of world are we living in that brings about such behaviour?"

I was brought up in a mining village (where I lived for four years) and then on a farm (another four years). During those first eight years of my life I had a comparatively sheltered existence except for the mental bullying of a youth named Brodie, a name I've never forgotten.

Moving to the town of Amble shattered my sheltered illusions when some cruel school friend informed me there was no Santa Claus. One always remembers the significant events – the exact time, day and year!

Just as bullying is on the increase, so is the use of the four-letter word beginning with F. The only time I heard any bad language, and I'm not talking four-letter words here, was in my schoolboy football days when we played against the Catholic School. I asked one of their team why they swore so much.

"Well," said the player, "we go and see the Father and he gives us absolution."

Mind you, I don't suppose he uttered that word then – we wouldn't have known what it meant! Bad language has been around since time began and the Anglo-Saxons merely enforced it here in Great Britain. However, the F-word was unheard of during my youth, and it was a culture shock when I started my apprenticeship as a painter and decorator. Every other word was Anglo Saxon on construction sites alongside hardened builders, which after a while became boring and monotonous.

Professional footballers are also prone to such language and this is often highlighted on close-up television. Much of it is in the heat of the moment but it can be upsetting to many sports lovers, especially young children.

A case in point occurred during my Port Vale days when we had crowds of between 20,000 and 25,000. Following a training session a lady, probably in her 40s, stood outside the main entrance of the ground anxious to speak with me. After the usual 'cat calls' from one or two players – "What's Kingy up to now?" – this well-spoken lady proceeded to question me about the bad language uttered by players during the matches at Vale Park.

She said her husband and 10-year-old son had attended the Sports Church Service the previous Sunday when the teams from Stoke City and Port Vale were in attendance and I read the lesson. Her son was a keen Vale fan and whenever possible positioned himself directly behind my goal. She said after the game her son came home bursting to talk about the match but was upset when the Vale players used bad language – he said because of the noisy crowd he couldn't hear but knew from the expression on their faces what they were saying.

I explained to her these words were said in the context and didn't really mean to be offensive. "In any case," I said, "what about the players from the opposition?"

She retorted immediately: "He's not bothered about them, only the Vale players!"

I left her saying I would do what I could but – and I have used the expression before – it will be like trying to stop a dog from barking and a cat from miaowing.

Nonetheless, nothing ventured, nothing gained. I decided to tell the lads what transpired between the lady and myself. If bad language on the field upset the young lad I was convinced he would never watch another Vale match if he continued to hear foul language coming out the mouths of the Vale players.

I suggested omitting the F from the offensive word so the lad wouldn't notice any lip movement. I know it sounds incredible but the lads reluctantly agreed to give it a go, all for the sake of one 10-year-old Vale fan.

The next home game was one I shall never forget. Even today the memory still makes me chuckle and if the lad in question reads this I do hope he has a sense of humour. To hear grown men 'ucking' on the playing field was bad enough, like a battery of hens, but when Tommy Cheadle gave away a free kick outside the box, he stormed up to the referee shouting: "Ucking ell ef, that wasn't an owl!"

I was always a compulsive giggler but when Tommy uttered those words players on both sides burst out laughing – the crowd behind the goal must have thought we'd gone bonkers.

Thankfully the story had a happy ending. I received a lovely letter from the lady I had met, thanking me for my co-operation – her son was delighted. What one has to do for the fans!

How long we carried on with this charade is was beyond my memory. I was 40 years old before hearing a member of the fair sex utter the F-word. That was shock enough for the system but to hear it twice in one day from another lady was a double whammy!

The year was 1964, when the Suez crisis threatened world peace once again. I was employed as a masseur by the American Air Force at Brize Norton in Oxfordshire. As I entered the officer's quarters that the commanding officer, Colonel Baine, had kindly allocated me, a young lady was loudly remonstrating with a male member of staff for some misdemeanour or other. After a lengthy confrontation the lad was visibly shaken, especially when she told him: "Eff off and don't come back!" I might say he wasn't the only one shaking!

Worse was to follow when I entered the dining room, where many of the young pilots were waiting for their lunch, obviously hungry having flown in from the US earlier in the day and displaying their impatience by banging spoons and forks on the tables.

This disturbance was nothing compared to the scene which followed. The cook, who was an enormous Irish lady, strode into the dining room, placed her hands on her hips and in broadly accented tirade boomed: "Roight you effin' lot, when I come back on this earth I'll be a flying cow and shite on the lotta yer. Now I'm goin' back to the effing kitchen to bring your effing dinners."

After a stunned silence the pilots all stood up and gave her a round of applause.

Twice in one day! I waited for the third but none came!

Nowadays of course it is commonplace to hear women using bad language and children too are embroiled in this familiar dialogue. Newspapers, radio and television regularly impart their powerful influence on the general public and just like the parrot are caught up in this sickening cliché.

And it is not only the F-word that is causing widespread offence. Other clichés that grate include 'Having said that', 'At the end of the day', 'At that moment in time', 'See ya later', and many, many more. But the most abused of all is 'basically'.

These words are often uttered by personalities on radio and television, even those in government, who ought to know better. Having said that, I am, at the end of the day, basically as sick as the proverbial parrot!

Money and Medals

I was most concerned when I read that Alan Ball, who was the youngest player in the England World Cup winning team of 1966, was to sell his medal from that famous victory. He said he is hoping to raise £120,000 in an effort to support his family – but why should such a situation arise for someone who was at the top of his profession, both as a player and manager for many years?

Granted, the money he was earning can in no way compare with the ridiculous salaries paid to players of today, many with a modicum of talent.

Tommy Lawton one of England's greatest Centre Forwards died in abject poverty, but again the question is why? The *Daily Mail*'s celebrated sports writer Ian Wooldridge told me some time ago that when he went to interview Tommy at his home in Nottingham he was appalled at what he saw: furniture which had seen its best years and floors with no carpets covered in old-fashioned linoleum – what a complete travesty.

Although my own league championship and FA Cup semi-final medals cannot compare with a World Cup medal, to me they represent a precious period in my football career. I was also presented with a commemorative plaque along with the other Vale players who created history for the club. I do know there are Vale supporters who would willingly pay huge sums to gain possession of these trophies, but unless I was in desperate straits they will stay where they are!

Drugs

Whenever I talk to young kids I warn them the danger of taking drugs, which is becoming increasingly prevalent throughout the world. It is not only the drug itself which causes the problems as on occasions other substances are being added, such as dextromethorphan – a drug used in over-the-counter medicines – which makes for a very dangerous formula. Drug takers beware!

In Thailand and other South East Asian countries there is no restriction on the sale of drugs – anyone who wants them can have as many as they like providing they have the cash. Rich kids are particularly vulnerable and consequently the drug dealers pinpoint them as lucrative targets. In no time at all they become millionaires at the expense of willing victims who in the process lose their young lives.

A case in point occurred when a 15-year-old boy, previously a student at my son's school in Bangkok, dropped dead of a drug-related heart attack. He had been 'sent down' from the school three weeks previously because of his drug addiction, but all to no avail. He was found in a hotel bedroom together with his girlfriend who was rushed to the intensive care unit of a Bangkok hospital fighting for her life.

The parents of the boy had five other children, one of whom went to the same school, where the mother taught. Following the cremation of the dead boy the family flew off to the United States for a memorial service before returning to Bangkok. Another family's life is torn apart, and how many more will suffer in this crazy world?

The Penalty Kick

As I write, there is much talk and tabloid coverage once again regarding the penalty kick. Quite recently two penalties were missed by the same player in a Premier League match. Players who are earning tens of thousands of pounds and more a week should never miss scoring a goal from a distance of a mere 12 yards. That is the view of course construed by most football followers, but human nature being what it is, penalties will continue to be missed whatever a player earns.

Temperament plays a huge part in this controversial issue, especially in situations when that one kick can mean the difference between winning or losing a match such as a cup final, winning the League or avoiding relegation. Even great players miss them occasionally – Alan Shearer, one of the best exponents of the penalty kick, and Peter Beardsley, in my opinion the best of all. Tommy Lawton, the great England centre forward, hated taking penalty kicks – he told me the last time he took a penalty was the one I saved from him at Goodison Park in the 1940s which broke my wrist.

Gareth Southgate, Chris Waddle and David Beckham have displayed the worst penalty kicks I've ever seen for England! As Southgate's mother commented when he missed in the 1996 European Championships: "Why didn't you just bend it?" A sound philosophy!

Anyone for Cricket?

As you know, I always inquired about the local cricket club wherever my football career took me. When I moved to Poole I didn't have to look very far as on my first day in the manager's office a young man by the name of Pat Butler came to see me. Pat was the secretary of Poole Cricket Club and he asked me if I played cricket.

That first meeting with Pat was the beginning of a warm friendship over the next three years and an association with the cricket club was the happiest of all the eight clubs I played for. Apart from Pat the names of David Robinson (captain), Peter Stuckey, Denis Broadhurst, Geoff Horsfield, Shay Seymour and Ken Grout come readily to mind. Others, whose faces I see clearly but for the moment forget their names, I remember with affection.

Playing at Poole Park was an absolute delight and on a pleasant day – which more often than not it was – deck chairs were placed around the boundary lines, creating a delightful atmosphere. At the far end of the ground a duck pond did at times cause an inconvenience when the water encroached across the boundary line, but thankfully it didn't often happen.

There are so many memories and amusing incidents which come to mind but that would require writing another book on anecdotes and my energy levels aren't quite up to that!

Although I enjoyed all aspects of cricket, whether it be batting, occasional bowling or fielding, I particularly liked the fundamental involvement of taking part in a game where the team spirit and comradeship was of prime importance. I enjoyed batting in partnership with Shay Seymour, a lovely West Indian with a typical swashbuckling style that earned him an abundance of runs. In contrast to me Shay counted every run he made, which he said helped him to concentrate (as well as not trusting the scorers!) He made his point on the day he was convinced he'd reached his hundred but when there was no applause his concentration was affected and his wicket fell on the next ball – in the scorer's book he was credited with 99.

Peter Stuckey, the team's opening strike bowler, also played county cricket for Dorset, and was involved with me in a knockout competition when I scored 50, all in singles. The soft wicket was not conducive to stroke playing, so we resorted to the type of game we played as kids: tip and run. Never have I had to work for runs as hard as on that occasion. Peter, apart from being a quick bowler, was also no sleuth between the wickets, backing each other up off almost every ball. In plain language I was absolutely knackered, which made me realise at the age of 40 it was time to slow down a bit. Can I really be double that now?

On the occasions that I did reach 80 with the bat my thoughts centred on accumulating those 20 extra runs to reach the coveted century. As any batsman will tell you, getting those 20 runs can be the toughest part of the whole innings. However, in terms of years, I have a feeling the cricket field bears no resemblance to that of mortality! My main concern is being around tomorrow!

I captained the team a few times when David Robinson wasn't available and one game in particular comes to mind which again involved Peter Stuckey. It has always been my policy to bat first and get some runs on the scoreboard, giving bowlers and fielders an extra incentive to get the opponents out – plus the first team to bat gets the best of the wicket! In this particular game I won the toss and opted to bat first. The Poole wickets were notorious for being on the soft side, especially if the tide was in (Sandbanks was a stone's throw from the ground – maybe a cricket ball's throw would be more appropriate). On this day we had great difficulty accumulating runs as the ball was not coming on to the bat quickly enough and at the end of our innings I wasn't happy with our total score. Even though Peter Stuckey was an excellent strike bowler I felt fast bowling was out of the question with the wicket in such a state against one of the top teams in Dorset.

A few eyebrows were raised when I decided to open with spin and Peter Stuckey proved what a good sportsman he was by agreeing with my unusual decision. Opening batsmen, so used to facing quick bowling, were caught completely off their stride facing a young left arm spinner who had the ability to turn the ball both ways. Half their side were back in the pavilion in no time with little to show for it.

However, like all good sides they had players with experience and ability to see them through against our modest total. The point I wish to illustrate is why don't more teams adapt themselves to the condition of the wicket instead of employing the same old format week in week out? Opening bowlers labour away until completing their allocated number of overs before the captain makes a change.

Because of my association with Homefield School the opportunity to link up with Hospital Services Cricket Club became available to me. A student at the school named Roger Baker, a tall lad who could bowl very quickly, was instrumental as he introduced me to his father Douglas, who was secretary of St Leonard's Hospital and also of the cricket club. I was at that time running the school cricket team in conjunction with Major Bob Broach, bursar at Homefield and wicket keeper of the team.

An additional member of our team was Derek Wilkinson, a former Sheffield United player who had previously held the position of sports master until my arrival, enabling him to take over the boarding school at Winkton, near Christchurch. Sadly Derek died at the age of 74 a few years ago.

The three of us added stability and experience by playing along with the team of young lads participating in a local Bournemouth league. I was then invited to play for Hospital Services, a team comprising doctors, administration staff and one or two guest players such as myself. Games were played on a Sunday to fit in with the availability of the players and the fact that the majority of opposition teams were in a similar category.

Most of these teams, based in Dorset and Hampshire, were unknown quantities and we often faced opposition which included several young players attached to county teams such as Hampshire and Somerset – quite a formidable challenge. Nevertheless it was most enjoyable playing on beautiful grounds and pristine wickets, some of county standard.

Unfortunately the same could not be said of our own ground at St Leonard's, although Doug Baker and his great friend John Hough worked extremely hard to bring the wicket up to a reasonable requirement. Doug and John were two remarkable men who played in the team almost up into their eighties, Doug as opening bowler and

John as wicket keeper, believe it or not still standing up to medium fast bowlers, resulting in many stumpings.

They were wonderful memories, all from playing the game I loved, with friendships to last a lifetime – but now they are just that, only memories to sustain those halcyon years.

Poole

The following years continued in a familiar pattern – there were good times mixed with the inevitable bad, all intertwined to create a more exciting life! My two years at Oxford United and a further two years at Luton Town were well documented in *"Hands, Feet and Balls"*, so I've no wish to comment on what were two episodes in my life best forgotten.

On the other hand my six years as a sportsmaster at Homefield School was the happiest period of my life – sadly the school is no more but those who were there both as teachers and students are left with wonderful memories.

One good decision Norma and I did make was to keep our house in Poole while I was away at Oxford and Luton. Even when I was out of work this did not concern me in the slightest – providing my hands were in good working order we weren't going to starve! Finding work as a painter and decorator was no problem and soon my physiotherapy work was in full swing, giving me the best of both worlds.

Norma and I were in our sixties by this time, and we were extremely happy living in Poole, having resided in the area for 26 years, the longest period in one place in our ever-changing movements around the country.

Apart from football memories there were many other aspects of our time that I feel compelled to mention, including some of those colleagues with whom I enjoyed an abundance of wonderful cricketing times, especially at Poole Park Cricket Club and Hospital Services CC.

Cricket was the love of my life and if my memory serves me right Brian Clough admitted he too preferred cricket to football. There were of course several top class footballers who also reached the heights at cricket, such as Denis Compton and Willie Watson. Brian Close and Freddy Trueman also combined the two sports although not quite to such a high standard at football. Both played centre forward, for Bradford City and Lincoln City respectively, and having played against both I was not particularly impressed. Ian Botham also had a go with Scunthorpe United but also fell by the wayside.

With so much football now being played most of the year round, any aspiring footballer or cricketer stands little chance of combining both sports – in my day most would plump for cricket if they were of a high standard but with so much money being floated around in the football world today, guess which game they prefer?

I am often asked why I haven't taken up golf as both my brothers Frank and George did. It's an easy question to answer – when I did play on the odd occasion I was bored to tears with the pedestrian style of the game, plus it is not played with the same team spirit as cricket.

Unless one plays regularly there is little chance of becoming proficient in any sport, and most certainly golf is a game which needs to be played every day – all that walking and so little to show for it! Rather ironic isn't it, the worse you are at golf the more shots you have – the good player spends much of his time walking! No doubt the dedicated golfers will pour scorn on my comments but that is only my opinion.

Return to Amble

It was the end of an era when we decided to embark on a new adventure, a return to our native north-east of England after an absence of almost 40 years. What has transpired since, to those who read of our unprecedented series of events, will probably conclude I am making it up as I go along – let me assure you every word and sentence I write is exactly how it happened. Not having kept a diary does make the task writing of events in years gone by much more difficult, but *"Hands, Feet and Balls"* was written from memory, so there is no reason why this shouldn't be as well.

Our first day back in Amble started off on the wrong foot when we were met by one of Norma's sisters, who said: "What are you doing back in Amble? It's a dying town!"

That was only the beginning. The house we moved into would perhaps be better described as a doll's house or, better still, a doss house. There was barely room to swing a cat, the rooms were filthy and outside the back door was a rubbish dump smelling like a sewer – in other words, an absolute nightmare.

Worse was to follow the next day when I was almost shot with an air rifle by a young lady firing from an upstairs window in an adjoining house – she said she was shooting at cats and birds – I can guarantee after I'd finished reading her the riot act her days as a gun-toting Bonnie (without Clyde) were over – she is now a respectable married lady with a family!

The saga continued when eggs were splattered over my car, the coping from my garden wall was pulled off and thrown into a neighbour's garden (whose own coping had been snatched for the purpose of smashing the local Co-op windows less than 50 metres away from my house). Ain't life wonderful?!

This was our introduction to 'little old Amble', the quiet town we left those 40 years ago – if the town was dying then the incidents we experienced in our first few days would suggest otherwise – Amble as we knew it had changed its image, and violence, as in most other towns and cities in the country, unfolded before us.

If brick throwing and burning and stealing cars wasn't bad enough the citizens of Amble also endured speeding motorists in built-up areas with a police force seemingly unable to cope. My house was situated on one of the busiest roads in Amble and speeding traffic was normal, drivers were completely oblivious to the danger. When I complained to the police they did some investigation with special instruments then informed me that traffic was well within the speed limit. A few weeks later a young man carrying fish and chips to his young family was knocked down and killed by a speeding motorist no more than 50 metres from where we lived.

We were desperate to move away to a more suitable area but did not expect to sell our property without the inevitable problems usually associated with such a project. However, we were astonished to receive an offer in a short space of time, which we readily accepted.

"As one door shuts another one opens" has long been a popular quotation, but there are times when the other door refuses to budge, and this causes complications. Fortunately for us we selected a good door and soon we were off to another area of the town which was more familiar to us both, having spent the earlier part of our lives there. I became more involved in the general run of things in Amble, particularly in sport, meeting up with old friends and remembering the good old days – at least that's what we believed, although the younger generations would probably disagree.

Getting together with several former Amble FC players, notably Jimmy Stewart and Jim Taylor and other willing helpers, we formed a committee with the sole purpose of inviting all the older generation of sportsmen to a celebration dinner. We invited the great Jackie Milburn as our guest celebrity.

Jackie and I had remained friends ever since my days playing for Newcastle United and this occasion could not have happened at a more appropriate time. His health was causing a considerable amount of concern and it was then he confided to me his eyesight had started to bother him. No one who was there that historic evening would have guessed Jackie had health problems, he was the same smiling and friendly lad whose fame hadn't changed him one tiny bit.

The evening was a great success which was especially pleasing for me as it was the last opportunity I had to honour a friend and former playing colleague.

My last words to Jackie as I said goodbye were: "Long after you have gone your fame will increase through the years."

His typical reply: "Oh, had away and shite!"

Newcastle United are renowned for the great centre forwards, and I am proud and privileged to have played in the same team as two of them, Albert Stubbins and Jackie Milburn, who were also my friends.

Norma and I gradually became accustomed to the Northumbrian way of life and change of climate, which is quite considerable. My acupressure therapy was taking off in a big way, then when I was on holiday in New York, staying with our son Gary, he arranged for me to attend a course on shiatsu, a Japanese form of alternative medicine – of all the other therapies I have experienced, shiatsu gives more benefit than any other – pressure on points of the body relieve pressure, particularly the feet.

When I mentioned to Harry Green there were an estimated 72,000 nerve endings in each foot, he commented in his inimitable dry style: "How long did it take you to count them?"

Off To Sunny Florida!

Resigned as Norma and I were to spending the rest of our lives in Amble, Gary rang us to say he was having a house built in Florida where it was hoped he would spend his retirement years. In the interim period he thought it might be a good opportunity for Norma and I to live in the property, apart from better security we'd also enjoy a warm and sunny climate. This really was a bolt out of the blue – it meant we'd have to sell our house, furniture and car, as well as dealing with all the other commitments necessary for moving to another country.

While we deliberated on the best plan of action, Gary rang us late one evening to say the builders constructing the house had demanded a considerable down payment. There was no time for deliberation, so we had no alternative but to place the house on the market and hope for the best, otherwise it meant taking a bridging loan, which was quite unthinkable.

Once again, fortune was on our side as an offer came the same week the house had been placed on the market – of course we accepted as time was of the essence.

Disposing of our household goods was the hardest part – everything went to the sale rooms, many treasures accumulated over the years were sold at knock down prices. It really was heartbreaking. It was also with heavy heart that we left Amble once again in completely contrasting circumstances, after all we had just adapted ourselves back into the fold. We had to ask ourselves what on earth we were letting ourselves in for.

It wasn't long before we found out. Loaded down with four large suitcases (our worldly goods) we were fortunate to have a friend, Gary Wilson, who offered to take us in his car to Newcastle bus station en route to London, from where we would fly to Tampa, Florida – this was where the real story began, even today I find it difficult to believe that the following events took place.

The bungalow, or house as Floridians prefer to name them, was situated in a new town called Springhill, 40 miles from Tampa. It was built to Gary's own specification – lounge, three bedrooms, two bathrooms and a swimming pool – a dream home in every respect!

Gary had flown from New York to greet us at Tampa airport where a car was hired to take us on the final stage of the journey to Springhill. As we drove through the countryside and villages, isolated petrol stations dotted at various intervals, I was bemused at the flatness of it all, plain boring land which created a feeling of utter depression – what a wonderful start this was going to be to our new life! Worse was to follow on arriving at our destination. As if I wasn't dejected enough, the situation which confronted us on looking at this beautiful bungalow surrounded by its quarter acre of garden was a mass of weeds at least 3ft high – visions of spending the next few months clearing that lot was paramount in my mind before we even entered the building.

What we had just witnessed was miniscule compared with the complete devastation which greeted us as we walked into the lounge, or what represented a lounge. The floor, fitted with thick carpet, was practically covered in bricks and mortar which had been gouged from the ceiling and walls, leaving big gaping holes in every direction. The bedrooms and bathrooms were similar and even the swimming pool didn't miss out, the hooligans who perpetrated the vandalism topped off their wanton behaviour by defecating in it, which to them was a better option than using the lavatory!

Shell shocked as we were, decisions had to be made quickly. It was obvious we couldn't stay in the bungalow which meant having to rent a holiday apartment. There were plenty of them, at a price! The police didn't want to know and our insurance company refused to pay out because the alarm systems hadn't been switched on. The estimated damage was in the region of £10,000. Welcome to Springhill, Florida!

It wasn't until much later when we learned the main perpetrator was a policeman's son who lived in the next bungalow to ours, 50 metres away. With his gang of bored teenagers it appeared they had terrorised the area for some considerable time and our home had been their headquarters for their vicious campaign. But please don't go away, there is more to come!

The temporary home we rented until our own property was restored to its former glory was quite modern and in immaculate condition. So was there a change in our fortunes? We soon found out.

Gary had gone back to New York because of his school teaching duties, hoping we would be comfortable. He hired a car for me which would give us the opportunity to explore the area and perhaps meet up with a few of the local residents. What a hope! We were completely exhausted after the long journey and the horrendous events which were bestowed on us. We were eagerly looking forward to a comfortable bed and a good night's sleep. Certainly the bedroom was adequate and the single beds firm and comfortable – surely nothing else could go wrong?

My past and current experiences should have taught me anything can go wrong at any time and this night was about to prove the point. No sooner had we got to sleep when we were awakened by the sound of running water emanating from one of the bathrooms. Weren't we lucky having two? Half asleep and distinctly not in a jovial mood my depression deepened even further when I discovered *two* overflowing toilet cisterns.

Never before had I wished so much to have served an apprenticeship as a plumber instead of painting and decorating – here we were in a strange country, which reminded me of the song, 'Who can I turn to with no one to guide me'. And oh no, the story doesn't end there, in fact it's just beginning to get interesting!

I'd given up on hopeless attempts at stopping the overflow and went back to bed resigning myself to a continuing nightmare.

Click, click, click.

The sound increased in intensity as we lay there still in a daze and becoming more and more curious as to where this new din was coming from I crept tentatively toward the bedroom door which led straight through to the lounge. I slowly opened it with a slipper in one hand, well prepared for action! Switching the light on, the scene which unfolded was one I'll never forget as long as I live. The entire floor was alive with the largest brown cockroaches I've ever seen, they crawled everywhere, walls, ceiling and furniture and all the time emitting this metallic sounding click, click, click.

Any effort to get rid of them was a non-starter – my trusted slipper would be as much use as a wet sponge! Our first reaction was to get out of the building as quickly as possible, but where would we go? I decided the best solution was to stay in the bedroom, seal the door, then sweat it out until first light when these vile creatures return to their habitat, wherever that is. Sure enough when I opened the door in the morning it was sheer relief to be greeted with blissful silence, not a cockroach in sight. The water problem also appeared to have resolved itself.

Nevertheless we were both in a foul mood. Having had little or no sleep my first priority was to get in touch with the firm who rented us their "luxury holiday house". As expected they were full of apologies – the house had been recently decorated and cleaned and their only excuse was it had not been lived in for several months – hence the cockroach invasion and water cistern flooding through lack of use!

I emphasised categorically that we couldn't possibly spend another night there and they promised to do what they could to rectify the situation. By late afternoon the phone hadn't rung to relieve us of the anxiety we were experiencing but of course this was nothing new to me, it happens all the time in England: "Don't ring us, we'll ring you." But they never do.

Eventually I contacted the person responsible for our predicament, only to learn that no other accommodation was available until the following day which meant we had to spend one more night in the haunted house! We were assured there would be no more problems with the cisterns and a special bug solution had been sprayed in various corners of the house, which in effect eliminates all infestation. Our thoughts focused on the fear of what damage it could cause our health – breathing in particular.

Uneasy as we were lying on our beds listening for any unusual sounds, morning came without any undue incidents, but I was still apprehensive as I opened the bedroom door to the lounge. Sure enough the special solution had worked its magic, just as we'd been told, but what a sight to behold. All visible floor space was a mass of dead cockroaches lying on their backs – our immediate reaction was to get out of that hell hole in the quickest possible time – I wasn't in the right frame of mind for my bowl of cornflakes with an army of dead cockroaches surrounding me!

The housing firm refused to refund us which came as no surprise – we were completely in their power until our own house was restored to its original condition.

Relieved as we were to be rid of the infested building, moving into another 'holiday home' did not exactly excite us but we just had to content ourselves and make the most of it. Thankfully there were no such problems in our next house and it was here, complete with our four suitcases, that we survived several weeks until the eagerly awaited day when we returned to the house we were supposed to be living in!

Having a car to run around in was a great asset, and even remembering to drive on the right side of the road wasn't really a problem. It gave us the opportunity to explore the area. The more I saw of Springhill, with its 10,000 inhabitants, the more depressed I became and thoughts of living the rest of my days there filled me with despair. To compound matters, Norma developed a cough prior to leaving our temporary home which became increasingly worse at night time.

Then for good measure her right hand became inflamed and swelled to more than twice its normal size. The only option was the local hospital which had only recently opened, so at least that was a bonus – if only the same could be said for the doctors! During the two hours or so we were there she was examined by at least four medics, not one of whom could diagnose the problem – the popular theory was some kind of insect bite even though I explained to them it was more likely to be osteoporosis, a condition she incurred as a legacy from the cancer which gripped her as a 50-year-old.

Return to Amble

Imust admit the lovely feeling of at long last returning to our bungalow and to see it for the first time in the condition we had expected on our previous visit seemed too good to be true. Now we had the opportunity to weigh up our situation, make an effort to look on the bright side and ease our way into the Florida way of life.

It has been a policy of mine since my sporting days ended to continue exercising, albeit on a more limited scale. Walking plays a big part in my repertoire, not only for health reasons but it is an ideal way to meet other walkers intent on keeping themselves in good shape. This then was my intended philosophy in Springhill. What better way to become acquainted with the locals, who perhaps are themselves on the lookout to establish new friendships?

The area around the bungalow was a residential complex with residents secluded from their neighbours in a quarter-acre garden and surrounding hedges, an ideal environment for those who wish to be alone. The garden, which had been littered with weeds, was now looking pristine having been landscaped. This was certainly a heart-warming sight for me as gardening was never my forte!

With that hurdle over for the time being I could now concentrate on my fitness schedule, starting with my proposed daily walk around the sizeable estate, with the prospect of meeting up with some of our new neighbours.

As I walked on that first day, the weather was pleasantly warm, sun shining, I felt at peace with the world, the nightmares of the past few weeks behind me. This was the beginning of a new dawn. I still remember that walk as though it were yesterday, the silence, except for the occasional bird twittering – not even a dog barking or a cat prowling. I began to wonder if anyone lived in these luxury dwellings as I continued on my way, but then I realised human life did exist because most of the driveways had cars standing outside their garages.

For a full week I carried out my daily routine, occasionally seeing someone mowing their expansive lawn with a motorised mower or trimming enormous hedges, equipped similarly with the latest electronic cutter – the whole locality reeked of wealth. My gut reaction after just one week was the same feeling I experienced on our arrival in Florida – the Sunshine State – utter depression!

In England and New York, where we have spent several holidays, joggers can be seen wending their way through parks, open roads and even housing estates – but not in Springhill. Transport was the order of the day. No one walked. Even residents who came to collect their mail at the boxes near our house arrived in cars, some gave a perfunctory wave but most simply picked up or posted their mail before returning to their cars. It was like living on another planet.

We were also now 10 miles away from the nearest beach, which we didn't find particularly appealing and Clearwater, a major attraction, was 40 miles away on a busy road with traffic lights every 100 metres or so, which was very irritating. Having spent most of our lives in seaside resorts we couldn't see the point in making long car journeys when before the beach was right on our doorstep!

Over the following weeks we did become acquainted with two of our near neighbours and visited each other's houses which was rather nice, but as so often happens we had only to become reasonably comfortable with our new lifestyle before some sinister 'being' was rearing its ugly head.

Looking out of the window one morning I thought I was dreaming or my imagination was playing tricks, the entire quarter-acre of land which had been beautifully landscaped, the lawn manicured like a bowling green, was covered in small hillocks of soil. Each hillock was a heaving mass of ants all working in their inimitable style to destroy everything in their way. The landscaping firm recommended a brand of pellets which they said would work quickly to eliminate the ants.

I cannot remember how long it took me to spread those pellets on every single hillock but I do know my back was almost breaking by the time I'd finished. They did the trick but my main worry was how long it would be before they invaded again. I was back in deep depression! For five long months we soldiered on – we joined the Brit Club, an organisation where Brits got together to make new friends, but we were bitterly disappointed to discover everyone already had their own little cliques, leaving us in the cold looking on from the outside. One visit was enough.

The swimming pool was an attraction of course but I wasn't much of a swimmer – living in the north-eastern corner of England wasn't conducive to sea bathing and as footballers we were advised not to swim because it tightened the muscles – what a complete load of rubbish! On the face of it having a pool appears to be rather glamorous, but remember it has to be maintained constantly and there are many things that can go wrong, only adding to the expense involved.

The car was our main form of escapism. Gary, on one of his regular visits from New York, thought it better that we buy ourselves a decent car at the second-hand centre instead of paying the earth for a rental vehicle. We were fortunate to purchase a Ford Mustang which looked brand new – the engine was scrupulous, the price was reasonable and being left-hand drive didn't bother me. The sales woman, delighted at making a quick sale, remarked in her broad Texan drawl: "You've got a r-e-a-l s-t-e-a-l there, R-a-y." In plain English I'd got a bargain.

The car's performance matched its appearance and I thought how much I'd love to have a car like that in England for the same price – little did I know at that point my exultation wasn't going to last very long!

As I said earlier Springhill was a comparatively new town, well named too, with properties and shops springing up everywhere, but neither Norma or I could feel any kind of affinity with the place. One afternoon, again one I'll never forget, we were driving along a road which had been recently built. It went on for mile after mile, concrete walls on either side and dust everywhere. After what seemed an eternity I turned to Norma and said: "What the hell are we doing here? Pretending to enjoy ourselves? In reality we're bored out of our minds."

I was grateful that she agreed with me and it was at that precise moment we made the decision to call it a day. Florida wasn't for us. We rang Gary explaining our reasons for this monumental decision. He was understandably disappointed after all the planning and work involved designing a home for us with every comfort, but he realised how unhappy we were and immediately flew down to help us make arrangements for our return to England.

First priority was to sell the car, which in itself was heartbreaking. There was no way the car firm would offer me what I'd paid for it, after all I'd only had it for a few weeks. I'd hoped for a reasonable settlement, but car sales people are the same all over the world, they are in business and sentiment plays no part – I was the loser!

I know many readers will be astonished by our apparently selfish attitude, especially as Gary had worked so hard to create a new way of life for us in a part of the world which radiates sunshine most of the year, with a house containing all the comforts one could wish for. However, look at it from our point of view. We sold our house in England, our furniture and everything else. It was a complete departure from the homeland. Our decision to give it all up caused us much heartache.

There are those who would love the opportunity that we had, but for me life has more to offer than sitting near a swimming pool and going to the beach. Yes, there was the lovely sunshine and the famous Florida Everglades – which to us was the most depressing place to visit – but there was also the constant threat and experience of hurricanes.

Had we stayed in Florida our destiny would have been in complete contrast to what happened when we returned to our home town of Amble, then at various intervals to New York and Thailand, which I shall reveal later in these writings – it is all to do with survival!

Four Letter Words

Four letter words play a prominent part in our lives, particularly the one beginning with F and its sexual connotations, but there is a more powerful word also starting with F which will affect every one of us at sometime in our lives – Fear! The great American President Theodore Roosevelt said: "There is nothing to fear but fear itself."

During my lifetime I have encountered anxiety and fear on numerous occasions. Our Florida house was once again being left vacant, and even though the security system was now in operation, what happened before filled us with apprehension. We decided the best plan was to put it up for sale and in the meantime let it out. Selling wasn't going to be easy with so many new dwellings on the market, but we were optimistic.

We were determined to stay positive and booked the first available flight to London – there was no direct route to Newcastle Airport at that time but we didn't care – at least we'd be in England! Saddled with our four suitcases again, we heard the 'great' news from one of the air hostesses that the airline we were flying with – Highland Express or something like that – had gone bankrupt, so this was its last journey! And it gets better! On arrival at Stansted Airport a coach was waiting to take passengers to Victoria Coach Terminal where a London to Newcastle bus would be available to whisk us back to the north east – just like that!

Another forlorn hope! The coach driver, who was hired by the Highland airline, was furious received the news about the company's demise – which in effect meant his job was in jeopardy. Instead of taking us to our required destinations as instructed he dumped us in the centre of London on a small island, traffic flashing past on both sides, rubbing salt into our wounds. His parting words were of such comfort: "There's an Underground station 50 yards or so on the other side. All the best."

For what seemed an interminable age we stood there, two lost souls, four suitcases and all the time in the world – if you thought we were having 'fun', you ain't seen nothing yet! Eventually a policeman hailed a taxi for us. Astute taxi drivers seeing us with four suitcases didn't want to know – without that policeman we'd still probably still be standing there!

When we arrived at Victoria Coach Terminal further good news awaited us: the last coach to Newcastle had departed half an hour ago, with the next one scheduled for 7am the following morning!

The thought of spending a cold night in a draughty coach station was all we needed to end a perfect day, but with circumstances as they were at that moment, and feeling extremely low in spirit, the hand of providence reached out to offer a ray of hope: a coach was on the point of leaving for Glasgow, so we made a quick decision that our best option was to have a word with the driver about our situation. Listening intently and sympathising with our dilemma he readily agreed to take us as several seats were available. He also pointed out the nearest he got to Newcastle was Carlisle – 60 miles away. We decided to go with him and take our chances, anything was better than sitting in that cold bus station and at least we'd be much nearer our destination.

The following scenario will remain in my memory forever, and it is to the Scottish people we have to thank for their act of kindness and consideration. I had never forgotten how generous they were when as a 17-year-old playing for Newcastle United at Aberdeen I was again indebted to those wonderful Scots. When those passengers travelling on the coach, all going back to Glasgow, learned of our plight they asked the driver if he could deviate from his route and take us to the nearest point to our home – once again the driver (also a Scotsman) readily agreed, which beggars beyond belief. I must hasten to add none of them had been drinking! And most of them were women on an annual day out! Apparently they didn't want it to end!

How we got there I'll never know but when the driver shouted: "That's as far as I can go otherwise we'll end up in the sea!" we were in Seahouses, 20 miles from our hometown of Amble! It is difficult to put into words such an act of kindness, when there is much greed and hate in the world instead of the love and compassion that all of us need at some stage in our lives.

One of the songs or ditties rendered by the ladies was Sir Harry Lauder's 'Keep right on to the end of the road' which I mentioned at the beginning of this book and which I held onto as a title for these memoirs as a tribute to those ladies and that wonderful driver.

We are not yet at the end of the road. There is still a fair way to go and the journey is continually beset with its winding turns and hidden obstacles, but isn't that what makes life so interesting?

Norma and I were now standing outside a small hotel in Seahouses in the early hours of the morning, once again filled with apprehension as to what lay ahead of us. I had telephoned our friend Gary Wilson, the young man who took us in his car to Newcastle en route to Florida, and he was soon on his way to collect us and our suitcases! Gary is a great fan of Newcastle United (poor soul) but I don't hold that against him (I say this with tongue in cheek!)

When Gary arrived we hadn't a clue where we were going to stay until he suggested a popular pub in Amble called the Wellwood Arms where he worked as head barman – and they catered for bed and breakfast. Ann, the landlady, gave us a warm welcome and we made the pub our temporary home until we sorted ourselves out.

The pub had been recently refurbished, with additional bedrooms to attract more patrons, especially as Amble was now flourishing as a popular holiday resort, so with more spring in our step we would face the future on a more optimistic level. The spring wasn't to last long when we viewed the bedrooms and discovered they were little more than box rooms.

We still had those four damned suitcases to contend with. Lying them flat in the room was out of the question as they took up most of the floor space. I turned to Norma in forced jocular fashion and said: "Well, this is another fine mess you've got me into!"

For all our appreciation of Ann's kindness, to stay there in such circumstances spelled impending doom, which somehow continued to cling on at every opportunity. Living in those conditions for almost three weeks was too much to bear, but we accepted responsibility for our situation and made the most of it.

Finding more suitable accommodation was extremely difficult until a long-term friend of ours, who lived in the historic village of Warkworth, a couple of miles away, gave us the address of a lady in the village who owned several small flats overlooking the church cemetery. My immediate thoughts were that we shouldn't get too close – we weren't ready for burial yet!

Beggars can't be choosers and after a brief survey of the two-bedroom downstairs flat we had little choice but to accept her terms – at least there was plenty of space and the extra bedroom was ideal to store our suitcases – were we now beginning to see the light? Light, or indeed the lack of it, was indeed the operative word. When the sun did venture out it never reached our flat because the upstairs flat had been built with a large veranda. It was dark, dismal and utterly depressing.

Our upstairs neighbour, you will not be surprised to learn, was our dear landlady, who hogged all the sunshine. She capped it all when on the advice of her agent decided to increase our rent quite considerably! All we had as income was our old-age pension, which as most people know is not a King's ransom (please excuse the pun).

We had to start earning to survive and the only way to achieve that was to inform my former clients that I was setting up my therapy business again – practising acupressure and shiatsu. The response was overwhelming and soon I was inundated with old and new clients, but as always happens dark clouds weren't far away!

To restart my practice I had to buy a car at enormous hire purchase repayments, although I managed over the following weeks to balance our budget to reasonable proportions. Feeling once again that life was just a bowl of cherries I left the flat as usual one morning, turned the corner 25 metres away into the square and to my horror discovered an empty space where my car had once stood.

It is a traumatic feeling. I'd had the same sensation years earlier in London having parked my car at Olympia and returned to stare in disbelief at an empty space. The first reaction, once over the initial shock, is to murder the perpetrator, or at least beat the living daylights out of the person or persons who had no compassion for the victim implicated in such a travesty.

Once the murderous thoughts left my head on that occasion I found the nearest police station to report the theft. That inconvenience alone was enough to make my blood pressure rise to danger level. Norma and my son Gary were waiting for me, expecting me to roll up in the car, but when they saw my face they realised it was red for danger!

I expected to spend the rest of the day in the police station while they conducted their inquiries. The policeman taking my details switched on his computer which gave a list of stolen vehicles and we were astounded to hear him read out the licence number of my car. It was in a compound at Pangbourne, just outside Reading in Berkshire –

40 miles away. Apparently four black kids selected my car out of the hundreds parked in and around Olympia and decided to have a joy ride to Pangbourne where they had recently been incarcerated in a remand home. Some of their mates were still in there so they decided to visit them, no doubt for a chat about how wonderful it was to be on the outside enjoying freedom, selecting any car they fancied – and it doesn't cost them a penny!

Unfortunately for them their intentions weren't fully carried out. As they drove into the grounds of the remand home my car ran out of petrol and as they got out to decide what to do, a police car rolled up, much to their utter chagrin. It must have been a hilarious scenario when the youths decided to make a run for it through some fields with the police chasing them before eventually bringing them down with rugby tackles, then marching all four back in handcuffs! This time, the police said, they will enjoy the comfort of a real prison!

Looking back, the incidents do have their humorous sides, but at the time they weren't funny at all. We were fortunate Gary had friends in London and one of them was good enough to drive us to Pangbourne where we were told the car was okay apart from its empty tank. Outwardly it appeared to be in much better nick than other stolen cars in the compound which were nothing more than wrecks. It must have been heartbreaking for the owners when they saw them. Some people had come from far flung parts of the country to either collect their vehicle or arrange insurance claims, which could take an eternity. This is why the law should be much stricter when dealing with these irresponsible thugs who care nothing for the feelings and distress of unfortunate victims caught up in a despicable society.

All those memories came to me as I stood and surveyed the vacant spot where my car had been parked in Warkworth. To go through the whole procedure of reporting the theft to the police and all that went with it was almost too much to bear! Once I had reported the theft my next problem was transportation, as many of my clients were spread over a wide area of north Northumberland. Hiring another car would cost the earth!

One of my clients who lived in Warkworth offered me transport which was little more than a fairy bicycle. I appreciated her gesture, but riding on such a small bike would be more than an embarrassment, not to mention the efforts struggling against the strong winds prevalent in this part of the world – walking was a much better option!

After two days the police called to tell me my car had been found in Ashington, 14 miles away. It wasn't so much the name of the town which intrigued me, it was the name of the road – Milburn Road – now there's a name to conjure with! My sense of humour was sorely being tried at this stage and there are times when I began to wonder if I ever had one, but when the police informed me the car was found in Milburn Road I had to admit a wry smile crossed my face, the idea that 'Wor Jackie' was behind it all, looking down and smiling at my predicament, made me feel just a little better.

Mind you, when the car was brought back to me I was wishing the thieves had burned it (as was their usual custom) then I'd have claimed from my insurance. It was filthy inside and out and driving it again filled me with disgust – my immediate reaction was to get rid of it at the first opportunity. I did exactly that in double quick time. Even though the financial return was poor, there was no way I wanted that soiled car.

Until I had the resources to buy a decent vehicle to enable me to visit my clients the proprietor of the car company I was dealing with offered me the loan of a car. When he said I could have it free of charge provided I pay the road tax – then £50 – I couldn't believe my luck, especially when I saw the car which to all intents and purposes was perfectly respectable.

I had to wait for the car to be delivered, and in the meantime met up with a former acquaintance of mine from Amble named Billy Young who I'd known from our early sporting days when he showed promise as a fine wicket keeper. His wife was having back problems and he contacted me to make an appointment with a view to a series of treatments. I told him about our housing problem and it was music to my ears when they told me about the house Billy had lived in as a young man with his parents. The house in Amble was close to a school that had been built on tennis courts which had long been discarded, leaving the land open for anyone who cared to make use of it. The area had been a great place for kids like myself, my brother George and all other sporty youngsters. For several years we played our football and cricket games to our hearts content, breaking several windows with the cricket ball in the process! It was always the King brothers who bore the brunt of those angry residents and who could blame them? We didn't dare own up to it, not because of those angry householders, but because our mother would have knocked the living daylights out of us.

Our mother was wonderful, but we never dared step out of line. In contrast, our father, an ex-Army Sergeant Major, never laid his hand on us – the voice was enough, which is as it should be. There should never be any need to smack a child if parents taught their children the meaning of right and wrong from an early age.

When the car was delivered I eagerly looked forward to driving it out on the road – all for £50. What a bargain! The engine turned over quite nicely until I touched the accelerator and from the increasing noise as I applied more gentle pressure people in the vicinity would have thought a Grand Prix was taking place in Amble! The horrendous din eased off slightly once I got the vehicle moving and picked up speed. What I had thought to be a bargain was in fact the opposite – at £50 I had been robbed!

Although I only held on to this monstrosity for a couple of days, I called out the garage mechanic at least a couple of times to sort out the problems. Starting it up in the morning was an absolute nightmare and such an embarrassment!

The car may have been a disaster but at least our housing problem was eased temporarily and living back in Amble where the majority of my clients lived was more convenient. It was essential to purchase another car, even though it stretched me to my financial limit, and as most car owners know, the second-hand car industry is a dodgy business.

We were settling nicely into Billy Young's house when out of the blue we were offered a one-bedroom downstairs flat in a pleasant area of Amble. It was in a recently built housing complex run by Anchor Housing for the benefit of older people – it was the 'older' bit I didn't care for very much, but then I never did care being considered old! When Norma and I mentioned old age to a young Indian lady in Thailand she replied with a smile: "Remember, old is gold." What a lovely way to put it. Although it did nothing for our aches and pains, our outlook on life itself was given a boost.

A lady called Betty Fender, who was working as a house agent for Anchor, heard we were having problems finding suitable accommodation. Her mother and father had gone into another home in Amble, leaving their flat empty, prompting her to offer it to us and I must say we were very grateful, even though we had nothing but our four suitcases. Help was at hand in a way I never thought possible, except in one's wildest dreams.

It was kindness at the highest level. We now had our own little home – it just needed to be completely redecorated, and just like a newly married couple we had to acquire all the usual household necessities. We realised the enormity of the situation and were grateful to be offered salvation from friends whom we'd only known a short time.

Edna Ormston had been one of my clients when I treated her for a neck problem which had plagued her for years, and we had befriended her husband Ernie, daughter Sarah and Ernie's sister Connie. Their support and kindness was overwhelming: they worked to make our new home as comfortable as possible bestowed many effects upon us to help us on our way.

When I was rushed to hospital pending my court trial, Ernie and Edna brought Norma the 30-mile round trip in their car every day for a full month to see me. Their kindness did not end there – Edna was one of the ladies who entered the witness box at Newcastle Crown Court in support of me, which was a most harrowing experience – to them I shall be eternally grateful.

It was wonderful having our own home again, free to do the things we wanted without interference. We also had friendly neighbours in this small housing complex. We acquired a car which was 100 per cent more roadworthy than my last monstrosity, so maybe we were at last back on the long rocky road!

My physio business continued to expand so it was essential to have a reliable car to take me on my rounds around north Northumberland. However, Norma and I were at an age when we did not want our lives taken over completely and I decided whenever possible to keep the afternoons free to do things together.

On one of those afternoons Norma had a hairdressing appointment near our home, and being a lovely day, although the hairdressers was only a short distance, I took her in the car where I would wait until she came out so we could toddle off somewhere. I parked a short distance from the salon and as I sat there decided to drive up to the local welfare field where I'd played football and cricket in my formative years. As I approached the welfare gates an enormous lorry came speeding towards me. As he sped past I thought briefly of the two bends he would have to negotiate as he entered Amble, but those thoughts left my mind as I strolled across the football pitch which held so many memories for me, then when I picked up a £1 coin it seemed this was indeed my lucky day!

I returned to my car filled with nostalgia, seeing images of those lads I'd played with on the football and cricketing fields. I was soon to be knocked out of my reverie in devastating circumstances. As I was driving back on the quarter-mile journey to the hairdressers, I was confronted by a police road block and was informed that a heavy lorry had crashed into some cars parked along the road, ending up in the exact spot I had vacated only minutes before. Its load of silage was still pouring out onto the car which had taken my place and the unfortunate woman inside was trapped with this horrible sludge covering her whole body.

The lorry had been well in excess of the speed limit when it had passed me and the second bend I mentioned was too sharp for such a heavy vehicle. It was a miracle the salon escaped and especially lucky since several customers were having their hair beautified, including Norma. It was a great relief to find her safe. I did say finding that £1 coin made it my lucky day! I am glad to say the lady trapped in her car wasn't seriously hurt but the humiliation of smelly farm manure being poured over her was a bit much. It was my sporting instincts which saved me from that fate!

My Son Gary

It has been our good fortune over many years to have a son in the teaching profession which has taken him first of all the beautiful island of Bermuda, on to the United States and then Thailand. Before making those journeys he worked in Acton, London, becoming a deputy head at the age of 25.

The school was a comprehensive, mixed sex and race, with ages ranging from four to eighteen. Discipline was extremely difficult to implement and Gary, a strict disciplinarian, got little support from the head of the school, which left him very frustrated. Matters worsened when two black lads of 15 murdered a shopkeeper. On another occasion two girls were at each other's throats in the toilets, leaving one almost strangled. One evening after school Gary left to find his first car vandalised. That was the last straw!

Gary was also making quite a name for himself as a singer, frequently performing in the London clubs. His big moment came when he sang at the London Palladium for up-and-coming stars. One of those performing was a young lad named Michael Barrymore, who was billed as a stand up comedian. Gary said afterwards he was dreadful and barely raised a titter from the audience but of course as everyone knows he went on to be one of the country's best entertainers, until his sad demise.

During one of Gary's performances he met up with a young lady by the name of Gina Swainham, Miss Bermuda and Miss World of 1989/90. Gina was impressed with Gary's singing and they got together, becoming an item on the London social scene. She invited Norma and I to her apartment and despite all the adulation she was receiving appeared totally unfazed by it all – her one aim was to get back to

Bermuda where her fame was in complete contrast to that in Britain – to the Bermudans she was just another pretty girl!

A record company attempted to get Gary and Gina to sing together but it was doomed to failure from the start – like me, Gina couldn't sing a note if her life depended on it! When her term as Miss World came to an end she persuaded Gary to go with her to Bermuda where she said he would be able to teach and have more opportunity to expand his singing career, as well as live on a beautiful island with glorious weather. Being disenchanted with the school it didn't take Gary long to make the momentous decision to go along with Gina's suggestion.

I wondered at the time if he was doing the right thing. After all at the age of 25 he was an efficient deputy head and his singing career looked rosy – he was due to perform on Hughie Green's 'Opportunity Knocks' but chose instead to gamble on the Bermuda Triangle! In retrospect I do think he made the wrong decision considering how subsequent events unfolded.

From our point of view, Gary going to Bermuda gave Norma and I the opportunity to spend six weeks on this beautiful island. He, however, was disillusioned and bored out of his mind with this new lifestyle. As a holiday resort it was great, but living and working there was a different kettle of fish. Although well paid for his teaching and occasional singing (no tax in Bermuda) he felt hemmed in, with little prospect of advancement.

Meanwhile, Gina had bought a boutique with the money she had earned as Miss World and being a home loving girl had no wish to leave Bermuda. This meant a parting of their relationship as Gary was intent on moving on, with his sights firmly fixed on the United States – New York in particular.

He applied for a teaching post there and with his first class honours degree in maths and chemistry from London University he was offered an interview in double quick time. Within a matter of weeks he was bound for New York City, where he spent 17 wonderful years – as he has found out, life is all about making decisions – some are right and others are wrong, but at least we create for ourselves an excitement which those who stand still will never experience.

If for instance Gary had not moved to Bermuda he may never have left England and would have missed out on those 17 glorious years in New York. He was extremely happy enjoying the delights of New York and it paved the way for Norma and I to visit the great city, where we too shared many wonderful memories. It became almost a second home.

Gary's apartment was situated in Greenwich Village and his school overlooked Central Park. It was ideal. Although his lifestyle was extremely comfortable, he couldn't resist an opportunity to buy an apartment in the prestigious area of Battery Park, overlooking the Hudson River, where exotic liners from all parts of the world sailed into New York harbour. The Queen Elizabeth was a regular visitor and to see it in the early mornings, lights blazing, was a joy to behold.

Across the water from his apartment the Statue of Liberty with arm aloft holding the torch was in our sights every morning. Looking out of the bedroom window, the promenade immediately below us was full of roller bladers, runners and walkers enjoying the freedom away from the frenetic city streets.

Further along the promenade was a dock where millionaires anchored their glamorous yachts, then further on a large forecourt where the imposing Winter Garden building stood, with its all-glass frontage shielding giant palm trees reaching up to the ceiling, 50 ft high. Norma and I would often sit on one of the numerous seats watching the world go by, speculating where everyone was going across the floors, up and down escalators – it was a constant stream of activity.

Directly behind the Winter Gardens stood the incredible Twin Towers, the World Trade Center, where several thousand people were employed from countries around the globe, then there was Wall Street which controls world economy markets. Every day during the summer Norma and I would venture onto the promenade for our stroll, often stopping to chat with the odd walker on their lunch break from the World Trade Center. Their normal procedure was to pick up a chicken sandwich from an Italian store, which we also often patronised, and some brought sneakers with them – more comfortable than walking in polished shoes.

Our normal holiday period in New York was late August to September when the weather is at its best, and but for a twist of fate, in all probability we would have been there when the World Trade Center was blown up by a bunch of religious fanatics, causing one of the world's greatest disasters.

Only a month or so before this tragic event Gary decided he needed a change of direction. Having spent a holiday in Thailand he was so impressed with an easier lifestyle and lovely weather all year round, plus the fact a former headmaster friend had taken over an international school in Bangkok, he decided to sever his connection with New York and move to the far east.

One of Gary's main reasons for leaving the United States was the severe winters when the temperature could drop as low as minus 30. Having experienced it once ourselves we knew what he was talking about. Many months before the World Trade Center was destroyed I had vivid dreams of planes crashing into tall buildings, but when the real event happened it came as a terrible shock, especially being so well acquainted with the place.

On the Tuesday of the disaster Norma and I walked into the hardware department of the Co-op in Amble just as one of the young lady assistants was shouting: "They're bombing New York! They're bombing New York!"

We were confronted by several television screens showing graphic live pictures of planes plunging into the Twin Towers. We stood mesmerised, thinking it was some sort of TV drama, thoughts quickly banished when the voice of the commentator was almost in hysterics as he described the unfolding drama. We recognised two areas where we had walked, shops we had frequented, but it was the thick black choking volumes of smoke pouring out of the buildings, along avenues and the promenade where we'd walked so many times, that brought home the whole gravity of the situation to us.

We briefly saw Gary's former apartment, where we'd spent many happy times, before the whole block was enveloped in the black cloud. Had Gary not moved to Thailand it was the time of year when in all probability we would have been there with his Siamese cats. More than likely many of those who worked in the Twin Towers spending their lunch break on the promenade would have perished, particularly those whose offices were in the upper half of the building.

For Gary it was normal procedure on Tuesday mornings to catch the 9am underground train situated between the Towers – around the time the planes struck. It hardly bears thinking about.

New York lost so much of its magic when those impressive landmarks of Manhattan were blown away and for the citizens still living there it will never be the same again.

Out of the Woodwork...

Following the publication of *"Hands, Feet and Balls"*, I received many letters of congratulations, including one from then Prime Minister Tony Blair's secretary who wrote that Mr Blair intended to read it on the plane during one of his trips abroad – I'm glad I did not write anything that may have offended him!

However, two significant events which occurred more than 60 years ago that I did write about resulted in the perpetrators deciding to crawl out of the woodwork and offer their apologies. Both were connected to injuries sustained away from the professional game. Those incidents still remain clearly in my mind and according to those three people (now senior citizens) it was all because I played for Newcastle United!

The first was during my Army days when with my arm in plaster (a normal procedure for me). I continued to play, but in an on-field position at inside right. The game in question was an Army Cup Final against another battalion and I captained the team, probably because I was the senior NCO (at 21). As the referee blew his whistle to start the game, the centre forward passed the ball to me and the next thing I knew I was lying on my back with blood spurting out of the top of my nose. Not long ago I received a phone call from an elderly gent recalling the game, asking me if I remembered it – how could I forget something so poignant? It was a special game which I'd so much looked forward to, yet it was over before it began. Lapsing in and out of consciousness I had intended to get back on the field, but I'd lost so much blood I was restrained from doing so.

My telephone caller said his captain gave him instructions to put me out of the game because I'd played for Newcastle United! As I received the ball he ran straight at me and butted me with his head – apologising, he said how much he'd regretted his action – at the time he thought I'd die.

It was some years later that I played my first game in goal after three years with my arms and wrists encased in plaster due to broken wrist syndrome. The Newcastle United manager at the time, George Martin, asked me to play for my local team, Amble, which was a member of the Northern Alliance, a league in which Newcastle United 'A' participated. He thought it would be a good opportunity to recover my confidence before I returned to United – after all, I was still only 22!

As I wrote in *"Hands, Feet and Balls"*, the match for me became a nightmare. Diving at an opponent's feet early in the game I got kicked on the jaw as he followed through, fracturing it in two places. Once again two characters emerged out of the woodwork after reading the book. Both were involved in the conspiracy to put me out of the game simply because of my connection with United. They intimated their "sincere regret" for their dastardly action.

The younger of the two was the player who delivered the kick but the older conspirator had instructed his younger player to cripple me! This now very old man, the former manager of the team, wanted to put things right before he met his maker!

Remember both of these were amateur matches, with no money involved, yet the desire was to win at any cost! Even today when I see so much hate generated in professional football, players earning thousands of pounds a week, I ponder their negative attitude. Watched by millions of people all around the world on satellite television, cameras at every angle, close-up shots and replayed over and over again, players still persist in pursuing stupid acts of violence, spitting and effing away at referees, who have a thankless task and in my opinion do a great job. Human nature determines they will at times make a wrong decision but players forget it works out the same for both teams. Refs are like goalkeepers – they can win matches and they can lose them – nothing will ever change that.

Wayne Rooney is a rare talent – at the age of 18 he had the world at his feet, but even then he behaved like a prima donna. Unless he controls his volatile temperament he will discover the world is not his personal oyster – life has a unique way of handling our futures that he has yet to find out!

I know, having been so close to the New York Twin Tower disaster, knowing many of those blown away, and then in Thailand for another catastrophe of gigantic proportions. Too many members of our society are so dissatisfied, grumbling and moaning of minor irritations. Give a little thought for those victims and families caught up in such tragic events. My son's school was on holiday at various locations in and around Phuket when the tsunami struck on 26 December 2004. I will expand on the full extent of those involved later.

When Gary made his unprecedented move to Thailand our immediate thoughts were of the distance: 12 hours on the outward journey and 14 hours return. My main concern was the embolism in my left leg which has a tendency to swell so having to sit in cramped conditions for such a length of time was a major concern. However, a lady called Jane at the travel shop in Amble made arrangements with the airlines to ensure every comfort.

From experience I know it is of paramount importance to exercise the legs whenever possible and I went one step further by going to the toilet regularly to indulge in callisthenics (a form of exercise). The other passengers must have thought I was suffering from some form of ailment, but at the end of that journey my only health problem was sheer fatigue!

Despite my initial concerns, it is always worth the trip. Thailand has many wonderful qualities: the temperature rarely drops below 30 degrees C, the people are so friendly and smiles are an everyday occurrence – mind you the weather may have something to do with that. On the other hand there are so many things which are not so pleasing to the farangs (foreigners) such as the excessive speed of motorists who think nothing of travelling well over 100 miles an hour – police are on hand to issue tickets, although it is common practice to take bribes.

Thailand

A few years ago Norma, Gary and I were involved in a serious car accident while travelling the 90 miles from Bangkok to Pattaya, a seaside resort. our driver, a Thai with a much experience of driving at high speed in the Volvo, braked suddenly and for what seemed an eternity the car skidded for a good 50 metres or so before crashing into a stationary lorry at the back of a long caravan of vehicles. As we hit, our car was still clocked at 70 miles an hour.

It is difficult to describe one's feelings when something of this magnitude occurs – a sensation of bewilderment, loss of reality, moments of silence, before gathering our wits to determine the extent of the damage to ourselves. Both Norma and I had been thrown from our seats (no belts in the rear). Fortunately Gary was wearing a seat belt in the front otherwise he'd have gone through the windscreen. The driver's air cushion probably saved him and thankfully the car was a Volvo, reputed to be the safest for lessening such an impact, although the front damaged so badly that the car was no longer driveable.

Norma received the brunt of it. Her head hit the back of Gary's seat at lightning speed. Incredibly her glasses protected her eyes but above eye level an enormous bruise appeared – it was a miracle we didn't break our necks although we felt whiplash for several weeks. After the collision we just sat dazed and bewildered, traffic on both sides of the roads screaming past, dust flying and temperatures reaching 38 degrees C. No ambulances were available so a taxi was summoned to whisk us off to hospital in case of complications. Although Gary regularly visits Pattaya as a break from his school work, we have not ventured back.

One of the more amusing sights in Thailand is older males from the western world walking around with teenage Thai girls, most of them young enough to be their grandchildren. Wearing shorts to show off their skinny and bandy legs, these men, usually with money to spend, are having the time of their late lives, indulging in the pleasurable pursuits of available kids – it is their only opportunity to sample some of the goodies otherwise denied them.

On one of our first visits here a friend drove us around Bangkok in the evening, when the traffic had eased a little, to show us some of the sights not normally seen in the western world. Night clubs are quite common and to see almost naked girls cavorting around poles in suggestive poses outside the clubs was indeed a sight for sore eyes! When we mentioned to our friend how beautiful these girls were, he laughed and said they were actually of mixed gender – lady boys – who wear the most glamorous clothes and can be seen in and around South East Asia. They work in banks, hotels and shops and no one would guess they were anything but good looking girls.

One of these lady boys had an English boyfriend in ones of the apartments where Gary lived. She was absolutely charming, spoke good English, dressed in the latest fashion and wearing stiletto shoes. I cannot imagine the shock some men get when they escort a lady boy for the first time.

Without a doubt the biggest problem in Thailand is the laxity on drugs. Walk into any chemist's shop and they are available to anyone, irrespective of age. One 15-year-old student at Gary's school was expelled on drug related incidents. Weeks later he was found dead in a hotel bedroom alongside his Japanese girlfriend, who was left fighting for her life on a support machine – it transpired later it was a planned suicide pact. Following this tragedy police raided every international school in Bangkok, determined to root out students involved with drugs. Those caught in possession were given 24 hours to leave the country and never return. Any who overstayed those 24 hours would be incarcerated in a Bangkok prison, which are reputed to be among the toughest in the world. Knowing that I doubt any student would be foolish enough to overstep the mark.

This was a devastating blow to the parents enjoying a lucrative lifestyle, now forced into a heartbreaking dilemma. During my writings and talks aimed at the young I have stressed repeatedly the dangers and consequences of drugs. To those who are currently indulging, stop now before it is too late – life, despite all its problems, still has much to offer!

Yield Not Unto Temptation...

The Michael Jackson child abuse case made headlines throughout the world because of his celebrity status, but this was just one isolated case – child abuse has existed since time began and has increased to such an extent because we are living in a pornographic society.

Seldom a day goes by without a newspaper proclaiming a cry of rape by some hysterical female, sometimes naming the alleged rapist. Even if the accusation turns out the be pure fabrication the damage done to the accused can be devastating.

During my time as youth manager at Luton Town FC I could quite easily have been caught up in a maelstrom had I yielded to temptation. It beggars belief that at the age of 50 a girl of 13 should attempt to seduce me. I was relaxing in the lounge of the small hotel managed by her mother, reading a newspaper, when the girl sidled up to me, grabbed my hand and placed it on her breast. It was performed so quickly that I had no time to prevent this spontaneous action.

To recall this incident more than 30 years later still brings me out in a cold sweat. Thankfully, there were no other guests in the lounge at the time. I took my hand away as if I'd touched a red-hot poker, hauled the young lady from her seat and demanded to know what she was playing at. She merely turned on her heel, smiled and walked away.

Incredibly, this young upstart didn't stop there. The following morning, still half asleep, I sensed someone was in the room with me – opening one eye, there she was staring down at me. Before I could utter a word she said: "Can I get into bed beside you?"

Words failed me. Jumping out of bed and pulling on my dressing gown I flew down to the kitchen where her mother was cooking breakfast for the other guests. When I told her the full story she smiled, just like her daughter, and said: "Don't worry, Ray, it's just a phase she's going through."

I left the hotel and spent the next night in my car.

In my school days kids were often subject to the unwanted attentions of dirty old men who were seen as pillars of society. One of these men, whom I'd always respected, was continually harassing me and a schoolboy friend of mine, Willie McKenna. We never told our parents because of the embarrassment it would cause, and also the fact that this man's family would be ruined if they knew.

Going to the beach also had its problems and quite often there were men lurking near the sandbanks watching kids changing into their bathing costumes. One had the audacity to bring binoculars, making his intentions rather obvious.

Even as a naïve 17-year-old being accosted before my debut for Newcastle United in the local derby against Sunderland at St James' Park still holds unsavoury memories.

Walking around a housing estate in Poole, where I had an appointment with a client, a girl of no more than three ran up to me and said quite disarmingly: "Mister, can I see your willy?"

Apparently the estate had a reputation for child abuse, fathers assaulting their own children and police raids on a regular basis. The sad part is any child can say they have been assaulted by someone who is completely innocent, and the problems it can cause are incalculable.

On another occasion Norma and I had gone to a supermarket shortly after we had moved to Amble. I went to the toilet where two boys, one about seven and the other no more than four, were in the process of adjusting themselves. The younger of the two was having to rely on his older brother to fasten the buttons on his trousers, and even he was having difficulty. He turned to me and asked for my help. I asked him where his mum was and when he said she was outside the toilet waiting for them I quickly said. "Right son, go to your mum and she will do it for you."

Imagine the scene if someone had come into the toilet while I was adjusting the boys trousers!

Ever since that day I will not go into a public toilet unless children are accompanied by an adult. I would also make it law that children up to the age of 14 should have their own toilet. Maybe it will be difficult to implement but in this day and age when child abuse is on the increase drastic measures must be enforced.

Thailand Terror!

Vehicle accidents are commonplace all over the world and are almost always related to excessive speed, as was the case with our experience in Thailand. When you are involved in a near death collision apparently sheltered by a safety zone then you know nowhere is safe! This happened to Norma and I quite recently during our customary run in the car to a beachside road. I parked the vehicle and we took our usual stroll, breathing in the keen seaside air.

On our way back, driving along the narrow road which leads into the town, I approached a safety zone for filtering traffic and as I did so I saw this enormous caravan conveyor coming towards us on the far side of the zone. It was not travelling particularly fast but the back end, which carried the caravan, was swaying from side to side and taking up almost all of the road. I had to pull in so half the car was on the pavement. As he approached I said to Norma: "This blighter is going to hit us!"

I was right. He hit us with a horrendous screeching, almost slicing the roof off the car – a shade lower and the windscreen would have shattered, which could have caused serious damage to our head and face.

As we sat there mesmerised I couldn't believe it when I saw the carrier continuing on its way to the caravan park less than half a mile away. With traffic front and behind it took me ages to turn the car round on the narrow road before setting off to confront the offending driver. As I caught him up I flashed my lights continuously to attract his attention, which he ignored completely.

It wasn't until he reached the caravan park that I was able to confront him. He jumped out of his cab door and made a beeline towards two men who apparently were there to sign the delivery papers for the caravan. A quick temper is not part of my makeup but at this point I was absolutely seething at the audacity of the man and without using one single swear word I berated him in no uncertain manner.

After listening to my outburst he calmly replied: "Steady on mate, I didn't see or hear anything but I'll give you the name of my insurance company and you can deal with them." No "sorry, are you both okay?"

He couldn't have cared less, which intimated to Norma and I he was accustomed to these scenarios. It beggars belief that my car was considered a write-off by the insurers yet this man could stand there and say he knew nowt about it. People living 100 metres away heard the loud screeching!

Life can be tough enough without idiots driving without due care and attention and the sooner the laws are tightened on speed limits, especially in built up areas, the better.

To Hell with It!

It seems I spend much of my dotage moralising on certain issues even at an age when I suppose it would be easier to sit back, watch the world pass by and say: "To hell with it – let them all get on with it!"

That thinking plays no part in my philosophy. Providing my mind stays active it is important to use it in the best possible way, passing on my experience to anyone willing to listen. In a society where greed and violence is the norm how can youngsters progress into law-abiding citizens? Make no mistake, there are some great kids who are determined to be successful, and I'm not talking sport here, there are opportunities in every aspect of our society, but they have to work and study hard to achieve their goal.

I had no academic qualifications yet learning to read and write had been of enormous benefit throughout my lifetime, it is indeed one of life's great pleasures and I am most grateful to those wonderful teachers who taught me – when I think back to my schooldays all I thought about was football and cricket, what time was there left for reading and writing? You will note I have not mentioned sums!

Education in Thailand is difficult for me to come to terms with. While in the western world children start school at the age of four or five at no expense, Thai families must pay for their kids' education: if they can't afford to pay the children will never go to school.

Many Thais live in abject poverty and resort to begging on the streets – one of the saddest sights is so many people without limbs, beautiful children running up to vehicles in queues or at traffic lights – their eyes tell it all. It really is heartbreaking.

This is one of the reasons Gary has set his sights on offering these kids free education. It is a major mission but one he is determined to accomplish and provided he receives the backing of influential businessmen it will be a breakthrough of monumental proportions.

Skyscrapers sprung up all over Bangkok when Thailand's economy recovered following a recession which left buildings derelict for years. The buildings from these two economic eras now intersperse, giving the city an odd appearance but at the same time a fascination more sophisticated cities cannot match.

Thousands of Thais still live in primitive conditions, scattered around the city in their little tin huts which must make them very envious when they see the wealth of westerners. A great many Thais are extremely prosperous, yet they never portray any hostility towards the well off.

Cleanliness too is part of the Thai philosophy, early mornings they are outside their houses or tin huts sweeping up and clearing any dog dirt left by the many strays that roam the streets. Personal hygiene is strictly adhered to and in a country where the heat factor is an everyday phenomenon there is never a hint of body odour.

Since the tsunami disaster many tributes have been paid to those Thais who played a major part in saving so many people's lives, and it was heart-warming to note the large number of Brits offering to come back to Thailand to help at their own expense.

Seven-year-old twins, a boy and a girl, students at my son's school in Bangkok, were victims of the disaster, while their parents were seriously hurt. The girl's body was found but the boy's is still missing – this is one isolated case among so many.

It is common practice in Thailand for farangs to employ a maid, full-time or part-time depending on the circumstances of the employers. Gary prefers to employ a full-time maid because of his twin Siamese cats, which although very resilient need daily attention and crave company, especially when Gary is away for stretches at a time.

Good maids are difficult to find, especially when there is a language barrier, although Gary has solved that by learning Thai. He has employed several maids since he began living in Thailand, some more useful than others. I once had the misfortune to be the unwitting victim of one of these maids, proving once again the dangers of a certain type of woman. The 'lady' in question had been appointed shortly after Norma and I arrived at his apartment for our usual holiday, but from the very beginning she was a complete disaster. All she wanted to do was play with the cats. Being Siamese they had a high level of tolerance which was just as well with the constant attention she was giving them.

It wasn't only the cats who were subject to the maid's loving nature as I was soon to find out! With a cat in her arms she would sidle up to me, push herself against me and kiss me on the cheek when no one else was around. Of course, at my age I should have been flattered, particularly as she was only in her early 40s and quite attractive. I do know there are men who would willingly take advantage of such attention, but it doesn't end there – she was determined to achieve her aim of seducing me!

On an afternoon when I was having problems with my back, Norma had gone shopping with a friend, leaving me to relax on the divan all alone, as I thought, with the cats. Unbeknown to me, the maid, who was supposed to be in another part of the building, ironing laundry, had crept back into our living quarters while I was dozing, knelt down beside me and started to stroke my thigh.

Bad back or not I shot off the divan in near panic and ran to the bedroom (a bad mistake) where my bathing costume was, thinking I had to get out of there quickly and go up to the swimming pool. As she followed me into the bedroom she gave my back a heck of a wallop which threw me on to the bed. I cried out in agony: "My back, my back!"

She was completely taken 'aback' when she saw I was in pain and stalked out of the room shouting in disgust: "Back, back!"

To be on the point of being seduced at my time of life still brings me out in a cold sweat when I think about it. Norma came home to see me lying on the bed barely able to move because of an amorous female's rugby tackle! Needless to say the dear lady was sent packing because of her incompetence – as Gary termed the reason for her dismissal – but remembering what happened to me when those other four members of the 'fair sex' tried to destroy me there is always the threat of such a travesty happening again.

Of all those maids Gary employed there is one shining light. Her name is Chifirapron Dendovng, Ji for short (pronounced 'G'). Ji came to us when Norma and I were staying in the apartment. It was to be her first employment as a maid and at the age of 22 we did not expect she would have the necessary experience to fulfil the requirements needed for the position.

I can remember clearly the first day she walked into the apartment, a tall elegant, good-looking girl with a smile that would melt the most hardened individual. It was obvious she was a cut above the usual type of maid sent out by the agency and not for one moment did any of us expect she would accept the job – but she did and it proved to be one of the best things Norma and I have experienced in our lifetime.

She spoke little or no English – the first words she learned were 'Two teas please' which heralded our request for the usual morning cuppa. Ji took to the job like a duck to water. Nothing was a bother to her and she did everything with a smile. She seemed too good to be true.

Her hours were 8am until 4.30pm and to get to us from her home on the outskirts of Bangkok (wait for it) she came on a small passenger boat (20 minutes), the Skye train (15 minutes), then a bus which normally took half an hour, but would often take up to two and a half hours because of traffic congestion, a serious problem in Bangkok. This meant starting off at the crack of dawn, but she took it all in her stride.

Instead of going home at 4.30pm she sat on the floor next to Norma's chair hoping to improve her English – it caused great amusement to think of Ji speaking broken Geordie. However I must say Norma stuck to the task every afternoon for months, patiently explaining basic words.

When Ji's father decided she should go to university for English lessons, her working time with Gary was cut by half – even then she ensured everything was pristine before leaving the apartment. Like all good things nothing lasts forever and it was a sad day when Ji's father gave her the word to start working in his office as a secretary, principally on the computer. It was only natural her father wanted better things for his daughter, being a maid was the road to nowhere and supremely competent on the computer it did seem such a waste of talent.

We thought this would be the last we saw of Ji but a year since leaving her maids job we became closer to her than when she worked here.

Her mother left Ji's father when Ji was only 16 which placed a tremendous amount of responsibility on her shoulders having to run the house and look after the needs of her father and younger brother. This we feel was one of the main reasons Ji became so close to us. She readily admits to loving us and considers us as her second mother and father – I would have thought more like grandma and pa.

She visits us at every opportunity which can take up to three hours on a bad day but she doesn't care so long as she is with us. When Norma and I visit hospital, which is quite often, she always accompanies us and as Norma has numerous problems with osteoporosis, Ji bathes her, washes her hair, indeed intends to all her needs.

She now speaks excellent English and every time she leaves to go home her final words are: "Take care Madame, if you need me at any time of the day or night ring and I will come!"

Ji is indeed our living guardian angel and we love her every bit as she loves us.

A Tribute to Amblers

I now turn to pay tribute to four wonderful (now deceased) residents who lived most of their relatively long lives in Amble.

Eric Wilson was born with cerebral palsy, a condition that rendered his whole body in total physical entrapment and affected his speech throughout his life. To be afflicted in such a way, not being able to participate in the normal things most of us take for granted, must be extremely frustrating.

I had known Eric from early childhood, and although I lived away from Amble for nigh on 40 years he never forgot me, nor me him. He would always greet anyone he knew with a ready smile and endeavour to hold a conversation, especially if it had anything to do with sport. As far as I know he never missed watching the local football or cricket game at the welfare field across the road from where he lived. Even if the games were held at the other end of the town he would make every effort to get there.

Throughout the years Eric proved his strength of character in such a way that no one could help but admire him – he achieved more in his lifetime than many of those who possessed all their faculties.

During wartime he could not be considered for active duty in any of the forces but he was determined not to miss out. He applied for a job at Broomhill Colliery, three or four miles away, and was given a position in the manager's office. By all accounts he performed his duties admirably, and continued to be employed there until his retirement. That word was a foreign language to Eric – to retire was the last thing he wanted.

Every day he would dress with the aid of his mother or helper, then walk from his house to the bottom part of Amble, almost a mile away, where he would enjoy watching the fishing boats coming and going in the harbour, then he would return home up the steep incline – which seems to get steeper as one gets older. Walking that distance is a mere formality to the average person but to someone in Eric's physical condition it must have seemed like partaking in the marathon.

I received a telephone call from his step-mother one day requesting me to call and see Eric as his neck and shoulders were in severe pain. The doctor had been to see him and had advised Eric's mother to call me in. I found this gratifying as doctors don't normally recognise someone like myself practising alternative medicine.

Treating Eric gave me enormous satisfaction as I was able to offer him hands-on therapy and conversation as he lay on the bed so helpless and fragile.

This was to be the beginning of Eric's decline and I advised him at that point to cut down on his long walk and if possible invest in some form of transport. Shortly afterwards he was to be seen in a natty invalid car which he would use every day on his jaunt to his beloved harbour – travelling in style!

When I returned to Amble 19 years ago and organised a get together for veteran sportsmen I invited Eric to attend, but he declined – his mother told me he didn't want anyone feeling sorry for him. I had also intended to write an article about him. His mother was enthusiastic but once again Eric said no. He died in his late 60s and I knew nothing about it as I was out of the country.

Eric Wilson was one in a million – never have I admired a person more than him. If anyone should have been honoured in the Queen's Birthday Honours List Eric would have been number one.

Father Hart is a name most of Amble's senior citizens will remember with ease. He was part of the community and although many of us who knew him were not Catholics he was held in high esteem as a pillar of Amble and District society. To meet him in the street with his ready smile and firm handshake was always a joy.

Whenever we got together the conversation quickly turned to sport, whether it be football, cricket or rugby he was an enthusiast of them all – religion never came into the equation. However I had to tell him the story of my schooldays when playing against the Catholic school, whose players were rather prone to swearing. When I asked one why they did this, he claimed that they got an absolution from the Father!

Father Hart's broad sense of humour was evident as he laughed out loud in response: "Ah yes, but what he wouldn't tell you about was the stinging rebuke I handed out to them which they won't forget in a hurry!"

The last time I saw Father Hart was way back in about 1948 on Blackpool promenade before he made his way to Manchester to watch the test match between England and New Zealand. I was going to the game with my Port Vale team mates which was of special significance as it was the first test match I'd seen and Brian Close making his debut at the age of 18.

Father Hart enjoyed a wee dram and the inevitable cigarette in his time, but it was his outgoing personality for which he is most remembered. It was a pleasure knowing him.

I now turn the spotlight on two ladies who dominated the Amble scene for more decades than I care to remember. Muriel Usher was the principal chemist in Amble long before I came on the scene – her father before her spent a lifetime in the business until Muriel took over and she too dedicated her whole life administering medicines and offering advice on every ailment, such was her knowledge in the medical profession.

It was a known fact that Miss Usher did not suffer fools gladly and her sharp tongue frightened more than one customer away – even her staff were subject to the occasional outburst. They were under strict orders not to use the cash register as she did not trust anyone!

I first met Miss Usher around about 1952 when I was back home in Amble during the football close season from Port Vale. Cricket as always was my main preoccupation, playing for Amble in the Alnwick and District League. On this particular occasion I was unable to play because of a weeping rash between my legs, apparently caused by athlete's foot, a common ailment among sportsmen.

My father, seeing the distress it was causing me, got on his bicycle and went to see Miss Usher.

"If anyone can cure it she will," said my father.

He came back 15 minutes later puffing like a steam engine and gasped out: "You'll never believe this, but when I explained to Miss Usher your trouble, she said, 'I'm sorry, I haven't got the medication your son will need but don't worry – I know where to get it.'"

Leaving her assistant in charge she got her bicycle out of a back shed, cycled all the way to Alnwick, 10 miles away over several steep hills, collected the drugs from a chemist there and cycled back in record time. Can you imagine that act of dedication from anyone in today's society? even with a car it is doubtful if they would do it.

The 'red dope' was indeed a miracle cure – within two days the condition had completely dried up and disappeared. I've never been troubled with it since.

I never forgot her and whenever she was out and about, which wasn't very often, she would put herself out to speak to me and inquire of my health. During her latter years it was sad to see the rapid deterioration of her whole body structure, from being a smart attractive lady she became an extremely hunched old woman although her face still remained unlined despite the obvious pain she must have suffered.

It was a surprise when she rang me out of the blue asking if I could call to see her at the address above the chemist shop where she'd lived most of her life. Knowing the state she was in with osteoporosis this was a cry for help, but with the prognosis not good I wondered in what way I could be of assistance.

My first visit to see her was an experience I shall never forget. A note was pinned on the front door: 'Raymond come straight upstairs!' On opening the door I was confronted with a scene of utter devastation. It reminded me of an Army assault course, obstacles on every step leading upstairs. It was a problem for me to negotiate but how on earth did she manage it in her physical state with two walking sticks? When I did eventually make it there was a chair strategically placed to plonk on, obviously for her benefit, but I too took advantage of it once I'd mastered the course. Two other chairs were placed along the landing which led to the lounge where she was sitting on the sofa with her legs bandaged from ankles to knees.

When I eventually found a chair in the gloom to sit on while we discussed the problem in hand it seemed as though I was enacting a scene from the film 'Great Expectations', with Miss Usher was taking the part of Miss Faversham. The whole room was a complete chaos, I couldn't describe it even as a sale room, there were cobwebs everywhere, and here was this highly educated, articulate lady sitting quite unconcerned in these incredible circumstances.

She told me her reasons for sending for me, which were quite flattering and rather embarrassing especially with her pointed views on doctors in general. In her words, she had no time for them, which I felt very sad about as Amble has many fine doctors as Norma and I know from our own experiences. However, Miss Usher had a stubborn streak and nothing was ever going to change that, she was her own woman and woe betide anyone who tried to cross her!

My first task was to determine the damage to her legs. I was appalled at the emaciated state they were in. Bandages which must have been leftovers from the war (I don't know which one) were embedded into the skin and congealed with blood, making the task of taking them off extremely difficult. I told her she must get a supply of bandages and gauze from the chemist before I could attend to her.

I asked for a pair of scissors and she intimated there was some in the bedroom on the dressing table. I couldn't find the dressing table never mind the scissors as the room was even more cluttered than the lounge and the bed had the contents of the large bowl which had adorned her shop window when she was in business strewn all across the covers. I couldn't possibly believe she would have slept in the bed even though she was pencil thin – my guess was her sofa in the lounge was her bed. Not being able to fine any scissors she then told me to look on the mantelpiece. Lo and behold there they were – covered in cobwebs. For how long they'd been there was anybody's guess!

She had the bandages and gauze delivered in double quick time and I then proceeded to make her as comfortable as possible. For several days I treated her neck and shoulders with extreme care, knowing her physical deterioration was so advanced that the benefits of the therapy would only be short term. She was grateful that I'd given her some comfort, though. I thought of that historic day when she cycled the 20 miles to Alnwick and back on my behalf. Nothing would have given me more pleasure than to effect a complete cure in the same way her 'red dope' did for me.

Some readers may be sceptical, but I can assure you every word is exactly as it happened, hard as it is to believe. Muriel Usher was an incredible lady, extremely talented and dedicated to her profession, which perhaps was carried to the limit as no social activities were on her agenda.

It was rumoured she had an ill-fated love affair as a young attractive girl, which was the reason for her rather cynical attitude to life – whatever it was, as far as I am concerned her whole life was dedicated to the needs of Amble and District and my admiration for this rather complex lady was immeasurable.

Helen Aisbait was Miss Tate when I first encountered the 19-year-old school teacher who arrived at Amble Council School way back in 1937. It was love at first sight – I and every other 12 or 13-year-old boy was captivated by the tall lady with the twinkling eyes, rose-coloured cheeks and infectious giggly laugh that remained for all of her 84 years.

Helen hailed from north Northumberland. "I was brought up in the 'sticks'," she would say, and coming to Amble, a town with 5,000 inhabitants, was a monumental change to the lifestyle she had been used to. However, she became so popular not only in school but in the town itself where she joined various women's groups. Her favourite activity was on the speaking front.

Keeping fit was her forte, she organised keep fit classes and dancing sessions and quickly became an integral part of Amble society. It was a bitter blow when our beloved teacher got married to Bruce Aisbit, another teacher at the school. Jimmy Pringle, a pupil at the time, said many of the boys were in tears when they heard the devastating news!

Bruce Aisbit became a hate figure for a while but I have to admit I really liked him as he was the one teacher who made me realise there was more to life than football and cricket. Up to that point, school was just a means to an end for me but his influence played a big part during my last year at school, as I began to actually enjoy it.

Helen had four children to Bruce, all of them making a success of their lives. Sadly Bruce died before he reached the 'old man' stage and she lost one of her sons who died in his early forties. With much sadness in her life Helen kept a brave face at all times and was never seen without her cheerful demeanour.

In the 19 months before my trial at Newcastle Crown Court – an interminable waiting time – she was a tower of strength. Her words to me, which remain embedded in my memory, were: "Raymond, everyone is 100 per cent behind you – evil women who are bored out of their minds have seen in you an opportunity to bolster their miserable lives – they will live to regret it."

As Helen got older, unable to carry on with active life, walking became her favourite pastime and together with a lady friend they tramped the roads and pathways of 'little old Amble', as she called it, and the surrounding district. There were times when it was difficult to walk because of her calloused feet and the pain they caused her. I gave her several treatments of reflexology but the pounding those feet had taken over many decades took its toll.

I said to her, with tongue in cheek: "This is all to do with your ballet dancing days, Helen."

Her sharp retort, as always with a laugh and spontaneous giggle: "More like clog dancing, you mean!"

However, there were more serious problems to contend with than her feet. She often commented to me about her love of food, although she had a dreadful habit of eating the wrong things – rubbish as she called it – and now she was paying the price. I'd heard she wasn't feeling well and planned to visit her when a former school pal of mine, Lew Bobb, rang me to say Helen was very poorly and asked us to call.

She was lying on the bed in her living room as we entered and quite a number of her friends were gathered around chatting to Helen as though it was a normal social afternoon tea party. When she saw us her face lit up with that wonderful dazzling smile, invited us both to sit on the bed beside her and held our hands.

"Look at my lovely colour," she said with her inimitable giggle (her skin was yellow). "But don't look at my horrible feet." She then remembered I knew all about them!

There was no hint of her illness as we talked and laughed at events of the past. When Dr McIlhinney arrived we bade her goodbye as she lay there still smiling. That was the last we saw of our wonderful Helen, as she passed on several days later.

As expected the church was almost overflowing at her funeral, such was her popularity. Legend tells us that Helen of Troy launched a thousand ships with her beautiful face. Whether that story is a myth or not, mine is pure fact – Helen of Amble broke a thousand hearts with her beautiful face which shone like a beacon in a troubled world. She was loved by everyone.

Bobby Robson

As I slowly wend my way to the end of the road there are still many injustices I wish to be resolved before my faculties give up on me. The football world as I knew it is heading at breakneck speed towards oblivion – players with a modicum of talent are earning thousands a week, fighting and screaming obscenities at each other and the referee – we even have players in the same team resorting to fisticuffs!

Bobby Robson, knighted for his services to a game he was highly paid for, received £2 million for being sacked by Newcastle United, the club that never offered me a penny when I was forced out of the game through injury. It just doesn't make sense!

Hundreds of players are dead and dying from the dreaded Alzheimer's phenomenon having headed the heavy leather ball of the 1940s and 50s. I have been campaigning on their behalf for several years to the Football Association, which admits there may be a link between Alzheimer's and the heavy ball and is conducting a survey which will take up to 10 years! I ask you what good is that to ex-players and their families who are in need of financial help now? Rich Premier League clubs and their millionaire players should put their hands in their pockets and contribute now!

Images continue to ebb and flow from the halcyon days as a young and impressionable goalkeeper playing for the famous Magpies, Newcastle United, was it a dream or just a figment of my vivid imagination? Did the following sequence of events really take place? Looking back those 60 years and more, the images are so real, not dreams or figments of the imagination, they actually happened.

The United players were standing on the platform at Newcastle Central Station waiting to board a train to Manchester for the game against Manchester City the following day. A voice came over the tannoy system saying the train was delayed by half an hour, which to us was a voice of doom. Railway stations are usually cold, draughty places at the best of times and this wasn't one of those – it was freezing cold!

Jackie Milburn happened to spot a small stone lying nearby and began to kick it around, and before long the whole squad of players joined in, with the exception of Albert Stubbins. When someone shouted

"Come on Albert, get stuck in here," someone shouted.

Albert, who never swore, replied in his quietly spoken manner: "Not likely. You lot are too rough for me, I don't want a broken leg!"

Can you imagine players of today displaying such a natural spontaneous reaction? They are more likely to pick the stone up and throw it at each other!

DOUBLE STANDARDS?

In today's footballing climate, one, question is consistently nagging me as I continue to watch the scores of Premier League matches on television. I beg the question, "Is there one set of rules for outfield players and other set for goalkeepers?" Recent events would indicate that there are.

If, for instance, an outfielder commits a two-footed challenge on an opponent he will immediately be given the red card. A goalkeeper, however, who commits a similar offense isn't even cautioned. As many a commentator indicates, "The keeper came off his line to block the attacker!" This situation seems to be happening with increasing frequency.

Two recent occurrences that stand out in my mind were not merely blocking but rather ferocious, full-blooded, two-footed tackles perpetrated by the goalkeeper. The keeper in question was Hahanamen of Wolverhampton Wanderers. On both occasions he should have been sent off. One of the attackers in question was badly hurt, had to be carried off the field, and took no further part in the game. On the other occasion, both keeper and opponent required treatment but managed to carry on playing.

As a former goalkeeper, I am well aware of the danger when confronted with one-on-one situations. I do, however, consider that the goalkeepers of today are overly protected. So many of them have only to be touched by an opponent for a look of absolute anguish to be directed towards the referee. This is absolutely pathetic!

No doubt I'll be criticized for comparing the game of today with that of the 40s and 50s. It was in this era that players such as Nat Lofthouse, Trevor Ford, Dave Hickson, Arthur Rowley, Tommy Briggs, Dickie Davis, Billy Roost and so many more players simply hounded goalkeepers whenever they fielded the ball. I personally enjoyed these confrontations. I wonder how many of today's keepers would relish such physical challenges. That is something I'd love to know.

Antics on the Touch-Line

Having watched so many televised Premier League football matches, I must say that I have experienced a complete spectrum of emotions. These range from sheer enjoyment at one extreme, to plain boredom at the other.

If a game was boring, I suppose I should have just switched off the television. What I did, however, was to focus more on the antics of the managers, who display their respective idiosyncrasies in their little marked-out zones at the side of the pitch.

Firstly, you have the gum-chewers like Alex Ferguson and Sam Allardyce, chewing away as though their lives depended on it. I noticed that the frequency of their chewing motion increases when refereeing decisions are made against their team. It baffles me how neither of them, at least as far as I know, seems to have swallowed their gum when such incidents occur. I remember a visit to my hairdresser (yes, I still have some!) a few years ago. A young female assistant was chewing a piece of gum voraciously. I happened to mention to her that chewing gum supposedly stimulated the brain. She promptly replied, "It does nowt for me. All it does is fill me full of wind!" Charming, I thought. If it does the same for Alex and Sam, then heaven help those sitting or standing alongside them on the touch-line!

Then there are the "Twitchers", such as Harry Rednap and Martin O'Neill. At least Harry stays mainly in his seat. His head, however, is constantly in action, twitching back and forth. Martine O'Neill struts around the allocated zone like a puppet on a string, and drinks gallons of water. He must be bursting for a pee at the end of each half.

Next we have Owen Coyle, who cups his hands around his mouth and appears to be shouting instructions to his players. Now enter into the equation a two-fingered whistle. Interspersed between these mannerisms is a kind of semaphore code, which probably translates as push forward, push back, close ranks and so on. How on earth can players who are supposed to be concentrating on the game take notice of seemingly incomprehensible instructions from the touch-line? It makes me wonder what role the captain plays!

Of all the managers whose antics I have watched, my favorite has to be Steven Bruce. This is not because he is a "Geordie", but because he seems to be such a nice guy. This certainly cannot be said for a small but significant number of football managers, who present themselves as foul-mouthed morons. Steve's biggest problem is his weight. He seems to get larger every time I see him. No doubt this is caused by all that comfort eating due to excessive stress.

The star of the show has to be Arsene Wenger. He is constantly up and down off his seat for the duration of the match, and displays a plethora of facial expressions and body movements, that are bewildering to say the least. Sometimes I wonder if he had a gun in his pocket whether he might shoot someone, just to relieve his obvious frustrations! I think the referee would be the first victim, should he award a decision against Wenger's team.

Perhaps managers should emulate Freddie Steele, my manager at Port Vale in the 1950s. He never watched a home match! When players left the dressing room for the field, he would slip into the shower room, turn on the water, and place a towel around his head so he couldn't hear what was happening. After the game, he would emerge and be able to sense from the atmosphere around him whether it had been a good or bad result. He would then walk around, picking up snippets of information that would enable him to discuss the game with the directors.

Without a doubt, managing a football team at a professional level is extremely stressful. Even though many of today's managers are multi-millionaires, the pressure of winning or losing definitely takes its toll on even the best. Great managers such as Jock Stein, Bill Shankley and Bob Paisley all died at a relatively young age. This begs the question, "What price is one's health?"

John Lennon

When I wrote in my book *"Hands, Feet and Balls"* about my meeting with another great man, John Lennon, I chose not to mention the intimate details of our conversation. As I mentioned in an earlier, many of my therapy clients divulged intimacies of their private lives to me – details that I have no intention of revealing. However, some of the details John and I discussed were hilarious.

Much of his Scouse upbringing was vividly portrayed, sending me into fits of laughter, but at the same tinged with mild embarrassment. To mention certain aspects of our 'heart to heart' dialogue would be much too revealing, but he was very interested in my form of therapy and expanded his curiosity when he blurted out: "Cor, you must have seen a lot of bare arses in your profession!"

Recovering from the shock of his unexpected outburst, I relied: "Surely John, with your worldwide fame, viewing nudity must be quite commonplace to you?"

His reply was straight to the point. "Everyone is under the impression we only have to snap our fingers and the 'tarts' will throw themselves at us," he said. "The main target they aimed for was, believe it or not, Ringo – whether it was his nose that attracted them or perhaps some other hidden agenda we knew nothing about, none of us could answer."

I got the impression that Paul McCartney and he weren't exactly soul mates, but he had a higher regard for George Harrison, the quiet member of the group. I managed to ask a question that I'm sure millions of Beatles fans would like to ask: "What was the real reason drummer Pete Best was cast aside for Ringo Starr when everyone knew Pete was much superior in that department?"

John's brief answer was straight to the point. "Ringo has star quality appeal – I couldn't argue with that. The 'tarts' spoke volumes!"

When John Lennon was cut off in his prime by an assassin's bullet the musical world lost a genius who inspired millions of fans – not only with his musical talent but with his perception of life itself – I shall always remember him for those qualities.

The Goalkeeper Spin

There are many qualities to goalkeeping – more than any other position on the football field. As I've said so often in the past, any goalkeeper worth his salt can make brilliant saves, but I wonder whether there is, or has been, any other keeper who has spun the ball when throwing it to a team mate.

I developed this art during my playing days with Port Vale and it worked a treat, except on one occasion which I will describe later.

When throwing to Colin Askey on the right wing I produced leg spin, which enabled Colin to take the ball in his stride without having to stop it. To Dickie Cunliffe on the left wing I produced an off-break throw. It was a unique brand of teamwork between Colin, Dickie and myself.

On the one occasion it misfired, left half Roy Sproson, who was principally left-footed, had wandered out to the right side of the field and shouted to me for the ball. Without thinking I threw him a leg spinner. As he moved to control the ball it spun away onto his weak right foot, causing him to lose control, almost resulting in a goal being scored against us. Roy's language cannot be reported here! Thankfully, he saw the funny side when I explained the routine with my two wingers.

Roy Sproson played a record 837 games for Port Vale, later becoming player-coach. He also had a brief spell as manager, but left the club under a cloud for reasons best known to himself.

Because of his services to the club he was given a testimonial game in which I played, travelling at my own expense from Oxford, where I was trainer-physio. I do not remember receiving a thank you message from Roy.

After he died the club planned to build a statue in his memory, but several years have passed and there is still no statue. I sent a contribution from the proceeds of *"Hands, Feet and Balls"*, but I've no idea where it went.

I had always got on well with Roy, or so I thought. Then some years ago I came across a book about Vale affairs which featured several columns taken from my book without my permission. In today's world any footballer connected to a club has their own agent who would sue people involved in such a blatant procedure.

In that book Roy Sproson labelled me as a loner, which I admit shook me to the core. A loner – someone who prefers his own company. Nothing could be further from the truth. Perhaps it was because I didn't go around shouting my mouth off, effing and blinding, that Roy categorised me as a loner.

He went on to say that Ray Hancock (a pal of his) would probably have been selected for England had he been in the Vale team, but he must have fallen out with the manager. What Roy failed to say was that Ray Hancock only claimed the number one spot while I was the subject of a witch hunt – a club chairman who instructed the manager, Ivor Powell, not to select me for first team duties under any circumstances because I refused to buy the chairman's derelict house.

I documented in *"Hands, Feet and Balls"* the reasons I was denied a first team place by the sheer prejudice of manager Freddy Steele. This was a time when I was at the peak of my football career. The reserve team coach, Bill Cope, told the directors of the club that Vale reserves had the best keeper in the country.

There was another time that I managed to ruffle the feathers of Roy Sproson. I had secured the number one spot on a permanent basis again and we had been involved in a cup replay against Southport at Vale Park, having drawn 1-1 at Haig Avenue. Southport gave us one of our toughest matches of a season in which we only lost four times in all competitions, including eight games in the FA Cup.

It was generally expected, as we were at home, that a win would be a mere formality. As events unfolded Southport played us off the park but incredibly we won 2-0.

In the dressing room after the fame the great Stanley Matthews, together with actor and comedian Terry Thomas, made a beeline for me.

"Kingy," Stan said (he always called me that), "that was an international performance. You saved your team today."

Terry, with his gap-toothed smile, said in his 'posh Cockney' accent: "Gor blimey, Ray, you've got more arms than a bleedin' octopus!"

I've never forgotten those words. I heard later from one of our players that Roy was livid that I'd been singled out by the stars of sport and show business. Sad, really.

Years later, living back in Poole, my son Gary was making a name for himself as a singer on the club circuit and *Opportunity Knocks* producer Hughie Green offered him a spot on the television show.

Port Vale's social club, knowing my son was a singer, invited me and my wife Norma to the club, where Gary would be given top billing. I readily agreed and asked the club secretary if he would invite Roy Sproson, then a coach at the club, as well as his players and their wives.

On the night of the event the club was packed to capacity but not one Vale player, director or any other member of staff made an appearance. The secretary told me he had passed on the invitation to Roy, who said he would bring as many as he could.

Thankfully, Gary gave a great performance and received a standing ovation at the end. A female member of the club committee, said of Roy Sproson's non-appearance: "Ray, it is pure jealousy. Don't let it worry you. We all enjoyed a wonderful evening."

I'd be lying if I said the failure of Roy and his staff to attend didn't bother me. Although all the players I'd played with had left Vale, surely someone could have attended to represent the club?

As I look back on those memorable days, good and bad, Roy Sproson plays a significant role, not only as an excellent footballer but as an entertainer and comedian in the dressing room.

I remember quite clearly him standing up on the bench, stark naked, with his peccadillo dangling. He launched into an impression of the singer Bryan Johnson, the brother of Teddy Johnson, who famously sang duets with his wife Pearl in the 1950s.

The words were: "On the road to Mandalay, where the flying fishes play." Roy displayed a remarkable impersonation of the singer, except of course for his dangler, which caused great amusement among the players. Those are the kind of memories I'd like to embrace, rather than harbour any resentment towards Roy Sproson.

2004
Modern Goalkeeping

It is ironic to think two of today's keepers received £100,000 each just for sitting on their backside during the 2004 European Championships when England once again failed miserably. Paul Robinson (then playing for Spurs) and Ian Walker, then at Leicester, were the keepers in question. Since then Robinson has claimed and subsequently lost the goalkeeper's spot – trading places with David James who has been lumbered with the unfortunate tag of 'Calamity', which I'm afraid will remain with him all his career. Ian Walker was never international standard, and must consider himself extremely fortunate to have donned an England jersey.

It proves how goalkeeping standards have fallen in this country. In recent times only Chris Kirkland has looked the part, but even he has now lost his way. Like myself he has suffered an alarming amount of injuries, and to survive he must be strong physically and mentally.

Concentration in any sport is paramount, but probably more so in goalkeeping than any other – one lapse can be disastrous. The five C's for superlative goalkeeping are: Confidence, Concentration, Control, Courage and Consistency. In *"Hands, Feet and Balls"* I wrote in extensive detail about the many aspects of goalkeeping but there is much I omitted, probably due to memory failure more than anything else. From time to time certain images appear in my mind which convince me that the power of positive thinking has much to do with mental stability.

Two other candidates for England's number one jersey – Scott Carson and Ben Foster – gained valuable experience from loan moves which were instrumental in elevating them to international standard – I shall be following their progress with great interest. Another keeper with great potential is Steve Harper, a Tyneside lad who inexplicably sat on the bench for almost a decade at Newcastle United, taking patience to the extremity of human endurance as understudy to Shay Given. Ten precious years of his football career have been lost, but with the sale of Given his patience has been rewarded.

I've written to Harper on several occasions offering him advice and he has responded with compassionate replies which portray the character of this unassuming young man. As I said to him – apart from the five C's – the world is his oyster!

2005
Discipline

Discipline is an essential ingredient in all our lives if we want to cope with the stresses and strains of life as a whole. To be able to enjoy the good things on offer just remember 'what goes around comes around' when the inevitable rough times hit you – enjoy the good times when you can!

Family values too are important during our growing up period, when we learn the difference between right and wrong, to treat the other person with respect – it costs nothing to say please and thank you, to say good morning or afternoon and to say it with a smile – what a wonderful world this can be.

Frank, George and myself were fortunate to have parents who taught us all these things at an early age and I trust we have carried out their teaching satisfactorily. One family in my hometown of Amble springs readily to mind when it comes to family values. Market gardener Joe Smailes and his petite wife were blessed with six sons, Jack, Billy, Bob, George, Alan and Joe. From the beginning of their lives they were raised in the way I have just mentioned, and every one of them progressed through life in fine style, not one black sheep among them.

Every afternoon after school they were each delegated little tasks in their father's allotment, all with their Wellington boots on. Like us they were fortunate to have parents who cared for their welfare, ensuring each one of them understood that life is not all about taking but also about giving.

Their second youngest son Alan sadly died in his early sixties, but during his time on earth he exuded a charming personality, always a greeting and an infectious laugh which dispelled a mistaken theory that all Geordies are miserable sods! Had they lived to ripe old age both father and mother would have been justly proud to witness their son's successful progress, no doubt through their early recognition of family values!

After watching both cup finals of 2005, the vast difference in class between the top three teams in the Premier League – at that time Chelsea, Arsenal, Manchester United – became more and more obvious. Chelsea, with their large contingent of foreign players, appeared to be unassailable in winning the Championship, which had eluded them for 50 years.

Arsenal, fielded only one British player, Ashley Cole, in the FA Cup final against Manchester United, who had only a sprinkling of foreign players in their side.

I have voiced my opinion over the last few years on the unfairness of a system which is taking away the ambitions and livelihoods of British players. At the same time I have to admit that Premier League attendances are at their peak and the foreign players, particularly at the top clubs, are genuine crowd pleasers. After all, football is big business and the clubs with the biggest bank balances are the winners in more ways than one.

My old club Newcastle United were completely humiliated in their semi-final against Manchester United that year, and it is painfully obvious that the squad weren't up to it, throughout the team. Shay Given was a good servant to the club and although his reflex saves were still in evidence he showed a lack of commanding goalmouth presence and his one to one confrontations were appalling.

Alan Shearer was the only one in my opinion who wore the black and white shirt with distinction. Alan retired at the end of the 2005/06 season, having been encouraged not to retire earlier by Graeme Souness. For me, his decision to carry on was foolish, taking into account his age and the number of injuries (some serious) he sustained during his illustrious career. He overhauled Jackie Miburn's scoring record but at what cost to himself? He may well ask himself if it was worth it.

My other club, Port Vale, continue to linger in the doldrums and rumours of every description from takeover bids to completed disbandment is freely discussed. For something of this magnitude to happen would be an absolute catastrophe considering the success the club accomplished from the 50s through to the 80s. Others from the successful team of 1954 Vale produced much local talent, two of whom, Harry Poole and Terry 'Smiler' Miles were included in the top players list over 50 post-war years.

Other well known names were the goalkeeping brothers, Ray and Ken Hancock, full back Jim Elsby, the 'Rev' Norman Hallam, Selwyn Whalley, keeper John Poole, Alan Bennett, Stan Smith, Stan Steele, Lenny Barber – he scored six goals in the first half in a match against Crystal Palace before the game was abandoned!

Many other young lads were on the fringe but never quite made it: Freddy Donaldson, Tommy Conway, Derek Tomkinson. The list goes on and on.

I end with the two most famous players of all, Bill McGarry and Ronnie Allen, who became England players with Huddersfield Town and West Bromwich Albion respectively. Both Bill and Ronnie succumbed to Alzheimer's and died recently. Bill, who lived out his life in South Africa, was a prolific header of a ball, whereas Ronnie, although spending much of his career at centre forward, hated heading the ball. Playing in that position he didn't have much choice!

There is no doubt many names do not come readily to mind and for that I do apologise. Suffice to say the local talent is there in every town, city, and village in this country – let that talent be given the opportunity to tread the green fields of professional football.

My physical aptitude is gradually diminishing, even though I continue to exercise every day, taking full advantage of my son's swimming pool in Bangkok. Thankfully my memory is still in working order, especially those now long gone – images of events which had long been forgotten are vividly portrayed.

When I was honoured along with Colin Askey, Kenny Griffiths, Derek Tomkinson and trainer Ken Fish at Port Vale's 50th anniversary last year, I was reminded of the old pro revisiting the ground where he'd displayed his talents many years before. As he stood looking around with tears in his eyes, he was approached by a young ground staff apprentice who asked him in 'impeccable' English: "Excuse guv, di yi mind telling us huw add (old) yu are?"

The old pro proudly replied: "I'll be 82 next birthday."

The youth retorted: "Eighty-two? I'd 'ate to live till that age!"

The old pro quick as a flash replied: "You would if you were 81!"

Whenever I see people deeply tanned, having indulged themselves under a blazing sun for hours on end, I'm reminded very forcibly of my years of sunbathing. Having been a sun addict most of my life, I am now 'paying the penalty' for those sun-drenched procrastinating days of my youth.

No one talked or wrote of the hidden dangers of sun damage, and having enjoyed the privilege of working or playing in the open air, it was 'shirts off' at the first glimpse of the sun! What a wonderful feeling it was to experience the heat those rays beamed on one's body – plus you got to acquire a lovely tan and display it at every possible opportunity!

Ten years ago, the first sign of sun damage appeared on my forehead, quickly followed with similar ugly red blotches on both my cheeks. My doctor speedily referred me to see a skin specialist, who told me those blotches were an early warning of skin cancer and they had to be removed before they spread any further. The operations were performed very successfully at both Newcastle and Alnwick hospitals, thankfully leaving me with nothing but minor scarring - but the dangers are still to this day continuing to 'bug' me.

Both ears and an eyelid have been operated on quite recently, and both my chest and back are covered in sores which aren't life threatening but are irritating, to say the least! These spots are known as Octinic Keratoses – I have another name for them, but that's best kept to myself! It does seem sad that during those days when the sun shone I'd cast my shirt at the first opportunity, but now I hate the sight of it – for me 'it can rain every day' – but then knowing my luck I'd probably become water logged!

The message is; beware of the sun and the dangers it portrays!

Alnwick Cricket Club

A necdotes are easier to come by on the cricket scene and there was one magical memory which occurred when I was playing for Alnwick CC in the Northumberland League. Fielding in my customary position at first slip, with my good friend Stan Anderson at second slip, an amusing but embarrassing incident took place. The opposing batsmen snicked the ball, which flew between Stan and I, and in reacting to a split-second situation we both shot our arms out but instead of one of us catching the ball our hands became entangled as the ball dropped gently to the ground. A wag sitting on a bench shouted out: "Hey, you love birds, instead of holding hands, why don't you get a bloody basket?" Red faces all round!

Stan Anderson remained a good friend so until his death a few years ago, another victim of Alzheimer's. He was an excellent opening batsman, quick between the wickets and a top class slip fielder – no basket required! His two sons, Geoffrey and Michael, followed in his footsteps and both played for village club Warkworth, a team of outstanding talent, until they retired from the game not long ago.

Five years ago, Ashington-born Steve Harmison, the Durham and England fast bowler was on the 'crest of a wave'. He was instrumental in the demolition of Australian batsmen, which contributed to a large extent if England winning the Ashes.

Five years on, the Australians came once again to England in a bid to capture those 'precious' Ashes – but this time around there was no Steve Harmison. Yes, this season, he has bowled probably better than he did those 5 years taking a record number of wkts.

There has to be a reason why he has been overlooked by England selectors. I can answer that in one word – 'LETHARGY'.

Allegedly, he was reporting for England games not fully fit and displaying the wrong attitude. This will never be tolerated at any level, and quite obviously the selectors have decided to discard him, which is a great shame. But Steve must know himself that not only has he let England down, but also himself! It is all right having talent, but fitness is the essence, as all great sportsmen will tell you. Stanley Matthews, the great England player, possessed both these assets right up into his 50s when he finally retired.

On a brief holiday in Blackpool I met Stan, walking along the promenade with his wife. He told me that although it was the closed season, he continued to train every day at Bloomfield Road, Blackpool's ground. He invited me along, together with Norma, to watch his training schedule – I was happy to do so, although Norma wasn't so keen! Watching someone train wasn't on her agenda, even though the participant was a living legend. Reluctantly she did condescend to make the effort, and watching the great man go through his paces all on his own was a sight to behold – even she was impressed, and she admitted later it was well worth the effort.

Sprinting at top speed over 25 to 35 yards, running the same distance backwards at speed – running sideways, again at speed, side stepping imaginary opponents, again at speed. This procedure lasted 45 minutes! Afterwards he wryly smiled, saying, "I never go out for the 2nd half!" Stan was then in his late 40's.

I would have liked to carry out the same type of training at the Vale, but our trainer's (coach's) idea of attaining fitness was more suited to that of cross country runners! Even goalkeepers were subjected to what could only be described as sheet torture – there were days when we never saw a ball, because the trainer's philosophy was that when Saturday came we would all be 'thirsting ' for the ball! Maybe he was right, but from a player's point of view, training without a ball every day was sheet agonising boredom!

When our son Gary reached school age we were living in Stoke-on-Trent as it was during my time with Port Vale FC. Two or three days before he was due to start Norma took him to the school gates and watched the children in the playground.

"Isn't it a lovely school, Gary?" Norma said to him, trying to ease his forthcoming ordeal.

"Yes it is," answered Gary. "But I shan't be going!"

She took him a second time, said reassuring words to him but got the same response – "I shan't be going!" When the day of reckoning came there were the inevitable tears but thankfully he reluctantly bade his farewell, trudged through the school gates then disappeared into the school itself.

The school did not provide meals so the children either took sandwiches or went home if they lived a reasonable distance from the school. In fear and trepidation when Norma went to bring Gary back home for lunch she was astounded to see a beaming face greeting her at the school gates. On their way back home, Norma told me later, Gary chatted nonstop, telling her everything that had happened at school in the morning session. He had no sooner finished his lunch than he was reaching for his coat, itching to get back again for afternoon lessons. For someone who was never going to school, Gary is still there after almost 50 years!

It is well known that memory makes the scholar and Gary has that in abundance. Once he heard something that interested him it was soon stored in his memory box, while anything that was of no interest to him was immediately discarded. We knew from early childhood his flair for figures, an aptitude for soaking in knowledge. Instead of spending his pocket money on rubbish he bought books.

His particular interest as a small boy was astronomy. At 10 years old, attending Poole Primary School, the teacher had given a lesson on the subject. Half way through his talk Gary interrupted him, saying he had not got his facts right! Completely taken off guard the teacher said: "All right Gary, if you know so much, you'd better take the rest of the lesson." So Gary did!

His knowledge of the stars, the Universe and anything appertaining to outer space is phenomenal. I have learned things from him which were never taught at school in my day and here I am in my eighties thirsting for information on the fascinating subject of astronomy. For instance I never knew there were more stars in the sky than grains of sand on Earth. If the Sun were a crater it could comfortably accommodate two Earths. The distances and times from planet to planet is beyond belief – the Earth is but one pale blue dot almost lost in a galaxy of stars.

There is so much more I could write about it. Oddly, all this talk of astronomy takes me back to my time as manager of Boston United. Veteran defender Dave 'Dusty' Miller remarked after a defeat, when the players were despondent: "No point being miserable lads, just think in 50 years time we'll all be grains of dust!"

That's enough of that subject. Gary went from Poole Grammar School to London University where he attained degrees in mathematics, chemistry and English. Maths is his favourite subject and he finds calculus as easy as the two times table. It is quite obvious he takes after me – the two times table of course! Having worked in London, Bermuda and New York, he now feels Thailand is where his true destiny lies.

A final word of advice to all youngsters aspiring to reach the top in their chosen career – you breathe, eat, sleep… wake up in the night, it's all you think about… like religion – to some it may seem like a selfish attitude, but as I have said many times, destiny is in your hands.

Amble Sportsmen

Whatever heartbreaks I have encountered in my lifetime they are more than compensated by moments of sheer joy and ecstasy – the friends and the places I have visited, not only in this country but many other parts of the world where English is the common language. Even in Thailand, which was once considered a third world nation, is rapidly becoming a powerful influence in the Far East, where young people realise that being able to speak English will open up opportunities that would otherwise be denied them.

In my home town of Amble there are citizens of my age group who continue to live their lives with dignity, exactly in the manner in which they were taught as children. Two well-known sporting figures, Ernie Bell and Ronnie Pringle, both well into their eighties, exemplify the generation in which they were born.

Ernie, although not a footballer of any note, decided at an early age he wasn't going to miss out in the game he loved. He decided that if he wasn't good enough to play then he'd do the next best thing and become a referee. With his love of the game and thirst for knowledge he was an ideal candidate to take on such a demanding role. Although he never reached the higher echelons of the Football League he became a key figure in the north of England and was recently honoured by the Referees' Association for services to the game.

These days he retains his enthusiasm, watches local youth games and offers valuable advice to young refs. We often talk together about the game as it is today, with emphasis on the verbal abuse directed at referees. Ernie, like myself, fears for the future of football and often feels like turning his back on the game, but as he says: "How can I when I love it so much?"

Ronnie Pringle, again like myself, has been involved in some kind of sport all his life. We played in the same schoolboy teams, cricket and football. Then in later years we teamed up once again for the senior Amble cricket team, in which one match was of particular significance to us both. Ron was captain the day I scored a record-breaking 143 although it wasn't such a joyful occasion for him because of an unfortunate incident: he collided with a team mate while running to catch a high ball, damaging an eye duct which still troubles him today.

Ron continued to play cricket for many more years and when his body had lost its sparkle he took up green pin bowling until finally it was time to call it a day at the age of 81!

His passion for Newcastle United began in 1932 when United beat Arsenal 2-1 in a controversial cup final at Wembley. Allen scored the winning goal from a pull-back that many thought had crossed the by-line. Controversies like this will last forever.

Like Albert Stubbins, Ron can still name the teams from that final but my guess is he couldn't name United's team from the 2005 semi-final. Nor could many others, including me. Ron's support for Newcastle United ended recently when hundreds of loyal supporters lost their regular seats in the ground because the greedy directors traded loyalty for financial gain. Those seats are now filled with lukewarm supporters who can afford to buy a season ticket without any qualms.

The supporters of years ago who stood in the pouring rain without cover at least an hour before the kick off, shouting at the top of their voices "Howay the lads", would not do the same today.

When Bobby Robson signed several players in his term of office with United I wrote that he would have problems with the players with chequered histories. And as the performances of the team suffered he lost his job. Just then, like Ron Pringle and his brother Jim, Newcastle United lost many supporters who had stood by the team through the good and the bad – and this was the thanks they got!

To end this unsavoury note, there was once a popular saying: "If 11 Newcastle United shirts were hanging on the washing line, 60,000 supporters would be there to watch them dry." Those supporters would have had more enjoyment watching that spectacle than those who watch the team now!

Writing these memoirs has given me the opportunity to relive my life once again on the swings and roundabouts and the long and winding roads, with all the obstacles life provides. When *"Hands, Feet and Balls"* was published I had hoped people in my home town of

Amble and District would buy a copy – after all it was merely pocket money to most people at £6.99. I was sadly mistaken.

It was the same story at Stoke-on-Trent, the city where I spent eight years with Port Vale. Only 1,600 books were published and yet rather than buy the book it seems many readers read it in the library or simply borrowed it! More than half the proceeds went to charity, even though it cost me £6,000 to publish. I did not have the luxury of a publishing company to support me.

In 1955 I walked around the perimeter of Port Vale in the company of my brother Frank, prior to Vale's match against Leicester City. As we walked and reminisced on various issues he took off a ring and asked me if I'd like to have it. It wasn't expensive in monetary terms but it is a ring I have cherished all these years. It was originally a piece of metal used to make a Spitfire, the successful Battle of Britain aeroplane which was dubbed 'the plane that always returned'. I have lost this ring more than half a dozen times, once for two years before it was returned!

Just as Frank's career was short lived as a professional goalkeeper, his vocation as a policeman did not last long either. I remember him saying the force was swarming with crooks in his time. Some of the tales he told me were quite alarming. When Metropolitan Commissioner Sir Robert Mark came into power he got rid of almost the entire force because of evil practices.

When I worked for a short spell as a security officer at Plesseys in Poole, the majority of staff were ex-policemen or fire officers. During the night shift it was common practice for officers to take their cars outside the buildings and fill their car boots with valuable materials before wending their way happily to their homes!

Policemen in my young days were both feared and respected, but one particular man in blue wore gloves both winter and summer. In these gloves were concealed two small ball bearings which he used to clonk misdemeanant rascals on the nut – needless to say the police didn't face many problems at that time!

Of course there are many fine policemen who have a very difficult task with so much lack of law and order in today's society. Amble is fortunate to have a locally born policeman by the name of Paul Stewart, the son of Billy Stewart, a former Sunderland centre half who died from Alzheimer's.

At 6ft 4in, Paul is a commanding figure in the town and his quiet demeanour belies his strength of character when dealing with local villains. To see him on the streets is to assure peace loving citizens, and all is well.

A Man Of Letters

At the height of my footballing career, way back in the 1940s and 50s, I received on average 25 to 30 letters from fans every week, requesting autographs or merely writing a letter 'hoping' they would receive a reply! It has always been my philosophy that if anyone who sits down to put pen to paper and buy a stamp (in some cases two envelopes and stamps), then it should be common courtesy to reply, however briefly.

However, I'm afraid that scenario does not apply to a lot of people, particularly professional footballers.

As I've already stated, Bobby Robson was my leading protagonist, failing to answer 4 letters I wrote to him – plus Bryan Robson and Gazza – mind you, I never expected a reply from those two!

For several years I have been writing a column in the local magazine called the 'Ambler'. It is a free issue, so none of us who contribute receive any remuneration, but certainly in my case, I do consider writing a wonderful therapy, both from the point of view keeping my 'brain' and memory box active, and most importantly to convey to anyone who reads it my sporting theme or other subjects, which I trust are of interest to the readers.

Due to the credit crunch, The Ambler is in danger of becoming extinct because of lack of funding. In view of this possibility, I took it upon myself to write to a number of professional football clubs and several well-known figures of stature.

On the sporting front, I set my sights on Newcastle Utd., Sunderland and Tottenham Hotspur. I directed my letters to Niall Quinn, Chairman of Sunderland, Alan Shearer (before his brief managerial stint), and Steve Harper, United keeper, with whom I'd formed a correspondence relationship offering him words of advice on the many aspects of goalkeeping. My last letter was written to Harry Redkapp of Spurs.

As a former pro myself, I did at least expect an acknowledgement of some kind, but none was received from either Shearer or Redknapp.

On the bright side, I did acquire an imposing picture of the 'Stadium of Light', Sunderland's football ground, autographed by Niall Quinn, accompanied with an excellent letter from Nialls Personal Secretary. I purchased an autographed Sunderland shirt at my own expense, so together with the shirt and picture, we at the Amlber plan to auction them.

Steve Harper very kindly donated his own personal cheque and the promise of a United shirt – but perhaps with all the turmoil presently within the club he may be reluctant to send one!

Prince Charles, the Duke of Northumberland and Sir Alan Beith MP were 3 high profile figures, who might have been forgiven had they not responded to my letters. Yet, as events unfolded all three wrote to me!

The Duke of Northumberland wrote his own personal letter, plus the promise of a substantial cheque. Prince Charles and Sir Alan corresponded through their secretary, but both letters conveyed a message of goodwill and understanding – in Prince Charles' case he is committed to a numerous amount of charities and organisations throughout the world. Sir Alan has promised that together with his 'team', he will give us the support in any way they can – which goes to prove the difference in breeding!

I've written to several other sources but as yet no response. In the meantime 'The Ambler lives on, unlike many footballers, regrettably.

When the announcement was made that Bobby Robson had died, no one could really be surprised, as he had endured several years with the dreaded terminal cancer. However, when that final curtain closes, it is then that the full impact of finality becomes apparent.

Superlatives from all over the sporting world came flooding in, depicting Bobby in glowing terms, both as a 'footballing giant' and as a person. But some of the comments from those who did not know him were way 'over the top'. There are those who knew him as a coach and manager, but how many really knew him during his playing days?

I can safely say I knew Bobby Robson, both as a player and as a manager, having played against him when I was at Port Vale and he played for Fulham. We also toured together on the 3 month tour of

South Africa with an England squad composed of full internationals and those on the fringe.

It was several years later when our paths crossed again. Bobby was manager of Ipswich Town, and I was Youth Manager at Luton Town – at that time both teams were in the 1st division, now the Premier League. Ipswich were renowned as, arguably, possessing the finest youth academy in the country.

With this in mind and with the blessing of the manager Harry Haslam (we were friends at the time), I arranged a series of games, taking my youth side to Ipswich not only to play, but learn the secret as to how I could implement the running of a successful academy. Apart from Bobby's managerial skills he was an accomplished administrator, an art very few managers embraced. It was during those get togethers, Bobby and I became extremely close in our sporting relationship, discussing issues on all types of coaching.

It was arranged he'd bring his 1st team to Luton to play a friendly fixture against Luton's 1st X1 at Kenilworth Road. As usual, manager Haslam sat in the director's box to watch the game, while Bobby and I sat on the touchline bench.

As the game progressed, a defender blasted the ball in an attempted clearance which flew close to me. Pulling it down with one hand and dropkicking it up the touchline with my left foot (some memories never fade!), Bobby exclaimed, "You haven't lost your touch, Ray; you should still be playing!" I replied, "I will if you will, remember you're much younger than I am!" Bobby was then 40 and I was 49! We continued our 'banter' all through the game; with nothing at stake we enjoyed every moment. These then were my fondest memories of Bobby Robson.

Somewhere along the line something went wrong, and I know that as Bobby has gone, I shall never solve the mystery unless we meet again on the other side, when I finally reach THE END OF THE ROAD!

Steven Mcmahon

Steve McMahon, a former Liverpool and England mid-field player, is now a pundit on Thai television, and writes a weekly column in the Bangkok Post. Steve is one of the few pundits I listen to and read, simply because of his obvious knowledge of the game and his interesting commentary and writing. Most of the time I agree but in his column on Saturday, April 17th 2010, I took issue with him, regarding his views on Ryan Giggs and Paul Scholes. Steve wrote that both these players should not be included on the Manchester United team, because of their lack of pace.

Those of us who have been in the professional game know full well that pace is an essential ingredient, particularly in today's footballing climate. This is especially true because the football that is used today maintains a constant weight throughout the game. This wasn't true with the old style of leather ball, that would become heavier and heavier as it soaked up moisture.

Although I will admit Giggs and Scholes are now lacking in pace, they are still world class players. Their tremendous skill and adroit passing of the ball more than compensates for any concerns. Scholes has always been a great favourite of mine, even though his tackles often leave much to be desired. After all, about 90% of them are fouls!

2010
England's World Cup Goalkeeping Dilemma

With the 2010 World Cup in South Africa looming, England had in no way begun to solve their goalkeeping problems. I have said many times that the position of goalkeeper is most crucial on a football team: No football club that desires success can afford to have a bad one. The main ingredients that a goalkeeper must have are, to use my definition, the "Six C's". These include: Confidence, Concentration, Control, Courage, Consistency and the most important of all, "Do not Concede".

As a young goalkeeper playing for Newcastle United in the 1940s, I was striving to make my mark. Those words, "do not concede", became etched in my memory. We had beaten Blackburn Rovers at St. James' Park 9-1, and followed up in the next game by trouncing Leeds United at Elland Road 7-1. As I sat on the dressing room bench just after that match, Newcastle's Managing Director, Stan Seymour, sidled up to me. He whispered, "Ray, if we hadn't scored all those goals, we'd have lost 1-0!" He then got up and walked away. That poignant and powerful comment remained with me all throughout my football career.

In the 1053-1954 season playing for third division Port Vale, I managed to create a defensive record, by conceding only twenty-five goals in fifty-four league and F.A. Cup games. This included only five goals at home in twenty-five games, with a total of thirty-four clean sheets!

Today, at the age of eighty-five, my physical attributes have long since gone, and yet I retain a plethora of crystal clear memories of

212

bygone days. I marvel at so many of the changes that have occurred since my playing days: millionaire footballers, pristine pitches, lightweight kits and boots, the new style ball, and worldwide media coverage to name but a few.

2010
Here We Go, Here We Go, Here We Go..!

"Let battle begin". No I'm not talking about action on the playing field; I refer to conflict in thousands of homes throughout the United Kingdom during the whole one moth of World Cup football.

Apart from the violence, it is estimated there will be more divorces than ever before in that space of time.

It's all a far cry from the 1954 World Cup held in Switzerland when I was included in the initial 30 players. There wasn't the hype portrayed as in today's sporting climate with its television, radio and newspaper coverage blasted at us almost 24 hours a day.

What are our prospects of winning the World Cup? We most certainly possess several world-class players in Gerrard, Rooney, Terry, Cole (full back) and Lampard, but to get the balance right is a matter of concern. Judging by the games I have seen so far, the team is not performing as a unit and to complicate matters the manager has not solved the formation of his final XI.

Goalkeeper, the most important position of any team, is also a problem which has yet to be resolved. I have stressed time and time again that a keeper must adhere to the six Cs: Confidence, Concentration, Control, Courage, Consistency and most importantly Do Not Concede. Of the three keepers, my vote would go to Joe Hart – he is less likely to make a vital mistake and blessed with their right temperament, an essential ingredient in what will be a daunting experience.

There is much talk about the ball the teams have to contend with, which swerves alarmingly, and keepers particularly will have to be vigilant to combat a problem they could do without. When I played in South Africa back in 1956 with the England squad, although the ball was leathered, it still moved through the air much quicker because of the thin atmosphere. All I can say is good luck to the keepers!

Hopefully, the team will perform well but in the event we are dumped out at an early stage, people will no doubt sob in the street, tear their shirt off and the nation will embark on national mourning. Let's hope there will be no cars upturned, windows smashed and general mayhem. Let us remember this is one of the world's greatest sporting events, which we should all embrace - win or lose.

England can expect – but only if we limit foreign imports

I have questioned the number of fouls committed during the run up to the World Cup Final on Sunday, - this game was to be the highlight, with two of the tournament's best teams, Holland and Spain, 'battling' it out as to who would claim the coveted trophy. As events unfolded, 'battle' was the operative word – before this game (conflict) I estimated almost 1,000 fouls covering every match, but this final descended into a blizzard of cards, most of them delivered to the Dutch team who were intent on preventing Spain from playing their normal attractive, passing game.

I was delighted to see Howard Webb referee the Final - his demeanor on the field of play is most impressive, what with his fine physique, speed in his movements over the pitch, and no nonsense approach I thought he was the ideal candidate to take on what was to be the most difficult match of this refereeing career.

Refs have always been categorized in a "no win" situation – they can never please both teams. I have constantly maintained that many matches are won and lost from wrong decisions, no matter how capable and experienced they may be, referees are only human.

To sum it up World Cup performances as a whole, I still stand by my prediction that Germany will be the team to watch for the future - which is being carefully planned. Almost every player has youth on their side and most importantly, they employ a system which is rigidly adhered to and have discipline, which English players never have.

England must start a new campaign from the grassroots – every young player with potential must be scrutinized now and groomed for international recognition. Every position in the team needs to be over handled and fit into a system which firstly players can understand and secondly that displays their respective talents without the need to waste valuable time thinking about what role they are employing. Teamwork is the essence; with any team desirous of success and employing both hard work and team spirit, England's future can be assured.

Here in our little corner of Northumbria I have seen some wonderful talent, but many players become disillusioned when they see the continuous infiltration of foreign players dominating our footballing scene. This has to stop. I would advocate four foreign players to every team in the Premiership, two in the championship, and none in the lower divisions. The team I played for at Newcastle United were all local lads except one (Joe Harvey), and at Port Vale only two were foreigners - of which I was one. Every one of these wonderful players has now departed to another 'playing field' except two. Colin Askey at Port Vale is the other, and he is now 77.

This is why I say to every youngster, enjoy every second of your sporting lives. Time waits for no-one - it is relentless, and before you know it, (providing you are blessed with long life) you too will become old like me!

The Modern Keepers

So many of today's teams have a legion of foreign players, who deny the opportunity to play at that level to so many young talented Brits. Goalkeepers have particularly felt the crunch. In the Premier League alone there are only at present six English goalkeepers: Green (West Ham), Robinson (Blackburn Rovers), Kirkland (Wigan), James (Portsmouth), Foster (not yet established with Manchester United), and Hart (Birmingham City).

In my opinion, not one of those keepers has all "Six C's. All are capable of making the brilliant save, but any keeper worth his salt can do that. Plus, there are many other aspects of superior goalkeeping that are just as vital as making the brilliant save. These include taking command of the eighteen yard line, by coming off the goal line to deal with dangerous crosses, as well as handling one-on-one situations that require diving at the attacker's feet. Stretching out of the arms to gather the ball and curling up in the foetal position, and thus not allowing the keeper to be penalized are also crucial skills to master. Keepers today seem to prefer to go in feet first, which is in my view, both a cowardly and ill-advised act, that often results in enabling the ball to go anywhere.

That brings me to one keeper, Steven Harper, currently playing in the Championship League with Newcastle United. Ironically, Steve was kept on the bench for ten years by Shay Given. Incredible as it may seem, Steve accepted that situation without any rancor, and bided his time. On the rare occasions when he did get the opportunity to play, when Given was injured he not once let the side down, and received "Man of the Match" on at least two occasions. Once Given was pronounced fit, Steve was ousted again.

During this period, I decided to write to Steve, in order to offer him some advice. He responded in a very positive way, and we have continued to keep the lines of communication open. When Given left Newcastle, Steve became the established first team keeper, and he continues to play with absolute confidence. Although Steve is now in his 30s, I would have absolutely no hesitation in booking him on that plane to South Africa.

I was very fortunate to visit South Africa in 1956, as part of the England team. My three month tour of South Africa and then Rhodesia was a highlight of my career.

Jo Hart has now currently emerged as the clear favourite to take on the number one keeper spot. He is well clear of any other rivals. Not only does he make the brilliant save, but his all round performances are extremely good. He is also less prone to vital mistakes, so it's Jo Hart for me!

Teamwork, Teamwork, Teamwork!

TEAMWORK is the most essential ingredient for any team who desires success – this has been portrayed by the German players during the build-up to the closing stages of the 2010 World Cup.

Before the competition begins, I doubt if any football supporter in this country could name any one player of the German team. I know I couldn't.

Household names such as Rooney, Kaka, Messi and Ronaldo were expected to set the World Cup alight with their individual skills – but as events unfolded they had all been 'dumped' before the main contest began.

This proves the theory that one man, no matter how brilliant he is, cannot initiate a successful formula for his team. In last week's Gazette, photographs of schoolboys with 'stars' in their eyes brought memories flooding back to me. As an eight-year-old, I too had those same stars in my eyes. I related to those boys who cherish an ambition to become a professional footballer. I just hope they don't emulate some of the tactics performed by the players during this World Cup campaign, watched by millions throughout the world. I would be interested to know the number of fouls committed by every team – they must be around the 1,000 mark!

The jury is still out, deliberating on what verdict they can come to – what was the real reason for such abject performances from England players? Was it the fault of the manager and his tactics, or player burn-out because of a long and exhausting season, or were they simply bored to tears? Being 'cooped' up for weeks (two) in training quarters, which were more like a concentration camp?

When I saw photographs in the national press of them laughing, drinking, smoking cigars and lounging on sun beds with their wives and girlfriends, it convinced me the reason for their failure was sheer boredom! In my day, whenever we lost players rarely smiled until the next match.

My first introduction into international football was being selected as Reserve keeper against Yugoslavia, in the capital Belgrade. The night before the game there was no restriction enforced on the players, they were free to come and go as they pleased, providing they showed commonsense!

The 1950 tour of South Africa was for a period of three months, the longest tour ever organized by the Football Association. During that period, there was never any possibility of us being bored, no one complained of being homesick, and we were treated to wonderful hospitality, invited to the homes of millionaires and met the cream of South Africa's society. There was no question of restriction the night before the matches, we were treated as responsible adults which was proved on the playing field by not losing one single match of the 18 played. The team spirit was superb – there was no sign of burn-out following a long, arduous league season!

We all enjoyed our football, which was proved by our performances and we appreciated how fortunate we were to perform our skills in the wonderful country of South Africa. My focus has naturally always been centered on goalkeepers, and this competition proves the importance of having a reliable keeper. Some were extremely impressive, particularly those from the African countries, but it was Switzerland's keeper who impressed me most of all, with his sure handling and control of the six-yard area.

It continues to baffle me why many keepers dive the wrong way before a penalty-taker has delivered the ball. It makes them look extremely foolish! When facing a penalty I wasn't allowed to move, and stayed on the line until the delivery, but I still saved more penalties than I conceded.

Cape Town, South Africa; the year was 1956. As I gazed down from the top of the exalted Table Mountain, my thoughts still remain visibly in my memory 54 years later. At the age of 32 here I was, one of the lucky 18 players selected by England to represent our country to tour this beautiful country of South Africa and Rhodesia (now Zimbabwe), and play 18 games over a three month period. It all seemed too good to be true!

On one side of the Cape there were the cold waters of the Atlantic Ocean, and on the other side the warm waters of the Indian Ocean, a remarkable contrast.   As I continued to gaze over the stunning spectacle of Cape Town, my eyes focused on the stadium where I was to play the next day, and butterflies began to invade my insides - a phenomenon which remained during the whole of sporting career. Anxiety also increased due to the knowledge I was to play my very first match under a handicap. Torn shoulder ligaments were incurred when I was injected with antibiotics prior to the African flight, which followed almost immediately after the last game of the season against Leicester City. To play eight games unable to lift my left arm above shoulder height was no fun, but there was no way I was going to be sent home.

We did not lose one of those 18 games, and it is ironic that the England World Cup side of 2010 gave arguably the worst display ever, on that same Cape Town pitch we played on all those years ago. Having watched most of the games already played, England players were the only team who displayed blatant fear on their faces – from goalkeeper right throughout the team, it was there for all the world to see.

The main focus has been directed at the manager Capello. Are the players afraid of him, or is there some other undercurrent among the players themselves? My firm belief is that they were staring defeat in the face, against a team who in normal circumstances would have been played "off the park".

There is no doubt about it - we do have quality players, but as I've said many times, the system is all wrong. First of all, right from the beginning there has never been a settled team - which is an essential ingredient for any side who desire success.

Then there are the various formations of 2-5-3 or 4-3-3 or 3-5-2. How many of the players understand the continuing changing of these systems? My guess is not many. Why don't they revert to the tried and trusted method of 2-3-5, the simple formation which brought great success to the team I played for and managed? Not only is the team perfectly balanced, but it is flexible where forwards can interchange at will. When defending, wingers move inside to create a funnel effect down the middle of the field when danger lurks. When attacking, wingers again move wide, creating width and at the same time restoring balance on all fronts. I called it my butterfly system - wings close in, then open to display a vision of beautiful football.

Those of you who saw Brazil v the Ivory Coast last Sunday witnessed football of the highest quality. Evidence of real team work - England must learn from that.

At the time you read these notes England's fate will be known, but I firmly believe they will reach the last 16. When I was in Cape Town I was befriended by a private detective who hailed from Brighton, and he took me in his car around an area where people were living in squalor. I remember that several boys kicked an object around which resembled a football. It was made up of rags tied together with string, but they were all happy and laughing together.

2010
Stop-Start England Slip Up

The eagerly awaited World Cup is off and running, and already there has been great excitement alternating with drama during the initial dozen or so games. There has been so much hype in the build-up to these games, with everyone speculating as to whether the football on offer would thrill the millions throughout the world watching events unfolding on the pitch.

The host country South Africa opened proceedings, with their match against Mexico and from what I have seen up to now, this was by far the best game. Both teams displayed bold attacking moves, with attractive build-ups from midfield. If this was a sample of football portrayed by those two teams, then the rest of the tournament could only be described as a huge success, should all other teams display their talents in similar fashion.

However, what a let-down it was when the following match I watched, Uruguay v France, was a case of 'after the Lord Mayor's Show'. During that game, I felt myself drifting off to sleep. I asked the question: "Was it old age catching up with me, or was it the boring football?" There was no way I was giving in to old age, and I plumped for boring football.

Of course, it is still early days for trying to analyse the merits or otherwise the teams who are likely to make the last 16. But the big question we all want answering is will England be one of the 16?

In their game against the USA, it was the same familiar display - stop and start, no tangible pattern and lack of a balanced unit. The left-wing position continues to cause problems. The England manager

Fabio Capello has been hailed as the new Messiah by tabloids and public alike - the man who will bring the World Cup to this country. He has been quoted as saying he does not make mistakes or wrong decisions. I dispute that in the strongest possible terms. Already he has made more mistakes than any other England manager, particularly in his selection of his final 23 players.

For a start, take my namesake Ledley King of Spurs, who has (like Michael Owen) spent more time on the treatment table than on the playing field. He could not even go to his local park with his five-year-old son to have a kick-about with him – so to then play him in England's very first match was beyond belief. James Milner, who I rate very highly, had been ill for several days with a high temperature. To play him in such a high profile game and with breathing a source of discomfort due to high altitude, meant he was a loser from the start. He spent the first 20 minutes of the game chasing the opponent right-winger, and was obviously distressed and had to be replaced.

Now onto my favourite subject – goalkeeping. This position has been a problem issue for some considerable time, and the catastrophe committed by Robert Green only exaggerated the problem. I have made my feelings on the need for a reliable keeper clear on many occasions, and my vote would have gone to Joe Hart. He has had a great season playing for Birmingham in the Premier League, and he is less likely than others to make a costly mistake. In Green's case, apart from not getting his body behind the ball, he grabbed at it instead of allowing the ball to fit cosily into his chest. Wearing those ridiculous frying-pan gloves only increased the dilemma. Wearing gloves was never part of my early years – I loved the feel of the ball, hugging it into my body and punching it as though I hated it – a love-hate relationship.

Robert Green appears to be a phlegmatic character, and judging by his comment on the radio, I don't think the whole episode will bother him very much. He will live it for the rest of his life. In my opinion and most certainly in the opinion of thousands who saw the game.

2010
England Burn-Out

Fabio Capello will resurrect England football back to world domination.

Wayne Rooney is the player England rely upon to play a major role in bringing the World Cup back to this country.

David Beckham's influence in the dressing room will also play a significant contribution in being supportive to every player.

These quotations were thrown at us from every newspaper, radio and television prior to the World Cup. What a load of rubbish! Capello has arguably made more mistakes than any other England manager, plus his English is difficult to understand. How do players react to that, particularly in the dressing room at half-time, when situations on the pitch require sorting out? On six million pounds a year he should know all the answers.

I have long been an advocate of Wayne Rooney – he is, without doubt, a wonderful talent, but sadly during the whole of his World Cup campaign he has been an abject failure. This has been brought about with too much hype, playing for Manchester United when he wasn't fully fit, and playing in an England team who has little or no direction. Like several other players, he is bordering on complete burn-out. I would have left him out of the Germany game and brought in Peter Crouch – his height alone could have caused problems for Germany's defence, who were vulnerable. I won't mention England's defence, if that's what it would be called.

What of David Beckham? I'm quite sure he enjoyed two weeks' holiday, all expenses paid with a whopping big pay-out.

As a former pro, I'd like nothing better than to support England players who must feel in the depths of despair, but in my heart I cannot do that. The weakness of the team's character has been visibly exposed, and dissension in the camp is rife. Moments of petulance spreading through the side, players moaning about being bored, and the manager too strict with his coaching methods. When morale sinks, players look for every excuse – they will accept no responsibility for the problems. They moan about the ball, the boss and the fans who have paid hundreds of pounds to come and support them, the altitude and exhaustion, the end of the Premiership season - my heart bleeds for them.

John Terry is a fine player but is he worth #150,000 a week? For a player who was not even captain, to demean his manager was unforgivable, but he describes himself as a big personality in the dressing room. As it happens the players did not support him and did not follow his lead. Terry claims he was driven to act by his determination to win, but others say he was motivated by the desire for revenge against Capello, after he was stripped of the captaincy. No man should think himself bigger than his club or his country. His pose as a heroic figure is absurd. This is a footballer whose career has been littered with incidents of squalor, seediness and sleaze.

Terry's Chelsea team-mate Ashley Cole, with his tawdry background, is not a favourite of mine either. He is another who thinks himself badly treated despite earning a fortune. When his former club Arsenal offered him £55,000 a week, he was ludicrously "being treated like a slave". For most Britons, 2.86 million a year would be riches beyond their wildest dreams, but for Cole such an offer was an insult. These players have no connection with the real world, they really think they are worth all their vast earnings.

The real heroes of this world are those lads in Afghanistan with their heroism, bravery and pride; two years of Army training would do present-day footballers the world of good.

I am a member of the Newcastle Utd Heroes Club. If baffles me that we should be labelled heroes, when we lucky enough to be born with a talent for playing a sport we enjoyed - and got paid for doing so.

Frolics in Thailand

Returning to Thailand, a country where Norma and I spent many happy holidays with our son Gary in the city of Bangkok, was a journey very much of extremely mixed emotions. I was of course looking forward to meeting up with my son again, but without my partner of 60 years. Of course, Gary also did not having the pleasure of greeting his mother when meeting me at the airport – it was an emotional moment neither of us will ever forget.

Gary's beautiful spacious apartment has windows which stretch from ceiling to floor around the living room area, plus sliding doors leading onto a balcony where we can occasionally sit sharing a glass of wine, to enjoy overlooking the spectacular views of Bangkok and fireworks displays which are much in evidence throughout the year.

With a swimming pool only 2 minutes walk from the apartment, my intentions were to spend every morning in the pool exercising my tired body, but my life has never at any time worked out the way I planned it – catastrophe wasn't far away!

I'd only been there a few days when, descending the steps leading from the building onto the path below, I missed a step which threw me off balance. In an effort to stay on my feet, the whole weight of my body transcended onto my right leg – to have landed on my left leg could have rendered me with more serious complications, having sustained an embolism some years ago. As it was, my right leg from ankle to hip joint was severely damaged, rendering me unable to walk without considerable pain, and confining me to the apartment for almost 5 weeks! Thankfully, during such a prolonged period, being incarcerated, I was never at any time bored with the situation I was forced into.

Gary has an enormous range of books of every subject one can think of – including many educational ones, such as "Calculus" – (I never got any further than fractions and decimals and even those were taxing to my limited brain power!) On the other hand, I am fascinated with his books on astronomy, and to learn about the hitherto unknown wonders of the universe. As a 10 year old pupil at his primary school in Poole (Dorset), the teacher was taking the class on astronomy when Gary intervened, by informing the teacher he hadn't got his facts right.

Where upon the teacher said, "All right, Gary, if you know so much, why don't you take the lesson?" And Gary did!

How many of us know there are more stars in the sky than there are grains of sand on our earth? And that if the sun was a crater, one million worlds could fit nicely inside? When one sees the world as a minute blue dot in the universe, then we can realise how insignificant the world is.

There should never be a time in our lives to stop learning – even at my age it is imperative to stimulate what little brain power I have, by reading and writing. Apart from my column in The Ambler, I contribute occasionally for The Northumberland Gazette, The Evening Chronicle and when I'm in Thailand, The Bangkok Post!

Several people have asked me if I'll be writing another book following the publication of 'To The End Of The Road', which was placed 'on hold' since I lost Norma. Certainly, I have enough material to write another book, but whether I've the stamina to do so is questionable!

When my hip and leg improved, I once again ventured to the swimming pool which is a mere 2-3 minute walk, but in my condition it was a marathon – I'd tried to make it on two occasions but failed miserably!

However, I did finally resume my exercises in the swimming pool and the Jacuzzi, where 8 powerful jets of water sprayed into the pool.

This, I found was extremely beneficial on my feet, legs and back, a routine which was carried on for several days, but once again disaster struck. Getting in and out of this small pool did cause me problems – there was no rail to hold onto for support, and with my lack of mobility I resorted to getting down on my knees, which again wasn't easy!

After two weeks, vanity got the better of me. To ease myself up into a standing position from leaving the pool meant standing from the kneeling angle first. However on this occasion, I decided to 'spring' straight up – a fatal mistake – as with both legs weakened considerably, they crumbled. I lost my balance and fell backwards into the pool. The water was only about 4 ft deep and I hit the tiled bottom, landing on my elbow which probably saved me hitting my head – had that been the case, I wouldn't be relating this tale.

Completely disorientated and floundering, desperately trying to regain my senses and stand up, my feet kept slipping on the tiled base, and the powerful jets kept pushing me back at least 4 times. Incredibly, a young Thai girl was on duty in the vicinity of the pool area. Hearing the commotion she ran to the pool, saw I was in distress and immediately jumped into the pool, dragging me up and screaming for help at the same time.

It was fortunate that a couple from Italy were on holiday in the hotel, and when they heard the girls screams and shouts for help they rushed to the pool and assisted the girl to drag me onto a ledge, then up to the main parapet, where I sat for some considerable time trying to collect my thoughts. I distinctly remember words imprinted in my mind, "What kind of games do you think you're playing at? Here you are, 85 years of age, your sporting life a long time gone, and you pirouette on concrete steps and perform 'back flips' into a shallow bathing pool – The mind boggles."

Finally, I regained my full senses and thanked those who came to my rescue, particularly the young Thai girl, who Gary and I ensured was well compensated.

It wasn't until the next day when I felt the full extent of my injuries – my left arm, which took the main impact, was black and blue from elbow to wrist but thankfully not broken. My left leg, which I'm always trying to protect because of the embolism, was swollen more than usual. My groin, a part of my anatomy I'd never had problems with during the whole of my sporting career, was also wounded. Apart from that I was "fine", except of course that I was incarcerated in the apartment for another couple of weeks!

As I have written on several occasions, to analyse the mysteries of life on our planet and one's own destiny is way beyond my mental capabilities – minds much greater than mine can find no answer either, nor are likely to in the immediate future.

An extended stay to recuperate in Thailand entailed going to Immigration, to have my passport stamped with an extension visa. It also required another passport photograph, which meant I had to go to the appropriate establishment to have it taken. In normal circumstances, this would have been no problem, particularly as the shop was no more than a 10 minute walk from our apartments. Ironically, at that time I couldn't even walk 10 yards without chronic pain in my hip joint ,and my breathing was causing me moments of distress if I ventured too far. The pressure between my shoulder blades was getting to the stage when I felt as though I was encased in a steel case, which was gradually crushing me into oblivion.

X-ray photographs of my lungs showed no sign of damage, and talking to my doctor we came to the conclusion my condition was caused by my sporting life, particularly as a goalkeeper where physical contact was the name of the game. If that is the cause, then I have no regrets. I enjoyed every second of my days playing with a ball – football, cricket and my favourite indoor game – table tennis – I'd do it all again!

With my son Gary heavily engaged in his business activities, my dilemma of getting to the shop was left to his housekeeper and myself. A taxi was out of the question, as there were grid locks all along the route. So the housekeeper (a wonderful Burmese girl) suggested I go on the back of a motorbike. Apparently, the Thai's use them regularly to get them from A to B more quickly. The last time I rode on the back of a motorbike was in 1939, as a 15 year old being transported to Stannington from my home town of Amble by Albert Michell, where we were working on the new mental hospital as painters and decorators.

After that experience, I said I'd never ride on the back of a motorbike again! However, it seemed I had no option, as it was imperative I got there, particularly as I had to go to the immigration the very next day, otherwise it would be too late. To describe my adventure on the back of that motorbike was sheer 'Fred Karno'. In the first instance, I had great difficulty raising my leg over the pillion seat, and my Thai driver helped me to get it over. He also instructed me, with sign language, to hold on tight to him as he weaved in and out of the almost static traffic, ensuring I kept my knees closed tightly in to avoid vehicles on both sides. It took perhaps only minutes to arrive at our destination, but it seemed a lifetime to me, and yet it was hilarious to watch the housekeeper walking briskly on the side walk waving and smiling to me – she got there before us!

If that part of the journey was a nightmare, you 'ain't' heard nothing yet! To get my leg over the seat was more difficult getting off than on, and my driver had to get off the bike, allowing me to slide forward and thus enable me to put both feet on the ground - what a performance! The housekeeper instructed the cyclist to wait for us, as the photograph procedure would only take 5 to 10 minutes. Sure enough, he was there ready and waiting, no doubt anticipating a large "payout"! If the first part of the short journey wasn't nerve wracking enough, the return journey paled in comparison.

As all roads in Bangkok are a one way system, my driver decided to direct his machine against the oncoming traffic, and even though vehicles were moving slowly towards us, the margin of error was paramount. My driver started realising his method was becoming more difficult, as we slowly weaved in and out. Without warning, he rode up onto the pavement, where pedestrians barely gave a second glance. Other motorcycles were coming towards us, which no doubt prompted my driver to abandon the pavement, and do a detour around the back of some buildings, including an impoverished housing estate (shacks really) where some of the Thai residents were hanging out their washing. Evading them was a work of art by the driver – all I had to do was duck my head!!

Arriving back at the apartment building, still in one piece but with my legs still shaking from a journey I shall never forget. Chei'r, pronounced Cha Char, Gary's housekeeper, asked the driver his charge and all smiles, he said 40 Baht – 80p in English money – the tip I gave him was much more than his charge! His smile increased 100 per cent, but I was left to reflect the hardships so many of these Thai people are forced to endure.

When I told Gary I'd been on a motorbike, he almost exploded – "What? You could have been killed!" It is a fact that hundreds of motorcyclists are killed on a regular basis throughout Thailand, particularly those who carry their children either on the front or on the back of their machine – many have no license or had any driving experience before negotiating the constant stream of traffic which prevails in Thailand.

Sitting up on the balcony of the 21st floor, I was watching the traffic ebb and flow in a constant stream and pondered the thought – "where are they going?"

The weather in Thailand was so wonderful – plenty of sunshine, which unfortunately is no friend of mine now, owing to skin damage incurred by years of sun bathing without protection – we were never warned of the danger.

However, sitting in the shade and a lovely breeze is everything I could wish for, except the missing link, and the pain for both Gary and I never eases – I doubt it ever will.

My thoughts often centre on my home town of Amble, where many friends send me their best wishes, often ending their words, 'mind what you're doing.' If only I could!

My next door neighbours Alex and Eadie Jobe have been wonderful both in their constant attention of Norma and my well being, and since Norma passed away they continue to see to my needs, and are taking care of my affairs while I'm in Thailand – they are the 'salt of the earth'.

As I wend my way ever nearer to 'The End Of The Road', there are still many issues in my life which need to be resolved, and my biggest wish of all is to give guidance to all those kids who are on the threshold of entering into an adult world. They are our future, and it is imperative they are taught the 'swings and roundabouts' which they will face during their lifetime. As I reflect on my comparatively long life, I leave you with the words of two of show businesses biggest names – comedian Woody Allen, says "I don't mind dying but I don't want to be there when it happens!"

Frank Sinatra on his death bed was more explicit. He said "Dying is a pain in the ......" We know what you mean, Frank!

My proposed return back to England was once again jeopardised, when a volcano in Iceland erupted, causing wide spread of volcanic ash over the whole of Europe. Consequently all aircraft were forced to cancel their flights to London and other European countries.

When finally normal service was resumed, the airline, Qantas, informed me a reservation had been arranged for me to travel back to London on Sunday 2nd May, a significant date which will remain with me for the rest of my days. Long distance travel, such as the long tedious journey to Thailand, has always been a source of concern to me because of an embolism both in my lung and left leg which I incurred 10 years ago, caused through the stress I had been experiencing at the time.

For seven years my wife Norma and I undertook the risk of making the long trip without insurance – insurance companies would not comply because of our ages and general health – and for those seven years we accomplished the journeys without any problem. When Norma passed away in September 2009, thoughts of going back to Thailand were but a distant memory. However my son Gary, who is now permanently domiciled in Thailand, persuaded me to embark once again so that we could discuss our affairs, and at the same time share our grief together.

Apart from my entanglement with the apartment steps and the Jacuzzi, I needed urgent treatment at the hospital to remove a malignant growth on my chest because of sun damage I had incurred during my youth! This of course was just another growth to add to previous tumours. For the 20 minute operation the cost was £400 and I didn't have insurance! I'm often asked why I don't stay in Thailand with Gary – perhaps the hospital charges answer the question!

Returning to my flight back to England, I experienced a foreboding several days before I was due to embark on the long journey, but if I had told Gary about my ordeal he would not have let me travel.

As the plane reached a certain altitude, I began to endure 'pins and needles' in my left ankle. Very soon, the ankle became swollen and extremely painful – pain is one thing which I have endured many times in my lifetime, but this was REAL pain – it became almost unbearable and how I survived 10 hours in this condition I'll never know. With another 4 hours before reaching London I knew something was terribly wrong, so as a last resort I called for the flight attendant, an Australian lady who had been very attentive to me during the flight.

When she saw the distress I was in, within minutes I was surrounded by a medical team who appeared out of nowhere; an Australian doctor who was on his way to London for the first time, a trauma nurse who worked in a intensive care unit in Melbourne, together with several flight attendants anxious to do anything they could for my well being – they were all absolutely wonderful. The doctors applied a breathing apparatus and gave me a morphine injection to quell the pain, while the nurse injected my other arm with a solution to calm me down.

The doctor was most concerned about the amount of swelling in my leg, particularly around my thigh, and if there were blood clots (DVT) there was the danger of these reaching my heart. They arranged for an ambulance to meet the plane on arrival at Heathrow, where I was rushed to a London hospital to undergo tests – it all seemed so unreal, as though I was enacting a film in which I took the principle part!

For two days I was subjected to various tests, needles, blood tests, scans and having to wait long periods for results – it was all so very boring. However it was a necessary measure, particularly when the scan exposed several blood clots behind my knee, which may have been life threatening – the story of my life!

Thankfully, following a needle in my tummy, the hospital decided I was out of danger and they allowed me to return home. Although there was a debate as to whether I'd be able to journey by plane or car, as the plane trip was only an hour by air, the doctors decided that was the best option. Nevertheless, I was gripped with fear and trepidation until those plane wheels touched down at Newcastle airport.

As I've said many times – life takes many twist and turns – before coming to 'The End Of The Road'!

Keep right on to the end of the road,
Keep right on to the end.
Though the way be long, let your heart be strong,
Keep right on round the bend.
Though you're tired and weary still journey on
Till you come to your happy abode –
Sing a song as you march along

We'll all meet at the end of the road.
Port Vale Honours King of Keepers

An amble ex-footballer was given a hero's welcome at Port Vale as the only surviving player from 1950 when the club moved to their new stadium Vale Park.

Ray King, 86, was invited to the home game against Aldershot Town a fortnight ago as part of the 60th anniversary celebrations for the ground then referred to as the 'new Wembley' or the 'Wembley of the North'.

Ray, who spent eight years with the club between 1949 and 1957, was also guest of honour at a dinner on the Friday night.

Ray said: "It was the best thing that has happened in my life, they called me a legend.

"I was given a five-minute standing ovation, which brought tears to my eyes."

Other guests at the dinner included Gordon Lee, the former Newcastle United and Port Vale manager, and Pete Conway, father of Robbie Williams.

Robbie Williams is a lifelong Port Vale fan and majority shareholder at the club. He had hoped to make it to the dinner to talk to Ray, but was busy and sent Ray his best wishes.

The acclaim continued the next day at the match.

Ray said: "I stood on the balcony in the director's box and was acknowledged by the crowd by people who had never even seen me play.

"It was absolutely out of this world and I will never forget it.

"Ever since I have been inundated with people coming to interview me."

Ray was goalkeeper in the Port Vale team that won the Third Division (North) title in 1953/4 conceding only 21 goals. The 30 clean sheets he kept in 46 games remains not only a Port Vale record but also a football league record.

It could have been very different for Ray though after an injury early on in his fledging career.

"My philosophy is you have to be positive. Life is a roundabout of good and bad.

"I broke my wrists early on but then my career really took off when I went to Port Vale," he said.

Ray recalls many of his experiences in his book Hands, Feet and Balls.

His second book, describing his life at Port Vale and elsewhere, called At the End of the Road, is due out next month.

By Ben O'Connell
ben.oconnell@jpress.co.uk
Thursday September 23 2010